BRIEF COUNSELLING

BRIEF COUNSELLING

A PRACTICAL, INTEGRATIVE APPROACH

2nd edition

COLIN FELTHAM AND WINDY DRYDEN

Open University Press

Open University Press
McGraw-Hill Education
McGraw-Hill House
Shoppenhangers Road
Maidenhead
Berkshire
England
SL6 2QL

email: enquiries@openup.co.uk
world wide web: www.openup.co.uk

and Two Penn Plaza, New York, NY 10121–2289, USA

First published 2006

A catalogue record of this book is available from the British Library

ISBN 10: 0 335 210 454
ISBN 13: 9 780 335 219 452

Library of Congress Cataloging-in-Publication Data
CIP data applied for

Typeset by YHT Ltd, London
Printed in Poland by OZ Graf. S.A.
www.polskabook.pl

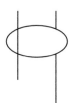

CONTENTS

FIGURES AND TABLES

Figures

Tables

ACKNOWLEDGEMENTS

The authors would like to acknowledge the following authors and publishers for kind permission to reproduce the following material as figures and appendices to the volume:

Figure 1. Expectations of psychotherapy duration: how long should psychotherapy last? Dr Jenny L. Lowry, Loyola College, Maryland, USA. Lowry and Ross (1997).

Figure 3. Counselling strategy selection chart. Dr Mary Lee Nelson, University of Wisconsin, Madison. American Counseling Association. Nelson (2002).

Appendix 2. Stages of change questionnaire, courtesy of J. Prochaska.

Appendix 3. Opinions about psychological problems questionnaire (Part 1: Causes of psychological problems). Chris Barker, Nancy Pistrang and David A. Shapiro, unpublished manuscript, Department of Psychology, University College London, Gower St, London WC1E 6BT.

Appendix 4. Opinions about psychological problems questionnaire (Part 2: Help for psychological problems). Chris Barker, Nancy Pistrang and David A. Shapiro, unpublished manuscript, Department of Psychology, University College London, Gower St, London WC1E 6BT.

Appendix 5. Possible reasons for not completing homework assignments questionnaire. Windy Dryden (1990) *Rational Emotive Counselling in Action.* London: Sage.

Appendix 7. Specimen 'goodbye letters'. A. Ryle (1990) *Cognitive-Analytic*

Theory: Active Participation in Change. Chichester: Wiley, pp. 43 and 47. Reprinted by permission of John Wiley & Sons Ltd.

Appendix 8. Case evaluation form. Professor S.L. Garfield (1989) *The Practice of Brief Psychotherapy.* Oxford: Pergamon, p. 132.

INTRODUCTION TO THE
SECOND EDITION

The first edition of this book was written just before brief and time-limited counselling started to become the norm in many practice settings in Britain. This edition is written at a time when it is common for counsellors to be working – in primary care, employee and student counselling – to strictly time-limited contracts of around six, eight or ten sessions. Although we would like to congratulate ourselves for being so prescient, a note of caution must also enter in here. Whereas at one time there was little sense of accountability for the efficient use of time and resources, the pendulum may have swung to the other extreme. We are now in the age of evidence-based practice in which much monitoring and research-informed practice characterize counselling and psychotherapy. This is probably a necessary development but it brings the danger of inflexibility. So, in this edition, although we continue to advocate a form or style of counselling that is efficient in the use of time and realistic about the funding implications of any counselling that remains stubbornly resistant to time-consciousness, we emphasize that a proportion of clients will still require longer term counselling or therapy.

In reviewing what we first wrote some 14 years ago, we remain pleased with our concentration on a down to earth, change and goal-oriented form of counselling that is explicit with clients about the process. We believe this approach is as valid today as at the time of the first edition. Many reviewers and readers have agreed with us and have reported finding the book of great practical helpfulness. We also realize that a certain undeniable accent on a *learning* approach was and is evident here; in other words, we have championed a belief in clients' ability to learn new ways of thinking, feeling and behaving. To some extent this betrays Windy's immersion in rational emotive behaviour therapy and cognitive therapy, but it is also in accord with Colin's belief in the relative modesty of what counselling can usually do. In our world, there are many reasons to be discontented and to suffer, and counsellors owe it to their clients to offer realistic, pragmatic, skilful help and not to harm them by creating or reinforcing fantasies that unhappiness can be totally overcome by counselling.

This book is not comprehensive but should be approached as a compendium of useful guidelines and pointers. It is healthy that you should read it critically and take from it what is genuinely useful. Perhaps one last caveat is necessary. We have, in this book, alluded to the non-linear nature of change, the tendency towards relapse and the dangers of perfectionism. Now, it is possible to read this book *as if* it offers a clear linear pathway to outstanding success with all clients. The nature of any text structured according to beginning, middle and end is that it appears to suggest a neat progression. Here we underline the reality that most counselling has some degree of uncertainty in it. We would rather trainees and beginning practitioners took from it what is genuinely useful and read it critically than imagine that it should be read and followed slavishly.

That being said, we hope that the purposeful, practical, flexible and integrative approach advocated here fits reasonably well with the current age and its consciousness of limited time, and that readers will take from it what can optimally help clients to accept themselves, gain some insight and move forward with their lives.

INTRODUCTION TO
BRIEF COUNSELLING

Purpose and structure of the book

As the title states, this is a book of practical advice. It is designed to help you examine and improve your work with clients in brief counselling. It is not intended as a definitive manual, as a theoretical tract, or as a new model of counselling. (For comprehensive treatments of brief psychotherapy, see Budman and Gurman, 1988; Wells and Gianetti, 1990.) We are interested in offering guidelines from a broad perspective. The ideas in this book are culled from our own experiences as seasoned practitioners of brief counselling as well as from our work as supervisors and trainers of counsellors. From the latter, we know that the kinds of questions raised here are frequently asked by trainee and beginning counsellors. Our aim is to raise these questions as issues to be discussed on training courses and in supervision. It is not our intention to convey a series of injunctions; rather, we wish to sensitize you to important issues in brief counselling. What you will find here is not what you *should* do, but what you might wish to consider in your work with clients. We have in some cases cited our own views and our own work with clients, but these are best regarded as our views, as illustrations and discussion points.

This book gives a process view of brief counselling. Where we have given examples of work with clients, this is in order to illustrate various points of the counselling process. We have laid the book out in six parts for practical reasons, but not to suggest that the counselling process necessarily follows such a structure. Also, we have presented a list of items in broad sequence, but we fully realize that in practice counselling does not easily fit into a neat ordered sequence. We suggest, then, that you use the book in a way that suits you, your point of development as a counsellor, and the issues facing you in your work with each of your clients. You may become aware that certain issues are relevant to different clients at different times. One of our hopes is that you will discuss these issues with your fellow trainees, other counsellors, and your supervisor.

The emphasis in this book is a practical one. We have reproduced some questionnaires as appendices and you may wish to use or adapt these for your own purposes. We realize that certain approaches to counselling do not readily lend themselves to particular interventions. The use of homework assignments, for example, is a topic which may arouse some dissent in certain quarters. The very word 'homework' arouses some indignation among counsellors, yet it is neater than 'between-sessions tasks', so we have retained it. We have not assumed that any particular counselling orientation is more fitting for brief counselling than any other, but of course we do bring our own views and orientations to this book. We have given various examples in the book of how practitioners from different schools might regard particular issues. We do suggest that you consider what role assessment, goal setting, homework and other issues might play in helping each of your clients effectively in a relatively short time. We recognize, too, that certain of the items listed will not apply at all to some clients. Use this practical advice flexibly in the service of your clients.

What is brief counselling?

We continue to follow the view that there is no essential distinction between counselling and psychotherapy and the incorporation of 'psychotherapy' in the title of what was before 2000 the British Association for Counselling (now BACP) underlines such a view. Both activities aim to understand and where possible alleviate human suffering, solve problems and help people live more satisfying lives. We disagree with commentators who define counselling as a superficial, brief, symptom-removing activity which compares unfavourably with the 'real' work of (long-term and 'in-depth') psychotherapy. One psychotherapist, for example (Storr, 1963: 2), suggested that 'psychotherapy which involves more than superficial guidance is bound to be of some length, often of very considerable length'. Length of treatment has been a contentious issue since the time of Freud (who himself conducted some very short analyses), and the debate continues to this day, not only within the psychoanalytic camp but also from a humanistic perspective. John Rowan, for example, in his interview with Windy Dryden (Dryden, 1992) regarded brief therapy as threatening to cheat clients of an opportunity to explore their lives in depth. It is psychoanalytic practitioners who have, in fact, been in the forefront of efforts to condense therapy (see Coren, 2001; Flegenheimer, 1982; Molnos, 1995) and these efforts have been helped by the emergence of behavioural and cognitive-behavioural methods, as well as by integrative models like cognitive analytic therapy (Ryle, 1990). For more detailed comparisons of brief and long-term models of therapy, see Budman and Gurman (1988: 11) and Malan (1975: 8). Please note that we are not claiming superiority for brief counselling and we address the subject of necessary referrals to long-term work within this book.

Brief counselling can refer to any counselling that lasts from one session to approximately 20 sessions. Malan (1975) cites cases of brief psychotherapy ranging from four to 50 sessions. The exact number of sessions to be cited as evidence of counselling being brief is not our concern here, and we shall assume that you, our readers, will be dealing with many clients who see you for anything from a few to six, 12, or 20 or so sessions. Shipton and Smith (1998) define long-term counselling as exceeding 25 sessions. We also need to point out that there are various patterns of counselling contract. Twenty sessions, for example, may either be consecutive weekly sessions, or spread over a year. Rosenbaum et al. (1990) present the 'challenge of single-session therapies' which recognize 'decisive moments of life' and call for the intensive use of therapeutic skills (see also Talmon, 1990). Many commercial, statutory and voluntary agencies offer a maximum of six or eight sessions. Mann (1973) pioneered time-limited psychotherapy consisting of twelve sessions, the non-negotiability of which reflected, in his view, the reality of life and death, and imperfection. Ryle's (1990) model offers 16 sessions, partly for economic reasons but also partly in order to maximize commitment and minimize unhealthy dependency. Budman and Gurman (1988) advocate a model of brief therapy which is phased out by the tapering-down of sessions; but they also conceive of therapy as a recurring process, to be used as a kind of 'mental health check-up' with reference to developmental crises. A technical distinction between brief counselling and time-limited counselling is that the former does not specify a limited number of sessions or an ending date, even though it may last only for weeks.

Why brief counselling?

Long-term therapy or counselling is not widely available through the National Health Service in the UK (or elsewhere), nor do private health insurance companies recognize its necessity. Private long-term therapy, particularly of the pure psychoanalytic variety (four or five times a week for several years) is very expensive and inaccessible to the majority of people. As Albee (1990) has pointed out, psychotherapy is so labour-intensive, so time-consuming and costly, that its impact on the mental health of the population as a whole is infinitesimal. Add to this the firsthand reports of some former consumers of psychotherapy (Dinnage, 1988; Sands, 2000) and their claims of wasted years in analysis, and you will agree, perhaps, that the length and cost of such therapy may require serious investigation. As Fairbairn and Fairbairn (1987: 22) put it: the way in which professional time, expertise and energy is used is one of the primary issues in resource allocation in all of the caring professions; indeed the justification of the way in which human effort is utilized is common to those who adopt a thoughtful stance in all of human enterprise.

Analysts like Malan (1975) and Balint et al. (1972) took up the challenge to reduce the length of therapy. They seemed to agree that 'focal' concerns helped to shorten therapy, and that attention to the use of time and judicious exclusion of certain kinds of client material were important factors in achieving change more efficiently. Focal concerns, as defined by Balint et al.

(as well as other writers) combine identified limited aims in counselling and identified conflicts in the client's life. The gradual emergence of behavioural and humanistic models of therapy stimulated research into therapeutic outcome and process and encouraged practitioners to experiment with other models and to integrate them into their own work. Many new schools of therapy appeared and developed around the 1960s and 1970s (including Gestalt therapy, primal therapy and transactional analysis), each often claiming to be briefer than previous models. From the 1980s, relatively short-term cognitive-behavioural and solution-focused therapies gained enormously in popularity. As Malan (1975) has suggested, there does seem to be a phenomenon of 'waning enthusiasm' on the part of therapists (who cannot summon the intense energy and interest they once had) which is perhaps responsible for originally brief therapies growing inevitably longer. Against this background of innovation and research, a combination of economic restraints and the growing popularity of counselling has led to an awareness that counsellors can help to effect personal change in relatively brief periods of counselling.

Budman (1990: 209) writes that 'of all the individuals who visited mental health outpatient settings in this country [USA] in 1980, nearly 70 per cent came for six or fewer visits'. Garfield (Garfield and Bergin, 1986: 217) demonstrated that various surveys revealed that clients frequently terminated therapy after six, eight or ten sessions. This is what Budman and Gurman (1988) refer to as 'brief therapy by default', since clients terminated without notice. It seems that clients who drop out of counselling 'early' may well have got all the help they perceive themselves as needing for the time being, within the first few sessions. Many student counselling services report that they see clients on average for only two, three or five sessions, by the client's choice; the service is free and there is no limit set to how many sessions are available to students.

There is also some evidence that brief therapy is as effective as long-term therapy (Carter, 2005; Shlien et al., 1962). Taken together, such research indications suggest that the reality is that most counselling and therapy is in fact brief; that clients wish it to be brief; and that its brevity does not detract from its effectiveness. For these reasons, many contemporary counsellors, including ourselves, advocate brief counselling 'by design', while also being prepared for that relative minority of clients who genuinely need long-term counselling.

Who is brief counselling for?

We recognize that there are people for whom brief therapy or counselling is not appropriate. We address this subject explicitly within the text. In general, it is not suitable for people with chronic disturbances including drug and alcohol addictions, personality disorders and serious mental health problems – although Ryle (1990, 1995) claims that cognitive-analytic therapy has been successful with people diagnosed as having personality disorders. Perry (1989), however, advocates 'intermittent continuous therapy' for clients with 'borderline' and 'personality disorder' diagnoses. Many time-limited thera-pists advocate strict selection procedures to ensure optimal prognoses for treatment. We believe that you can afford to be less selective than many of these practitioners (Feltham, 1997). Interestingly, Holmes and Lindley (1989) suggest that brief therapy, although more appealing to working-class clients because of its goal-directedness, is also less likely to be offered because working-class clients are commonly seen (so Holmes and Lindley claim) as being less articulate and as exhibiting their disturbances in more of the addictive and suicidal categories of behaviour (and are therefore more likely to be prescribed medication).

We believe that candidates for brief counselling should not be severely disturbed. They should preferably be in the 'neurotic range' of life crises, mild anxieties and depressions; they are likely to be people experiencing what Budman and Gurman (1989) refer to as 'interpersonal-developmental-existential' (IDE) problems or concerns. This implies that clients' problems are not necessarily rooted in their pasts. Your brief counselling clients should preferably be functioning reasonably well and be able to benefit from a therapeutic process that will last weeks rather than years. They should be capable of formulating and articulating their problems and goals reasonably succinctly. Thus, applicants for counselling who are either seriously psy-chiatrically disturbed or preoccupied with metaphysical questions about the meaning of life may need to be referred to alternative appropriate services. (However, on this last point, see Strasser and Strasser, 1997.) Brief counselling lends itself best to what Nelson-Jones (1989) calls 'pragmatic existentialism', which suggests a concern of client and counsellor alike for dealing with matters in a finite, problem-solving manner.

'Who or what is best for this individual?'

The above question is put by Lazarus and Fay (1990). We wish to underscore the importance of this question. On no account try to fit your clients to what is in this (or any other) book; pick from the book what meets your clients' needs. As an example of flexibility, Budman and Gurman (1988) are willing to include significant people in clients' lives in therapy sessions in order to facilitate needed change. However, unless you have had training in couple or family work, or a fair amount of experience, we do not recommend that you make this normal practice, even though it can be helpful. On the other hand, we do not believe that evidence-based practice guidelines [Roth and Fonagy, 2005] are yet sufficiently advanced to warrant your withdrawal from contact with many clients, simply because, for example, little concrete evidence has yet been gathered to support humanistic counselling with anxiety attacks.

So use this book as a reference for raising issues. Note anything that pro-vokes something relevant to your clients. Take to your supervisor any issues about which you are uneasy, unsure or excited. You will note that we advo-cate throughout the book that you invite your client's feedback on the counselling process. This will enable you to fine-tune your work. It may also be that you are not the best person for certain clients. We wish to make this point clearly: since the success of counselling rests at least in part on the relationship between client and counsellor (Feltham, 1999), and since you are often in a more powerful position than your client, do consider whether you are the best resource for the client.

We have made this last point in various ways throughout the book and it is not intended to be demoralizing. It applies to experienced and inexperienced counsellors alike. Perhaps this is a good point at which to state, too, that the success of brief counselling depends not only on the therapeutic relationship, but also on your understanding and using skilfully a range of techniques (see Hill, 1989; Rosenthal, 1998; Thompson, 1996). We hope that this book will be an aid to you in developing your skills further. Finally, we want to make the point that one of your best assets as a beginning counsellor is your level of enthusiasm. Durlak (1979), reviewing research on the effectiveness of para-professionals (such as students and volunteers) and professionals, concluded that paraprofessionals were perceived as at least as effective as professional helpers, and in some cases more so. Although some commentators have queried these results, our view is that if they hold true it is likely that the degree of enthusiasm of paraprofessionals and trainees is a beneficial factor for work with clients. So an overarching guideline might be: retain your enthusiasm, be open to new ideas, but temper this with a healthy scepticism! We wish you well in your work. Finally, if you are aware of areas of concern for which you would like to see practical guidance provided in any future editions of this book, we would welcome your comments. If so, please send any ideas to us, care of the publisher.

PART I
ORIENTING THE CLIENT
TO COUNSELLING

1 Recognize that the client reacts to you from the first contact

When is the first contact with a client made? Although some people regard the first meeting in person as the first working contact, we take the view that the first contact is usually, and significantly, that made by telephone or letter. Let's deal with the telephone first. Assuming that you're not exclusively a telephone counsellor, this is the way in which most of your clients do their initial reaching out for help. It's a big step for most people. Most are 'first-time buyers'; they may be very distressed, unsure of what they want (and need) and nervously unfamiliar with counselling. They don't know you and may have only the barest of information about you. Alternatively, but less probably, they may be informed consumers, ready to question how you work. What is going on in this apparently short and simple phone call, and how might you, as the counsellor, best be prepared for it? Brandt (1982) contends that counsellors are quite likely to be involved in various activities and thoughts when the phone rings, which will colour the way they respond to a new client's call. Brandt believes that this is the point at which slightly distorted mutual impressions begin to form and subsequently to affect the relationship.

Our preference, and recommendation, is not to become involved in counselling as such at this stage. Some, like Talmon (1990), take the opposite position. Don't invite lengthy explanations of the (potential) client's problems. However, do be courteous and welcoming. The person on the other end of the phone may become your client, and therefore this stage will form the beginning of the therapeutic alliance between you. (Even if she or he doesn't become your client, you may be able to help in a simple humanitarian way by offering information. Also, in some way you are an ambassador for the profession of counselling, and the way in which you respond may well influence the person's view of helping and helpers.)

Be prepared with what you will say about your availability, your fees, if you charge any, and your way of working. If enquirers don't ask about fees, for example, it is a good idea to give them the opportunity to do so by saying, 'Would you like to know how much my (or "our" in the case of an agency) fees are?' This makes it easy for the less assertive client to ask and it clarifies for them whether or not they can afford your fee. If this is more than they can pay (and you do not operate a sliding scale) it is advisable that you have some idea of where they can look for a counsellor or counselling service that is within their price range. If they don't ask about your way of working, you might want to elicit enough information to determine whether you are the right kind of counsellor for them or not. There can be misunderstandings about who you are, what counselling is, and so on, and this may be apparent at this stage. If it is, identifying it will save time and confusion. On the subject of what counselling is, or how it can be best explained, see Appendix 1 for suggested wording for simple leaflets.

If you have a telephone answering machine, record a message that is clear and welcoming and not offputting. Any client who is tentative might easily be put off by a message verging towards the cold, clinical and businesslike or, alternatively, the sloppy and unprofessional. When you do receive messages from people enquiring about counselling (and, of course, ensure that no one besides you or your professional associates can access these messages) be sure to respond with as little delay as possible. The moment when people decide they really want to do something about a problem is a significant moment and holds a great potential for change. Again, when responding be as courteous and helpful as you can. As far as urgency goes, try to offer an appointment quickly, a place on a waiting list if appropriate, or a referral to another counsellor if timing is crucial and you cannot see the client yourself. Everything that has been said about telephone contact applies to letters except, of course, information conveyed by tone of voice and dialogue. But if you do receive letters asking for counselling or for information about your service, reply promptly, clearly and fully. If you have any literature that explains what you or your agency do, this can help the client to make a more informed decision.

If you work from an office or in an organization, your potential clients may well speak first to a receptionist before speaking with you. Depending on the setting, the individual receptionist and her or his understanding of counselling, clients can receive a variety of messages about the kind of counsellor you are and the kind of counselling experience that may be in store for them. As far as possible the receptionist should elicit the same kind of information and convey the same sort of welcome and sensitivity as you would. If you have any influence over this procedure, try to ensure that receptionists put across clear, warm messages and minimize any misunderstandings. In an agency where there is a team of counsellors, it is appropriate to ask applicants for counselling if they would prefer to see a man or woman, someone from a particular ethnic background or sexual orientation (if available) and so on (Lago and Smith, 2003). You may need to ask whether they have any special access needs and give clear instructions about appointments, including the request that you be informed in advance of any inability to attend or decision not to attend.

Ensure that clients know where to find you, where to wait, and whatever they need to know to feel reasonably comfortable. If you work in a particular way, for example with Gestalt, it is a good idea to explain, at least in the first session, the presence of large floor cushions or any other 'props', and in general to put clients at their ease (see Rowan, 1988; Sklar, 1988). On first meeting the client it is again, of course, extremely important that your welcome is as natural and courteous as possible. While some therapists, for therapeutic reasons, refrain from shaking hands or making eye contact or engaging in any 'chit-chat', we advocate an initially reassuring, warm welcome. Some clients may prefer some emotional distance, and some may prefer not to engage in any opening conversation, but we believe that most (certainly first timers) will be helped more by a friendly welcome and naturalistic lead-in to counselling. You may want to consider what your building, consulting room, furnishings, and so on, convey to clients in terms of comfort, stimulation, fantasy or neutrality. It is common now for counsellors in primary care to work from rooms with medical furniture and this can certainly affect perceptions of counselling. There is a view that a lighter, brighter room with upright chairs may be more conducive to brief counselling than a room that is dimly light with a couch or armchairs that encourage too relaxed an atmosphere! You need to judge these matters yourself, where you have any choice. For an interesting description of one therapist's view of 'the first five minutes' of a meeting with a new client, see Hobson (1985).

Summary

Be prepared for telephone enquiries about counselling. Be courteous and helpful, but avoid beginning counselling at this stage. Ensure that answering machines or intermediary staff are welcoming. Consider the messages conveyed by all aspects of the setting in which you counsel.

---

2 Be ready with your approach to contracting

The need for greater clarity about the subject of contracting has been emphasized in recent years. This is partly due to increased awareness of the potential for complaints and legal action from clients and also awareness that clients may well make better progress when mutual expectations have been aired and clarified from the outset. It may also resonate with the increasingly professionalized status of counselling. We use the term 'contract' and acknowledge that, like 'homework' (see later sections), it is sometimes disliked and risks being misunderstood. By contracting we mean the explicit discussion and agreement on certain matters, such as exactly what is being offered, appointment times, cancellation policies, emergency contact, length of sessions and overall therapeutic time available, confidentiality and its limits, and so on. Time and monetary factors are dealt with in more detail later. We wish to stress here the importance of being explicit, of setting some ground rules in the interests of fair treatment, ethical clarity and a good therapeutic alliance. What is it that you really must impart to your client at the outset and what might your client need or want to know?

Of course, you are likely to be more ready than your clients about such matters. You know what counselling entails but the client doesn't. The onus on counsellors is to be informed and to act professionally (BACP, 2002).

Less attention is paid to the subject of helping your clients to be informed consumers. Now, this is understandable for two main reasons: (a) you will not, especially in brief work, want to take up too much time on things that may sound very formal and legalistic and (b) you need to be sensitive to the client's mood, level of distress and needs on presenting for the first time. Here we encounter a paradox. Trainees are now generally taught the necessity for good contracting, yet they are acutely aware of wanting to be attuned to and remain within the client's frame of reference. A bombardment of information about the nature of your counselling service – your theoretical orientation, specialisms, training, policies, supervision, tape-recording, preferences for a few sample sessions and reviews, and so on – is not likely to impress the client (unless she or he is an especially legalistic person). It is possible to make an exhaustive list of what you might tell the client at the beginning (boundary issues, for example, can be extended almost indefinitely as a topic) but it would be absurd to try to convey all this. So decisions must be made about which items are crucial generally and which may be crucial for each client. Your particular therapeutic orientation may also affect these decisions: person-centred and psychodynamic counsellors are likely to spell out fewer items upfront than, say, cognitive-behavioural counsellors. But you cannot make these decisions unless you have previously worked through the range of contractually important items for yourself.

Sills (1997) outlines many of the issues involved in contracting, some of which are practical in nature and others therapeutic. We advise you to consult such texts and to arrive at your own preferences. There are two major considerations. First, it can certainly save time and awkwardness if you produce and send out in advance (or hand out at the first session) a leaflet explaining the details of what the counsellor and counselling service offers and what the client will be 'buying into'. Second, you need to consider what the minimal amount of information that must be imparted is. Obviously, it is important to clarify from the outset matters of confidentiality and its exceptions, time boundaries and any fees involved. This doesn't necessarily have to be in the form of a bombardment before the client even speaks! But certain information should be given by the end of the first session. Use your discretion and sensitivity to the client's moment-by-moment emotional state and needs to decide exactly when to impart or agree more minor contractual aspects.

Summary

Think through the wide range of potential contractual items and consider what is essential for you to impart and agree in the first session. Time and expand on any such items according to the client's need.

3 Consider and introduce the subject of tape-recording

We place the subject of tape-recording here because you may need to discuss it with your clients at the outset. You may or may not be familiar or comfortable with tape-recording your counselling sessions. It is an established trend in counselling and a great deal has been learned by counsellors and researchers from listening to audiotapes. We are aware, however, that many people are unhappy with the practice, claiming that it upsets clients, inhibits spontaneity and threatens confidentiality. Also, some counsellors say that their clients are unwilling to be tape-recorded.

Let's look at this closely. First, let's consider the value, if not the indispensability, of taping. You can learn a lot from listening back over the session, with an ear to your manner, timing, intentions, clarity in responding and overall effectiveness. You can learn by comparing earlier with later sessions. You can even, if you wish, give copies of tapes to your clients for them to learn from. Even more important is the use of tapes in supervision. Without tapes, all your supervisor (or supervision group) hears, however astute she is, (or they are) is your inevitably selective account of your counselling. (We are not, however, advocating that you dispense with case discussion.) Research suggests, too, that even process recordings written soon after a counselling session exhibit selective memory and are a poor second best to audiotapes. Most people who do work with tape-recording attest to its benefits.

Second, let's look at how the issue of tape-recording is presented to your client. If you are convinced that taping will be beneficial and ethically sound, you are unlikely to encounter resistance to it from your client. Frequently, counsellors who are wary of using tapes convey their unease to the client and receive in return, ambivalence or refusal from them. So our advice to you is to consider your own attitude carefully! Once convinced and ready to go, what will you say to your client? Be as honest and clear as you can.

All counsellors are required to be supervised. I have found that one of the best ways of having work supervised is by listening to tape-recordings of actual sessions. The focus in supervision is on how I work, rather than on you. Naturally, everything heard or discussed is confidential and remains between the supervisor, who is a professional colleague, and myself.

Try some variant of that, to suit your own style. Perhaps the trickiest bit comes after this. Do you say. 'Is this OK with you?' or 'How do you feel about that?' (A closed versus an open question.) You need to consider how important taping is for monitoring the quality of your work and therefore how firm or negotiable you will be. After all, most counsellors are firm about time boundaries and fees, so where do you draw the line? Note, however, that if a client is genuinely reluctant or reticent about tape-recording it is better not to press the point.

You may work in an agency with a 'no taping' policy. Such a policy may be well founded, or simply a tradition. Where it is the latter, we suggest you present the benefits of taping and negotiate for the right to do it. You may want to mention that one of the pioneers of such recordings was Carl Rogers.

Another issue you need to address is how long you will keep each tape, how you will arrange to keep it secure, and when you will erase or destroy it. Some counsellors tell their clients that tapes will be erased after they've been listened to, or after a period of six months or so. Some counsellors offer to give the tapes to the client. If you do this you may well need to stress that confidentiality applies both ways. Decide what to do on the basis of your own developmental needs and your ethical sensitivity. Some things cannot be left to chance, and protection of tapes, particularly where, for example, you may send them through the post to a supervisor, is one of these. (For reasons of geographical remoteness or where a counsellor practises a specialized form of therapy, and therefore has a specialist supervisor, supervision by post is sometimes practised.) Ensure that you have safeguards for any such transactions. It is now quite common practice to include such matters in a written contract that explains all relevant details.

On the practical front, be sure to use a good quality recorder and check that batteries work and everything is switched on! There is little as frustrating as finding that a fascinating, learning-filled session has yielded a blank, fuzzy or inaudible tape. Try rehearsing the whole thing before actually doing it. Having said all this, we assure you that once you get into the habit of recording your work in this way, it will become as normal and non-intrusive as opening the door for your clients, telling them their time is up, invoicing them, or helping them to monitor their daily anxieties!

Summary

Consider the value of tape-recording your work, and any reservations you may have about it. Tapes offer you a wealth of material for supervision. Explain their use to clients: reassure clients about confidentiality: seek clients' permission to record. Check the practicalities of taping.

4 Discover why the client is seeking counselling *now*

Counsellors are trained not to ask 'why' questions, of course, but one such question that inevitably arises when the client presents for counselling is 'why now?' Budman and Gurman (1988) make this a central consideration in their brief therapy model, and it is evident in many other approaches. But why ask it? We believe that the client's choice of when to seek counselling probably indicates something important: and that if you can understand why she has chosen this particular time you may be in a good position to understand and exploit her motivation.

Budman and Gurman believe that timing is highly significant. They present an I-D-E schema, which stands for interpersonal, developmental and existential issues. What is happening in the person's life right now, in her relationships? How old is the client? Has she just had a birthday – for example, has she turned 40 and is she wondering where her life has gone? Is it an anniversary of someone's death? What compels her to think about the meaning of her life now? What accidents or incidents may there have been in her life recently? People do not simply find themselves in counselling by chance. Often there is a crisis, precipitating a sudden inability to cope or a sudden need to reflect on life events. Sometimes it seems as if there is no obvious crisis at all. When asked what's brought them to counselling some clients claim they 'just don't know' or 'the doctor sent me'. But later they may refer to a divorce, death or other crisis. So don't take your clients' 'I don't know' at face value – listen carefully for the precipitating factors.

As Budman and Gurman point out, many clients claim that they've 'always' been this way (depressed, lethargic, aimless). Sometimes a little probing and focusing reveals, however, that they have enjoyed quite different moods and experiences at other times, and that the present state can be identified as specific in time. This 'searching for exceptions' is common practice in cognitive and solution focused therapies. Having in mind the question 'why now?' helps you to press for such specifics. Often people cope fairly well with adversity until 'the straw that breaks the camel's back' arrives on the scene. When you maintain a focal perspective (identifying and working on the client's specific concerns), you are looking for the straws. What is it that makes this client think she can't cope? This isn't to say that everything was fine before the crisis, but that there is a crisis, and by identifying it you may have access to a mine of useful information.

Part of the 'why now?' is the client's declaration of discomfort, pain and need for change. What has happened? Have family dynamics changed? Is money a problem? Is the client no longer able to pretend to herself that she's going to become a concert pianist or run a marathon? There is richness in the timing of seeking counselling, but its reasons are not always obvious. Some people put up with terrible suffering for a long time. Colin knew a woman who was sexually abused for years as a girl, which led to self-mutilation, shoplifting, alcohol and drug abuse. But she finally started to tell her story: she could bear it no longer. Exactly why this was the time that she chose, it's hard to say, but if she had been regarded as 'just another shoplifter' or 'just another addict' the emergence of her terrible story might have been delayed. The originator of the concept of I-Thou encounter, Martin Buber (1947), tells the story of how he once had a casual conversation with a man who soon afterwards killed himself. This shocked Buber into realizing that when people sought him out for 'casual' conversations, their motives and timing were usually far from casual.

One way to look at this question is 'why not before?' If your client's story is true, that everything has always been awful, then why has she not sought counselling earlier? It may be because she had become habituated to the bleakness of her life, but even so, why should she bother to try to change it? Amato and Bradshaw's (1985) study of delayed helpseeking lists reasons for delay, which range from the client thinking he could solve his problem himself to lack of money.

You may also come across the client who has had counselling before (once, twice, or countless times). In this case, to ask the question 'why now?' carries a different meaning. 'If you have had counselling often and over a long time span, then what might counselling do for you now that it hasn't done before?' would be a good question to ask, or to bear in mind. Exactly how you put these questions depends on your style and on the context. It is not always wrong to ask 'why?' but there are ways of investigating that do not make the client feel fired at. 'I'm really interested to know what got you to come for counselling at this point in your life' conveys warm interest, for example. By taking seriously your clients' present predicament and present needs, you are respecting their frame of reference and using the time economically. You may reflect on all such developmental needs by reading Sugarman (2004), who also poses challenging questions to the counsellor about their own developmental transitions.

Summary

Consider, and find ways of asking, why your clients have come for counselling at this particular time in their life. What is the significance of it? What does it tell you about their motivation and about the best way to help them?

5 Find out what the referral agent said

By a referral agent we mean anyone who has been involved in advising the client to see you or who has actually made initial contact with you in person, by telephone or letter. Often this will be a doctor, psychiatrist or other medical or helping professional, but equally it may be a friend of the client, a family member, a boss or colleague. You will want to know what the referral agent said to the client to be clear about what preconceptions the client is bringing to counselling. These may be accurate and helpful, but they may be inaccurate and could get the counselling process off to a bad start if they are unknown..

For example, the client may have been told that you work with particular problems (for example, sexual dysfunctions) and you may not. The client may have wrong information about who you are. Windy has been telephoned by women who thought he was Wendy, for example, and who needed to be asked, on discovering the error, if they were willing to see a man or not! A friend of the client may have recommended that she sees you because he saw you and benefited enormously. However, that does not necessarily mean that you are the best person for your ex-client's friend. Indeed, some psychoanalysts refuse to take any such referrals. Sometimes people are given the wrong information completely – for example, that they will be attending group therapy – and may arrive in a state of high anxiety. Let's now look at the kinds of expectations clients may arrive with, based on what they've been told.

What did the referral agent say about why he thought the client needed counselling? Some clients may arrive with the idea that there is something dreadfully wrong with them, based on someone else's exaggerated view. Some clients come to counselling only because they've been told they ought to – some GPs, for example, well meaningly adopt this practice – and this is usually not the best way to begin. In this case you will need to elicit whether, in spite of this, clients want to make a genuine commitment of their own. A referring agent may have told clients exactly what they need from counselling (for example, 'to boost your self-esteem' or 'to learn to relax'). The client, if compliant, may try to go along with this. You, as the counsellor, are at risk of mistaking the referral agent's views for your client's views if you don't elicit the client's own, live agenda. It is worth saying here that some referral agents, particularly established helping professionals, may prescribe the treatment your client is to receive on your behalf. Ironically, this might be a negative spinoff of evidence-based practice guidelines: professionals come to think they always know best because they read the latest guidelines. You may not agree with their assessment; you may not want to be pre-empted and you may not even be equipped to offer certain interventions. Sometimes, therefore, you may need to address, in a tactful or an assertive manner, these issues with other concerned professionals. But the most important question here is why the client has come. In her own mind, why is she here?

What did the referral agent say about counselling? Here we are asking what ideas the referral agent has implanted. Are they accurate or not? Are they biased? Are they exaggerated? Are they overprescriptive? In other words, what expectations has the client brought to counselling that have been engendered by someone else? It can be a very useful way of opening up a discussion to ask this question and to lead into what the client thinks counselling is or can be. It is then also an opportunity for you to correct any misperceptions.

What did the referral agent say about you, the counsellor? Have you been presented as a medical expert, a friendly soul, a cheap psychotherapist, an advice giver, or as someone who never gives advice? Discussing these points allows misunderstandings and fantasies to be aired and, hopefully, allows the client to engage more directly with you, thus establishing the beginnings of therapeutic work. You may need to correct erroneous ideas about who you are and what you can offer. This might also apply, by the way, to written information about you or about counselling methods that the client has read and that may be inaccurate, partial or out of date.

Your client may have been told by a friend, say, that she has a serious problem in relating to men. She may have been shocked and impressed and started to have all sorts of fantasies about the meaning of this. Her friend may exert a lot of influence over her. She may come into counselling with this agenda. Now, her friend may have accurately pinpointed a problem, but it may not be the problem that the client is primarily concerned with, or it may be just one of many ways in which an underlying problem manifests itself. It can help to ask the client how she reacted to her friend's assessment of her concerns. Does she agree? What did the friend mean by it? Can she recall how she reacted at the time? And what has she made of it since? Has she been brooding on it? What thoughts lead from it? Getting back to the point at which she began considering coming for counselling is a valuable exercise because it enables the client's various motivations to be teased out. It is an important shift for people to make between entertaining the vague idea of counselling and actually seeking it. Another vital point is that people often feel motivated to consider making changes, yet realize that this feels threatening to them (see Section 10 regarding client fears). So it can be enormously important to examine how they felt on first entertaining the idea of seeking counselling and how they feel now.

Summary

Ask clients who has encouraged them to come for counselling, and what advice or impressions they have been given. Allow any misconceptions and inaccurate information to be aired and corrected if necessary. Elicit the client's own perceived needs.

6 Consider the scope of assessment and your own views on it

The broadly humanistic base of counselling and much of its anti-medical tradition has, we believe, led many counsellors to regard the practice of assessment with suspicion, as if it is synonymous with everything negative about evaluation, diagnosis, labelling and depersonalizing. Contrary to this view, we suggest it is an integral part of the counselling process and of counsellors' growing maturity as practitioners. One of the problems of our field is that rigid adherence to one's original training orientation can sometimes overshadow clients' needs. While this problem waits to be addressed at a macro-level, we suggest that you consider what your own stance is to be *vis à vis* the setting in which you work and the clients you tend to see. You may or may not conduct an initial assessment of your clients but you always have a responsibility to make a conscious decision as to whether counselling, and counselling with you, is the best option for each client. This responsibility overrides managerial decisions and your own need for business or for accumulating hours toward accreditation.

In certain therapeutic approaches the view is adopted that each client is unique, an irreducible whole and an expert on her or his own needs and aims, therefore an assessment made from an external, clinical point of view, is counterproductive. This may be true, or true of some clients. But the point has been made that if clients are such experts, how come they got themselves into difficulties and impasses and turn towards counsellors for help? At the very least, a *collaborative assessment* seems indicated here (Neimeyer, 1993). It is especially true of time-limited counselling that great lengths of time cannot be expended on misunderstandings about the client's concerns and needs or on waiting for the client to articulate these clearly. It is also clear from many consumer views that clients often want to know their counsellors' views and gain from their knowledge (Feltham and Lambert, 2006). In some approaches the view is taken that if the client is sufficiently psychologically minded and well motivated and there is a good match or rapport between counsellor and client, then counselling can proceed. In yet others, the practitioner may assess according to personality theories, modalities and so on. Again, we simply ask you to consider these critically. They don't automatically add up to an optimal assessment followed by optimal therapy. Quite often, the mere fact that the (proposed) client has an appointment, or has been referred by a GP, seems to imply that counselling is the natural way forward. Below, we suggest some of the questions you might ask yourself, perhaps along with your client if appropriate, before becoming immersed in counselling:

- What are the clients' own assessments of their own situation? Do they seem to have a realistic grasp of their situation, their personality, how they come across to others? How clear or 'befuddled' are they? To what extent are they coming from an adult ego state in a working alliance with you as opposed to a confused and needy state?
- To what extent is it clear that counselling has something to offer this person that will make a significant difference? In other words, is something being presented that is within the typical 'zone' of counselling rather than economic, political or philosophical in nature on the one hand or severely pathological on the other. Counselling may sometimes be superfluous, inappropriate or inadequate.
- Do you need to conduct a formal assessment with an hour or longer devoted to it, using paper or questionnaires, or is it a better fit with your approach, your agency and clientele that you assess informally? Do you conduct a collaborative assessment, sharing all your thinking openly with the client, or a covert assessment? Is it written down or noted mentally?
- Is the client's presenting state actually troublesome or fleeting and likely to pass of its own accord? A notorious television programme of the 1990s exposed, by use of hidden cameras, counsellors faced by a person seeking counselling whose 'problem' was that their girlfriend had gone on holiday for a week and they felt sad and lonely. This normal feeling was taken by some counsellors as an automatic sign of a need for in-depth therapy and had the effect of making counsellors appear foolish or greedy to the viewing public.
- Might the client's problems be best addressed by some down-to-earth, commonsense advice? For example, basic information on healthy dietary habits, exercise, hygiene, alcohol control, statutory benefits and social skills is what certain people need instead of, before or alongside counselling.
- Are there any indications of problems that may be outside the counsellor's domain of competency? Those with speech and communication difficulties, including autism and Asperger syndrome, are usually best helped by speech and communication therapists, for example. Those suffering from the effects of head injuries are probably best helped by clinical psychologists with special knowledge of that field. Some conditions are best addressed by medication.
- What risks might the client face if proceeding with counselling? For example, are self-harming behaviours or suicidal intention evident? Might the client endanger others (including you) or be in danger from others? Is there a risk that your way of working might exacerbate the client's condition? Are any physical risks present? What steps might be necessary to address any risks noted? Which other professionals are involved?
- Does the person have deep-seated, severe and/or multiple problems? This need not rule out counselling but it does require very careful thought. Such clients may need experienced practitioners with unbroken time and specialist skills available to them.
- Are you aware of the latest evidence-based clinical guidelines and what they may mean for each of your clients? One of the most powerful tests of your professionalism is your readiness to consult these and weigh up their

recommendations even if you come to disagree with them. Alternatively, you may judiciously integrate techniques from another approach into your work where necessary.

- On the basis of whatever assessment methods you use, what tentative hypotheses do you come up with? This includes not only a grasp of the client's problems, concerns and needs but a sense of all the above points and your own honest assessment of your readiness to address these competently.

Of course, one of the difficulties here is that you do not always know what you do not know; you may not recognize certain syndromes or specialized clinical problems. All health professionals have areas of ignorance – and this is the best reason for supervision. Even when you recognize something that you have not worked with before, you may reason that you may as well have a go – you need to expand your competency by taking on a challenge, there is a long waiting list to see a specialist, and so on. In all these cases, be sure to discuss this in supervision. The worst possible scenario is one in which counsellors foolhardily take on a client, perhaps passionately believing that they can understand them where others have not, and then find themselves far out of their depth. But we have also worked with anxious supervisees whose low self-esteem leads them to assess too many clients as having severe clinical problems and being in need of specialist interventions that they cannot provide. This extreme is also to be avoided!

Let's not forget that collaborative assessment is probably best and even when you may have much more experience of a wide range of problems than the client, you can still seek their comments on any hypotheses you are formulating. Where multiple problems or difficulties in articulating exactly what the problem is are concerned, try asking clients to come up with one word or sentence to encapsulate it. Develop your own assessment practice according to your stage of development, your agency setting and client base. If you recognize that you have a strongly anti-assessment stance, examine the reasons for this and question its wisdom; reflect on this in supervision and link it with your continuing professional development needs. See Feltham (2006), Nelson (2002) and Palmer and McMahon (1997).

Summary

Think carefully about what is involved in assessment and what your own attitude to it is. Consider the range of presenting issues that may or may not benefit from counselling and from what you have to offer. Use supervision accordingly.

7 Assess whether brief counselling is the most appropriate form of help

As we have noted in our introduction, most counselling in fact turns out to be relatively brief. You will eventually make your own decisions about how you prefer to work and you may come to discourage very short counselling contracts. Or you may do mostly long-term work, interspersed with briefer contracts. However, when confronted with a new client you need to assess in some way whether brief counselling is appropriate or not. Does the client have obvious focused concerns, or does the client have broad issues that can readily be broken down into specific areas of concern? Where clients have a broad 'personal growth' agenda, this can be addressed by brief counselling provided that they are willing and able to focus on specific concerns or aspirations within that agenda.

How do you help your client to focus in this way? When a client says, 'I don't know. I just feel generally unfulfilled', you need to be able to help her to make this concrete. Asking 'can you tell me one or two of the ways in which you feel unfulfilled?' or 'I'd like you to tell me about a recent, specific example of this feeling' helps to make things workable. Arnold Lazarus, the multimodal therapist, sometimes asks clients to try putting their concerns into one word or one sentence. At this early stage of counselling, however, we are looking at how you assess the appropriateness of brief work. In this example, if it seemed clear that your client could not answer in a focused way, then another form of help may be indicated. You may decide to work in a longer term, more exploratory way with her, or to refer her on. See Elton Wilson (1996) and Shipton and Smith (1998) for further views on how to judge the appropriateness of short-term and long-term counselling.

Opinions differ on how close a match is possible between client presenting condition and optimal length of therapeutic time to be offered. Figure 1, based on an American survey of 234 therapists' expectations of 'how long it takes', by Lowry and Ross (1997) gives one useful view. Even some British sources have adjusted their expectations upwards from a slightly unrealistic six towards 12 or 16 sessions for many fairly 'simple' presenting complaints. In general, the more complex, chronic and psychiatrically oriented conditions are likely to require between a year and two years rather than a few weeks. Remember, too, that research into the so-called 'dose-effect curve' suggests there are very real diminishing returns as the period of counselling or therapy grows longer: about 62 per cent of clients are effectively helped within the first 13 sessions and a minority need relatively long-term work (Howard et al., 1986).

Another good indicator of whether a client will benefit from this kind of brief model is the nature of his pre-therapy relations. Has he had some good relationships with significant others? Has he spent a lot of time living alone? Has he had a very disrupted history (for example, being taken into care as a child, being hospitalized, divorced, isolated, dislocated from his country of origin)? Let us make it clear that these considerations are not intended as labelling exercises. What we want to convey is that the client's history of relating to other people is probably going to indicate the level of difficulty he

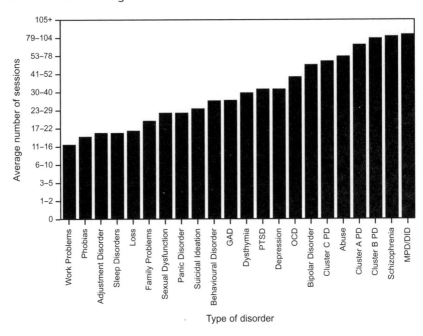

Figure 1. Mean number of expected psychotherapy sessions by disorder. With kind permission from Dr Jenny Lowry.

will have in relating to you. If he has had good relationships, then he has an internalized experience of a joint alliance, and what he needs to have with you is just such a working alliance. So the chances are that if he says he is unable to get on with people, lives alone and rarely socializes, then you will probably have some difficulty in establishing a good working relationship within the limits of brief counselling. At the very least, you can expect that such a case will be a long-term prospect, and it may contain a lot of challenges. You have to decide whether you want to offer the time and whether you have the expertise. Strupp (1980) presents an interesting comparative study of such cases and their outcomes.

A further, and crucial, indicator of how successful brief counselling may be is the stage of change clients have reached. Here we refer to the work of Prochaska and DiClemente (1984), which sets out the pre-contemplative, contemplative, action, maintenance and relapse model of stages of change (see Section 21). For our purposes here, pre-contemplation refers to that phase in which people do not consider they have a problem, or may dimly and distantly feel some discomfort but have no specific idea or intention regarding making changes. They may have been 'sent' for counselling. Contemplation is the phase in which a problem or problems are in conscious awareness. Not only do people realize that there is something uncomfortable and pressing but they are considering doing something about it. This is of course the stage in which people frequently enter counselling. It is important to note that this may be a tentative time. People may slip back into the pre-contemplative stage. They may certainly take their time to be fully committed to change. But evidence of a contemplative level of motivation is crucial when considering whether a client will benefit from brief counselling. You could well be wasting your client's and your own time if you try to persist with counselling when he is clearly not ready.

In looking at these issues you will be getting some idea of your client's level of motivation. Is he here because he wants to be? Is this time in his life significant enough to push him into counselling? And does he have an understanding that he must be an active partner in the process, rather than a passive consumer? Can you see evidence that he will be able to stay the course? If the answers are predominantly 'yes' then you can feel reasonably confident in moving ahead with brief counselling. If the answers are negative then you may need to take more time to help the client towards readiness and commitment, or alternatively consider referral to other resources.

Your clients' future goals are tied in with the ability to specify what their current problems are. Elicit at this stage how your client envisages change. Unless there is some idea of where she wants to aim there is a risk that the counselling process may become bogged down in work that is interesting but not progressive. Having goals (which can, of course, be modified) helps to serve as a bridge between past and future, between problems and solutions, and between counselling and self-realization. Unfortunately, some counsellors and clients forget at times that counselling itself is not the goal, but that change and autonomy for the client in her everyday life is what counselling is for. Does your client have goals, and can she realistically head towards, modify and attain her goals? Remind yourself (later in the process) of why the client entered counselling in the first place, if you are tempted to protract counselling or if you and your client run into impasses.

Lastly, as an indicator of the appropriateness of brief counselling, consider the everyday networks in which the client lives. Does she have a good supportive environment? Are there friends or family who will support her efforts at change and be available in times of difficulty? And conversely, are there significant others in her life who may be destructive, eroding what the counselling may be building, undermining the new energy and strength she is gaining? It is common to find that some clients are still living with or near an abusive partner or parent, for instance. In discussing such scenarios, both you and the client will be able to assess and anticipate any potential setbacks. If she has little support, or has friends who are antagonistic to her coming for counselling, she will face more obstacles. Has she the strength to deal with these? Is there some way she can find other resources for support? How can you best help her through such obstacles? Such discussions will help cement an understanding of brief counselling and its appropriateness for the client.

Summary

Consider whether brief focal counselling is something you are happy to practise. Discover whether your clients have well-defined concerns and goals. Consider what stage of change they are at – whether they have had good enough relationships previously (as a sign that they can relate to you) – and what social supports they will have during this process.

8 Refer if appropriate

If necessary, we commend the practice of referring a client on, either at the telephone stage or soon thereafter. There is a danger that some counsellors can come to think of themselves as God's gift to clients and therefore arrogantly dismiss the idea of referral; or have economic reasons for not referring clients on (they need the business); or a rationale that their way of working prohibits prejudging clients and the seriousness of their difficulties (and that they must therefore take on everyone for counselling). Let's remember that clients are consumers who have a right to the best possible service and also that they are often distressed, which means that the sooner they receive the right help (rather than hit-or-miss treatment) the better. You may well be the best choice of counsellor for many or most of those people who come to you, or you may be as good as many other counsellors (or you may not be!). In reality, many counselling agencies can offer to clients no choice of counsellor. Your client may live in an area where there are no other counsellors, in which case the idea of referral may be irrelevant. But do give proper thought to your ability to provide each client with what he or she needs.

Do not succumb to the idea that you are a failure as a counsellor if you feel a need to refer. You may well not have the experience to deal with particular clients and you will be acting responsibly if you refer someone on if you are in doubt. Arnold Lazarus considers referral to be a crucial skill in itself (or set of skills – involving assessment, knowledge of different conditions, evidence-based practice guidelines, local knowledge). Referring on implies, of course, familiarity with other counsellors and their work, and with other local services. We certainly advocate that you familiarize yourself with colleagues locally, (for example by joining the British Association for Counselling and Psychotherapy (BACP) and other organizations, and their local branches). It is a good idea to know something about local (or even national) agencies offering specialized services. There are specialist agencies working in the areas of mental health, marital distress, eating disorders, sexual abuse, and many others. If you can't help particular individuals, try to refer them on, or at the very least direct them to the reference section of the local library, or give them the phone number of BACP, Relate, Cruse, or whatever is appropriate.

There may be various reasons for referring on. It may emerge that someone's problem would be better addressed through couple counselling or in group therapy or the client may want and benefit from long-term psychotherapy. It may become very clear that the client wants a particular kind of therapy. You may think of a colleague whose experience and/or orientation closely matches the needs of this client. You may feel that a counsellor of the opposite sex, or someone older, or someone who can speak another language may be more appropriate for the client than you are. For example, your client may have clear signs of an obsessive-compulsive disorder, and you realize that he'll be better off getting some medication and behaviour therapy than psychodynamic counselling from you. A woman client may tell you that she is being beaten by her husband and you may suggest she seeks a refuge. Since some people perceive counselling as a kind of befriending; you may have to refer this kind of person on to a befriending scheme. Some people, let's say with agonizing headaches, may be afraid of doctors and believe that counselling is what they need. You may have to encourage them gently to see a doctor (perhaps helping them to explore their fears but without trying to substitute for medical attention). Or a client may not be able to afford your services for very long and you may not offer a free counselling service.

All of the above not only implies familiarity with other services but also implies a readiness to act in the interests of the client. It is unprofessional to ignore such issues. Besides that, we believe you will work more effectively and more happily if you learn to identify people with whom you work well, and learn which people are better referred on. Some counsellors no doubt worry that some clients will feel rejected if they are advised to go elsewhere. Look at it, rather, as being in the client's interests that she gets the best service. It may well be you, but if it isn't don't hesitate to let her know. ('I appreciate how you feel about these problems', you might say, 'and I might be able to help somewhat, but I happen to know someone who has particular experience in this area, and I think you would find that she is best placed to help you.') Also remember that while you refer on to colleagues, they may well refer people on to you, and this is a persuasive reason for knowing your local colleagues and their ways of working.

A more difficult area, perhaps, is when your client does indeed need counselling, and perhaps even the kind of counselling that you offer, but for some reason you realize that you are not going to get on. In theory all counsellors treat the first session as an opportunity to decide whether they can work together with new clients, but in practice it is probably rare that any counsellor or client would say 'no, I don't like you', or 'I'm sorry, but you remind me too much of my mother' or even 'I can't relate to someone who is sexist, or who has an obvious public school background'. Sometimes such interpersonal obstacles can be explored and used to good effect in subsequent counselling. There are research findings suggesting that a good fit between client and counsellor is optimal for a good outcome, so if you notice doubts on your part or your client's part relating to these sorts of issues, or even more subtle personality factors, raise them sensitively for discussion.

Obviously if you are just beginning to counsel it will often be hard to know if you are right for each client, and if you are inclined towards self-doubt you may want to refer every client on to a more experienced counsellor! This is not the message we want to give here. We simply suggest that you don't feel obliged to take on everyone, that you bear referral in mind, and that you prepare yourself by becoming acquainted with colleagues and other services. See Leigh (1998) for further examples.

Summary

Don't automatically take on everyone for counselling who makes an enquiry. Consider the kind of help most appropriate for each client and whether you can offer it. Assess how good the fit is between you and the client. Familiarize yourself with other colleagues and services. Don't interpret the need to refer on as a failure on your part.

9 Consider and spell out the limits of confidentiality

We consider it essential that clients are made fully aware of the nature and limits of confidentiality at the outset of counselling. Some counsellors may not give much explanation of confidentiality or other practicalities and boundaries. We are in favour of explicit discussion of certain matters and confidentiality is one of the most important of these (Bond and Sandhu, 2005).

Confidentiality needs to be clear to you, the counsellor, from the very beginning. Suppose, for example, that before you've even seen your client for the first time, his mother telephones you and wants to talk about him. You must make it clear that you will not discuss her son with her because he is your client and your work with him is confidential. Or suppose that you are seeing two people who know each other, each for individual counselling. Your contract is with each one, and confidentiality should remain with each one. You may be given information by one about the other, which you may find taxing to 'put aside', but you are obliged not to share it. (It should be noted that some counsellors would not see both people under such circumstances, but you must decide where you stand on this.)

Is it enough to say 'counselling is confidential'? We think not, because it says very little and is usually not entirely true. What is usually meant is that counselling is confidential within certain limits. These are as follows. All counsellors must be supervised, so they must discuss their work with supervisors, and therefore clients will be discussed. Some people prefer to talk about their clients anonymously in supervision, or to refer to them by initials or some other disguise. This is up to you. What is important is that you let your clients know that this is the case. They should, however, be reassured that all discussion remains confidential at that level and is for the purpose of professional enhancement only. Related to supervision is the expectation that you sometimes submit written reports on a client. In this case, it is best to discuss it openly with the client and ask if there is anything they would prefer you not to include.

An instance in which confidentiality may be tested is where you as the counsellor have grounds for believing that your client is a danger to himself or others. Put this straightforwardly. Windy says to his clients, 'If in my judgement you became a risk to yourself or to others and you didn't realize it, I would need to confer with other professionals. Is this acceptable to you?' We recommend some variant of this statement in the interests of clarity and honesty. Some counsellors, in fact, attempt to guarantee total confidentiality, including immunity from this kind of instance. We advise you to consult BACP's (2002) *Ethical Framework for Good Practice in Counselling and Psychotherapy* and Bond (2000) to help yourself decide where the line is drawn. Consider your own position. How will you deal with it in those probably very rare instances when it occurs? For example, if your client admits to having recently sexually abused a child it is appropriate to confront him and ask him either to take appropriate action himself, or to give you permission to do so on his behalf. But it is advisable to have forewarned him of the possibility of this latter eventuality. See Bond (2000) for further clarification.

Now, this may seem like a lot to get across without alarming your clients. We don't suggest you read them the Riot Act, as it were, either at the beginning of counselling or later. Rather, find your own way of putting it, and present it sensitively. If the client is in distress and needs to talk, you will not choose this moment to go over this but it is best to make it clear at a very early stage. Some agencies have produced quite comprehensive leaflets that explain confidentiality among other matters and that thereby reduce the pressure on the counsellor to explain in great detail. You cannot necessarily assume that clients know exactly what confidentiality means and where it ends. It can be very containing to be told clearly what the ground rules are. It gives clients the opportunity to decide, if there is anything extremely delicate or bordering on violence or criminality, whether counselling is the right place for them to bring their problems.

Summary

Introduce the subject of confidentiality at the very outset of counselling. Talk explicitly, clearly and honestly about the limits of confidentiality. Present the subject sensitively but be prepared to confront the client and take appropriate action if necessary.

---

10 Explore the client's fears about counselling

In discussing confidentiality we have touched on one of the fears that clients may well have about counselling. But there are others. Several research studies have revealed a number of common fears:

- Is counselling what I need?
- Will I be treated as a 'case'?
- Will I be taken seriously?

- Will the counsellor share my values?
- Will the counsellor think me a bad person?
- Will the counsellor think I'm more disturbed than I am?
- Will the counsellor discover things I don't want him/her to?
- Will the counsellor be competent?
- Will I be pressurized into doing things I don't want to?
- Will my friends think I'm crazy?
- Will I find out things I don't want to know?
- Will I lose control of myself?

(These items are taken from Pipes et al., 1985. See also Feltham and Lambert, 2006)

It is very evident that clients fantasize about what their counselling and counsellor will be like, what the setting will be like, and how they (the clients) will handle, or fail to handle, their anxiety. Anxieties are sometimes elicited by certain settings (such as psychiatric hospitals) or by certain professionals and their status and power. A common element throughout, however, is vulnerability. The client is distressed or confused and is about to acknowledge this to a stranger. He is hopeful of a solution and is putting himself into a stranger's hands. He probably does not know the ropes, although he will probably imagine various things about counselling based on images received through the media or stories heard from friends, or from books.

It is clear from the list above that people do not want to feel dehumanized or stigmatized. They feel that they are putting themselves on the line, baring their emotions, and in order to do that there is a need to feel some assurance that the counsellor is competent and has integrity. Perhaps people sense that the counselling situation is one in which honesty and emotional freedom is respected and even expected, but on first going into the situation they cannot know what will come up, what surprises may emerge, and how they will be affected. In this sense, then, it can look, and feel, very frightening.

You may remember from your own first experiences as a client how frightening it can all be, but because you may work with raw feelings and intimate stories day after day, you may forget some of the strangeness and vulnerability involved for the client. So, in being aware that people do bring these fears, and often other, more personal, idiosyncratic fears, how will you deal with them? Obviously time needs to be allowed for the expression of these fears, but will you just leave it to the client to come out with them, or elicit anxieties by questioning? We are in favour of putting it to clients that they may well feel a little unsure and may have some question they want to ask of us. Anything that conveys the idea that we are listening, interested, understanding and non-judgemental will be helpful for the client. Sometimes a statement to the effect that counselling can be a daunting experience, including reference to the kinds of common fears listed above, can relieve a client of the fantasy that he is the craziest and most undeserving person in the world. You need to find a way of putting this that does not ignore or minimize the possible enormity of his fears. Clients' recurrent questions about the normality of certain symptoms may indicate that there is a particular severity of problems. But remember that a certain level of anxiety often promotes therapeutic movement in counselling. So we are not advocating a pacifying exercise but a sensitive attunement to the individual, and readiness to explore his particular fears.

These fears have been found to be commonly experienced among clients, but identifying which fears your client has and what exactly they mean to him is likely to throw up rich material for your work together. It can form the basis for future work on irrational beliefs, for example. Or it can help to strengthen the trust between you, which can then be generalized into other everyday situations.

Summary

Recognize that clients commonly enter counselling with fantasies and fears. Encourage them to air these and if necessary offer examples of common fears. Be alert to acute fears and anxieties. Use what is discussed to focus on concerns.

---

11 Find out the client's idea of how long counselling will last

Some clients are totally new to counselling and their ideas of how often they will be coming and for how long may not accord with your own. In some cases people will expect counselling to compare with what they get from their GP, which is to say, perhaps, ten minutes today, with perhaps a follow-up two weeks later. Others may have seen television dramas showing people lying on couches day after day, and may expect to come and see you for some years. Some people certainly expect to see you for only one or two sessions. If you are working with the kind of brief model we are talking about here, then there could well be a mismatch between your idea and your client's. We would advise that this issue be aired and resolved.

You might ask 'have you thought about how long you might come for counselling?' This gives you the opportunity to hear some of the clients' perceptions of counselling and perhaps to gauge how difficult they think their problems are, but it also allows for any misconceptions to surface and be resolved. For example, it may be that you will need to refer on if the client wants to come three times a week for some years. Or you may decide that you will see them for a longer period after all. Or if they have in mind only a few visits, you might want to suggest that it would be fairer to them if they gave it more time. It can help to say that often a minimum of four or six sessions is advisable in order to assess matters or to let the counselling process begin to take effect, and that many people undertake counselling for a period of several months. (See section 89 in this book on different kinds of endings.) You might arrange a specific contract for a series of sessions followed by a review. Whatever you decide, it will unfold better by opening a discussion on expectations. It is also fair to the client when you give some picture of what may lay ahead in terms of time and financial commitment. Elton Wilson

(1996) gives some useful examples of different lengths of therapeutic contract.

Summary

Help your clients to talk about their impressions of how long counselling will take. Look out for any discrepancy between the client's and your own views on length of counselling. Address any practical implications.

12 Value the occasional one-off session

It is sometimes the case that a client will attend only once. It is commonly assumed that this represents a 'drop-out', a discontented, uncommitted or fearful client. But as Talmon (1990) has shown, many clients feel positively helped by just one session and do not necessarily report this to their counsellor. The level of help may sometimes be quite dramatic (see Feltham, 1997: 41–3 and 87–8), depending on the client's previous circumstances, the timeliness of receiving counselling and the intervention offered. A certain amount of evidence exists, for example, in support of behaviour therapy and neurolinguistic programming phobia cures in one session, and eye movement desensitization and reprocessing (EMDR) cures for post-traumatic stress disorder in one session. It is well know that a fair number of people who have booked a counselling appointment recover from their crisis before even attending, and some of these consequently cancel or fail to turn up. But some attend and are ready to use just one session optimally. Often this is for the purposes of making a major life decision, such as anything relating to abortion, critical health issues, marriage and job changes. Here, we are talking about single-session counselling by default, when neither the counsellor nor the client has predicted it. Consider, too, the options of single-session counselling by design (the client may intimate that one visit could be enough); single-session counselling whose very intensity and roundedness makes itself clear during the actual session; and single-session counselling that is enough for now but where the client may seek further counselling next year or at some further point in the future (Cummings and Sayama, 1995).

Talmon (1990) suggests that creating expectancy is crucial in making single-session therapy work effectively. The main strategies are: fostering readiness to change, telling people about the benefits of a single session, focusing on pivotal chords, concentrating on client strengths, practising solutions in-session, allowing for last minute issues and giving final feedback. Pivotal chords are outstanding refrains that one can pick out from the client's presentation, perhaps using a 'captivating metaphor' to feed it back to the client and carrying it through the session. In many ways, Talmon's methods resemble those of solution-focused therapy, although his own approach is heavily existential. Bear in mind that Talmon may extend the session to an hour-and-a-half if that is useful (either having prearranged it or if it is fortuitously possible at the time). He also talks about leaving an open door and offering a follow-up session later. So, you may be creative in your use of time, remembering, however, to be contractually and ethically clear about this. Or you may have an occasional session that is characterized by emotional intensity and *kairos* (meaning that the time is right for the client to have major insights or make major decisions).

The astute reader will have noticed that certain risks are involved. How can you know that what looks like authentic intensity and readiness on the client's part is really that, and not a transient high; and may not clients then need further help but be wary of asking for it because you seemed so pleased for them in their sudden success? These are real possibilities and you should be aware of such traps. Also, how can we know who is suitable for single-session counselling? Talmon has some useful suggestions for this last question:

1. Patients who come to solve a specific problem.
2. The 'worried well' who come for a mental health check-up essentially to ask whether they (or their significant others) are 'normal.'
3. Patients seen with significant others or family members who can serve as natural supports and 'cotherapists.'
4. Patients who can identify (perhaps with the therapist's assistance) helpful solutions, past successes, and exceptions to the problem that occurred prior to seeking therapy.
5. Patients who have a particularly 'stuck' feeling (anger, guilt, grief, and so on) toward past events and are fed up with it.
6. Patients who come for evaluation and need referral for medication, medical exams, or other nonpsychotherapy services (legal, vocational, financial, religious, or similar counselling).
7. Patients faced with a truly unsolvable problem. Acknowledging the impossibility of change and aiding patients to cease useless or compulsive attempts to solve the impossible may help them attain a measure of equanimity and acceptance by letting go of further treatment and attempts for 'cure.'
8. Patients who will be better off without any treatment.

(Talmon, 1990: 31)

Summary

Don't write off one-off sessions as inferior or unhelpful. Consider the reasons why some clients benefit from either planned or fortuitous single-session counselling and work accordingly. Look out for any obvious or subtle risks.

13 Explore the client's past history of being helped

Many clients have had help with their problems before, some from counsellors and other professionals, and others from friends and family. We believe that there are good reasons for explicitly asking about clients' previous experiences of seeking and receiving help. Your client may have had a successful or unsuccessful experience. ('Neutral' or bad experiences of help are sometimes called 'attempted solutions' or 'negative outcomes'.) Bearing in mind our suggestions about sensitively adjusting your questions to each client and the frame of mind they are in, we suggest you try to obtain the following kinds of information.

Find out whether your client has previously seen a counsellor, therapist or other helping professional. When was this? Under what circumstances? Ask these questions with natural interest, avoiding an interrogative or clinical style. As rapidly and skilfully as you can, you need to elicit the client's experience of whatever help she has had. The purpose of gathering this kind of information is to learn what to capitalize on and what to avoid. So ask the client what she found helpful and unhelpful about any previous counselling. Such a conversation might go something like this:

You: Have you had any counselling or similar help in the past?

Client: Well, I saw someone once or twice a few years ago, yes.

You: Can you tell me something about that experience, perhaps?

Client: Well, it was just that I was having a bad time then and I went to this 'drop-in' place and talked to a lady, a kind of psychologist, I think.

You: I see. I'd be interested to know how helpful that was for you – I mean, if you were having a bad time, in what way did this psychologist help?

Client: She listened to me. She was quite kind. She told me I should be more assertive.

You: And did that help?

Client: Yes and no, really. I mean, it helped in a way, to have someone interested in me, but it wasn't that easy for me. I mean, I couldn't just go out and be assertive.

You: And so, what happened? Did you stop seeing her?

Client: Yes. I meant to get in touch with her again, but I couldn't see how it would help.

What do we learn from this kind of dialogue? First, that our client has had a 'bad time' before, in life and perhaps in a helping situation too. (We can pursue this later.) Second, that she sought professional help and was offered some definite kind of help. At this stage we don't know if the 'psychologist' actually recommended that the client 'should' be more assertive or if this is what the client heard, but it still gives us some valuable information: it will be important not to come across as prescriptive. The client appreciates having interest shown in her. She is expressing a belief that assertiveness was or is difficult, but probably meaningful as an avenue for exploration. Evidently things did not work out; she was disillusioned and did not return. These pieces of data contain many warnings! However, they need not be read as facts and her feelings may have changed since that time. This kind of information is useful, but requires intelligent analysis and operationalizing. Let's look at one way it might go:

Client: I just couldn't go out and be assertive.

You: That was too much for you at that time?

Client: Yes, I was very shy. I still am. Things have improved a bit, but recently, well, I just can't face some things.

You: So there have been some changes since then, but things are not as you'd like them at the moment. I wonder – is there anything the psychologist could have done that might have helped you more in the long run?

Client: Mmm. Well, I suppose if I hadn't felt so rushed. Maybe if there had been longer to talk, to unwind...

You: Taking things at your own pace might have felt more helpful?

Client: Yes. I know I'd have to make some effort, but it takes me a while to ... to unwind, I suppose.

You: Yes, I can see how important it would be for you to relax in the beginning – have some space to ... just to talk?

Client: Yes, that's it. That's right.

Going along this path with the client helps her to disclose some very useful pieces of information. She has identified shyness as a problem, then and now. She believes her life has improved somewhat. Already we have a problem focus and a sense that she experiences some hope. We learn that something has probably happened recently to set off an old pattern of behaviour. Most usefully, we discover that she didn't want to be rushed and still doesn't. (Perhaps she wasn't assertive enough in the past to tell her psychologist this!) As we elicit all this, we are also empathizing, and in doing so we are beginning to form a therapeutic alliance. We do not wish to collude with any intention on the client's part to blame the psychologist. Rather, we wish to (1) obtain valuable information, (2) make links between previous experience of help attempts and the present, (3) demonstrate our concern for the client's welfare, (4) sensitize ourselves and the client to new hopes, and (5) tailor our counselling approach to the client's situation.

The key here is to encourage the client to spell things out. Push gently for more than vague answers. You want to know not just that a previous counselling experience was helpful or unhelpful, but how it was helpful or unhelpful, and beyond that you can ask how it could have been even more helpful. As you receive these answers you can begin to build up material for the kind of approach you will be using. If the client tells you, for example, that her previous counsellor talked about himself too much and that this was unhelpful, you will note this and watch any tendency you may have to do likewise. You can ask, in this example, what it was about the counsellor talking about himself too much that was offputting. If, on the other hand, the client reports that her previous counsellor's self-disclosures made her feel more relaxed, you may decide to take note and do likewise. This kind of data gathering helps you to formulate what has been called a kind of 'bespoke counselling', calculated to fit the client as elegantly as possible. Note, however, that if you learn that a previous 'unhelpful' counsellor offered much the same as you have to offer (and if you feel you cannot offer a significant variation on it) you may well consider making a referral.

Most of what we have said here applies equally to previous help offered by friends, partners, relatives, clergy and other people in the client's life. Whether such help has been given professionally or not, and was helpful or not (or came in shades of helpfulness and unhelpfulness) you can ask questions like these and gain valuable insights. In a pilot research project conducted by the authors, we put many such questions to a number of people, covering successful and unsuccessful experiences of counselling. We asked questions covering pre-counselling expectations, memories of first contacts with the counsellor, and many issues concerning the quality of understanding between counsellor and client. We framed the research around the idea of helpful and unhelpful aspects of counselling and psychotherapy. Everyone's experience is unique, and the good and bad vary enormously, but all those interviewed, whether they had had successful or unsuccessful experiences, appeared to learn from the exercise – about themselves, their counsellors, and about the nature of help. We also discovered much, and therefore recommend such a research attitude to counsellors (see Dryden and Feltham, 1995). You may rightly object that counselling is not research and that you have been trained not to ask too many questions! No, you are probably not a researcher as such, but you are hopefully client centred in the best sense of that term and interested in giving clients of your best. We suggest that you do, therefore, need some of this information, and that you can obtain it sensitively without the client feeling that she is being interrogated. Psychodynamic counsellors may be particularly attuned to unconscious messages to the counsellor, about a rough dentist or rude colleague, for example, which are thought to always refer to unhelpful treatment from the present counsellor. This may be the case, and certainly be alert to such unconscious messages, but we suggest you do not rely entirely on this approach for feedback. Solution-focused therapists stress the importance of 'doing something different' (from what obviously hasn't worked well) and we agree but caution against *automatically* doing something different.

Summary

Find out about your clients' previous helpful and unhelpful experiences of formal and informal counselling. Use this line of enquiry to build a picture of what the client will probably benefit and not benefit from. Do not offer more of the same bad experiences. Stress the dissimilarities between those and what you intend to offer. Note and use elements of previous helpful experiences.

14 Elicit the client's view of counselling and explain and demonstrate yours

Most people have some kind of preconception regarding counselling even if they cannot immediately articulate their views. One of the commonest ideas is that counselling is a form of advice giving. Conversely, many people have heard that 'counsellors do not tell you what to do'.

Also, people may have in mind an 'as seen on TV' version of what counselling will turn out to be. It can conjure up pictures of couches, psychological assessments, Rorschach tests, and therapists with diplomas hanging framed on their walls as they sit smoking a pipe and looking piercingly at their clients. In other words, clients can and do have all sorts of expectations derived from various sources that may or may not match the reality of seeing you.

'What do you imagine counselling is like?' you might ask. Your client will then proceed to tell you, perhaps, some of the above. 'I expect you'll ask me about my childhood', she might say, or 'you probably want me to say whatever comes into my head.' If you get these sorts of responses, what will you say? We advocate a gently probing, exploratory approach. You might say, 'if I did ask you about your childhood, would that help?' And you might press the point further and ask how it would help. Now, what you will also get as a response sometimes is the familiar 'I don't know'. The client claims not to know at all what to expect from counselling; she has no pictures in her mind at all. Try pressing a little. 'What do you think it could be like?' you might venture to ask. Another blank? Persist. Try this: 'well, some people think of counselling as a chance to reflect on their life, to take time out and get a perspective on what's happened to them. But other people have firm ideas about changing things they're very unhappy with now, so they want some action. Which of these means more to you?' By working towards a focus you are likely to elicit some specific ideas from the client.

The kinds of answers you receive may not only tell you a lot about your client but will also be instructive for how you decide to work. If your client says, 'well, I know you're not going to tell me what to do', you may ask 'and are you happy with the idea that I may not tell you what to do?' thus eliciting information about her goals in coming for counselling and preferences for counselling style. Another route forward from this kind of statement from a client is to consider explaining the way in which you work. This is, in fact, something we commend. It is helpful to think deeply about how you can describe the way you work, as a well thought-out explanation can be therapeutic for some clients. Many clients, for example, are bewildered by the principle of 'abstinence' presented by some psychodynamic counsellors. If you do work psychodynamically, we suggest that you explain this to your client, simply but clearly, or alternatively offer a pamphlet that explains it. We strongly advocate that you respect the client's right as a consumer to know what she is 'buying'. Do not present counselling as a magical mystery tour or guessing game! If your way of working involves giving plenty of space for exploration, for example, you might explain: 'Because I believe that you have your own answers within yourself, I prefer to give you time to stand back and look at yourself, and arrive at those answers in your own time; for that reason, I often leave silences.' In saying this, you let the client know that silences are therapeutically purposeful, rather than disconcerting wastes of time.

Don't be afraid to give structure to your counselling sessions from the very beginning. There is a common belief in counselling that you must follow your client's material at all times. While it is true that the client's story is important, it is also important that the client is seeking counselling (not friendship, or a passive audience) and that you are a counsellor, with some responsibilities towards your client. We believe that there is almost always a directive *element* in counselling and that it is advisable to recognize this and use it to help the client. Both clients and counsellors have preferences about the amount and kind of structuring in counselling, but it is better to face this issue squarely rather than to fudge it. Day and Sparacio (1989) outline the issues involved in structuring, including practical, ethical, methodological and philosophical considerations. When you are explaining your approach it is advisable to avoid jargon altogether. Use the language and concepts appropriate to your client. It is a highly instructive discipline to think over your work and theoretical stance in order to clarify your purposes and to test your ability to describe your service without mystification.

There is still the possibility that after discussions such as those above, your client will remain unsure about what counselling is, whether it's what she wants and exactly what her goals are. If so, then the next step is to offer to demonstrate the process. 'Are you willing to agree to meet for, say, three or four sessions so that you can get the feeling of how I work, and then you may be able to tell if it's right for you?' This demonstrates to the client that she is not making an irrevocable decision or spending a huge amount of time or money for a service she may regret paying for. She is paying as she goes and is free to decide that it is not for her. When you offer this way forward, be sure to remind the client that her goals and preferences are what are important. 'Some counsellors and clients are not the best match for each other, but by working together for a while, you'll be able to make up your mind about how well we work together', you might say. (As with the issue of tape-recording, by the way, it is important not to convey a message that is self-doubting and hence negatively self-fulfilling!) Show what you have to offer and demonstrate it well. Using brief explanations of your method of counselling, perhaps suggesting brief material to read on counselling (for example, Preston et al., 1995), and allowing the client to experience it, all add up to an inviting beginning. These kinds of invitations and pieces of education are sometimes called 'role induction'. You need to decide for yourself how valuable they are both for your client and for yourself, but we recommend that you try them out.

Summary

Discover what your clients expect counselling to be like. Consider how their expectations may colour the actual process. Be ready to give an account of how you work in clear, consumer-friendly language. Provide the beginnings of structuring. Give your client an 'introductory offer'.

15 Deal with practical agreements

We have already looked at confidentiality. There are certain other matters that have to be agreed before proceeding, and these are practical and business arrangements: scheduling, frequency of sessions, length of sessions, duration of counselling, and fees.

By scheduling, we mean the arrangements made concerning the times you will meet. Many counsellors and therapists like to offer a regular appointment time, for example, 4 p.m. every Thursday. There are theoretical grounds for setting and maintaining a time that does not vary: it is thought to symbolize containment, reliability and safety for the client. If that is how you work, that's fine. Both of us prefer some flexibility in scheduling, for different reasons. Your own working life may be varied and regular meetings may not be possible. But you also may not believe (as we do not) that regularity is sacrosanct. Many clients are quite happy to make appointments from week to week, and it can even add to the working alliance between you when you negotiate mutually convenient times. Some clients definitely prefer appointments that are not in their working time, either so that they do not have to reveal to others that they are having counselling or because they might lose money by taking time off work. We therefore advocate that you negotiate the best mutually agreed times.

Counselling is usually offered on a weekly basis. The reasons for this, apart from simple convention, probably lie in the identity of counselling as neither crisis intervention nor psychoanalysis. We believe that counselling focuses on recognizable problems, or clusters of problems or concerns, and has a problem-solving and meaning-making ethos. Brief counselling recognizes the relatively small part it plays in the client's daily and ongoing life. It is one hour out of 168 hours in a client's week, and most of her obstacles and learning opportunities are to be encountered in her everyday life in the remaining 167 hours. So counselling may be conceived as the catalytic or the oasis hour. However, there is nothing sacrosanct about this weekly hour. At times you may want to fit in an extra session, for example if there is something particularly stressful going on in the client's life. Alternatively, you may decide on fortnightly meetings, or a changing pattern of frequency as the client improves. Budman and Gurman (1988) purposefully vary the frequency in order to emphasize the need for clients to confront issues in daily living. Overall, it is probably better to adhere to weekly sessions at least until you are sure of your way of working.

We have already alluded to a weekly hour. Some counsellors work to a full hour, but many work a 50-minute hour. Nothing more is involved in this but practicalities. If you see one client after another, then you obviously need a short break between them (for a stretch, a sip of tea, a trip to the toilet, or in order to make a few notes). You may see each of your clients for a full hour and be able to schedule breaks as well. It depends entirely on where you work and what your workload is. Some counsellors see people for 45 minutes. At the other end, some humanistic therapists prefer to offer longer sessions, sometimes of two hours. This is the case, for example, with Mahrer (1989) and others who aim in their work at releasing deep feelings that may not fit neatly into 50 or 60 minutes. These are matters for you to decide, but whatever your decision it is vital that you make it clear to your clients in advance. You may want to let your client know when there are, say, five minutes left at the end of a session. Our practice is to bring the session to a natural close and to terminate promptly but politely. See Feltham (1997) and Perraton Mountford (2005) for further views on session lengths.

The question of the duration of counselling is rather more problematic. Sledge et al. (1990) compared time-limited therapy, brief therapy and long-term therapy. By time-limited therapy is meant a therapy contracted to last a prearranged, non-negotiable number of sessions (say, 12) ending on a definite date. Brief therapy may be defined in advance as lasting 'about three or four months' but no finishing date is set. Long-term or open-ended therapy is just that. (Interestingly, Sledge et al. found a drop-out rate from time-limited therapy that was half that of each of the other two.) We have outlined our views on brief counselling in our introduction. What is important here is that you decide what you are going to tell clients. You may have already explored their expectations or fantasies regarding the duration of counselling, but make these explicit agreements. There are some advantages to clear time limits. Clients can know in advance how much they will have to pay (if they are paying). They may find the notion of set limits more acceptable than an open-ended commitment. They may feel very contained by the time structure. Also, many time-limited theorists argue that the finiteness of such counselling maximizes commitment and discourages dependency on counselling (Ryle, 1990).

What shall I charge? Every counsellor working privately must ask this question – and answer it! How do you decide? Rowan's (1989) rule of thumb is 'to charge fees which are high enough so that I don't feel exploited, and low enough so that I don't feel like an exploiter'. In practice there is always a 'going rate' that you will know by asking around. The going rate varies according to the area in which you practise, your experience, any specialities, and so on. It is usual for counsellors to charge a little less when beginning, but there are no hard-and-fast rules. It may be true that if you charge too little you will arouse suspicions about your competency. Another consideration is your policy on reduced fees or a sliding scale. For political or humanitarian reasons, some counsellors offer one or two low-cost or even free places. Some offer a sliding scale (for example, £1 per hour for every £1,000 of income) and some offer two or three fee bands for the client to choose from (such as £40, £30 or £20). There are advantages and disadvantages in each of these. Colin learned from experience the pitfalls of wanting to offer the lowest possible deal. He found at one stage that he had several clients paying a minimum fee and that when he became freelance the earnings from these were not realistic. You need an overview of how much money you need to live on and what this means in terms of your realistic hourly fee. Equally, it is crucial that the client can afford counselling. Windy often says, 'I don't want to create financial problems for you at the same time as we're working to help you deal with your personal problems.' (See Clark, 2002, for further examples.)

You may well have debated with colleagues the merits of clients paying and not paying for counselling. There is a notion, with which neither of us agrees, that clients do not truly commit themselves to counselling if they receive it free. Orlinsky and Howard (1986) were unable to find any evidence to substantiate this idea. You may work in an agency that offers free counselling and which may or may not encourage donations. It probably is true that some clients feel uncomfortable 'taking without giving' but it is not true of all or even most human beings that payment increases commitment.

Summary

Make clear agreements about when you will meet, how often, and over what period. Negotiate suitable mutual arrangements. Consider, discuss and agree to fees, again taking into account your needs and your clients' ability to pay.

PART II
ASSESSING THE CLIENT'S
CONCERNS

16 Allow the client to talk

One of the features of counselling that distinguishes it from everyday conversation is the quality of listening. Many people seek counselling precisely
because there is no one in their life with whom they can speak and hope to be
attended to without constant interruptions. Most counsellors are acutely
aware of this because counsellor training courses devote a lot of time to
developing active listening skills. These skills, as you will know, include
empathic responding. You give your client plenty of space, but you also
communicate your interest and understanding. So when clients come into
counselling and begin to tell you their life story, it is entirely appropriate to
hear them out. It may be the first time they have had the opportunity to feel
really heard. In giving you their story, they are doing at least two things. One
is the giving of information – their history, circumstances and feelings about
all of it. Another is the process of unburdening, which can in itself be cathartic and therapeutic. Don't, then, underestimate the importance and power
of simply letting clients talk from their frame of reference.

Now, clients vary enormously. Some like to talk a lot and need little
prompting. Some will talk about their whole life. Others will talk specifically
about a current pressing problem. Some will talk effusively but aimlessly,
perhaps out of embarrassment or avoidance. Some clients simply have a style
of talking that is unfocused and rambling. So we do not want to give you the
idea that you must let all clients talk at great length without interruption. You
need to be sensitive to the nuances involved and you are faced with a seeming
paradox: how do you allow clients to talk, as we suggest, while at the same
time deciding when talk is cathartic and useful, or defensive, or rambling? In
the case of someone who is genuinely and acutely distressed you will
instinctively listen without a need to intervene. In the case of someone who is
trying with difficulty to disclose significant information, your ability to
respond empathically is a key skill but you will also need to initiate some
subtle structuring. Egan (2002) writes about the counsellor's role in 'helping
clients tell their stories'. He suggests that clients frequently display either
choice or change issues. People may be aware of choices in front of them but
may not feel ready to act. Others may desire changes in their lives but not
know how to begin. Egan advocates that you be flexible, collaborative and
action oriented. Facilitate your client's need to talk, but give some shape to it
too. From the very beginning you will be making an assessment (even if this is
intuitive and informal) and part of this is to ask yourself if the client's needs
are initially or primarily for catharsis, for relationship building with you, or
for gaining clarity and problem identification.

A word on assessment. If your way of working involves taking a history of
all clients, we do urge you to be ready to put this aside when it is obvious that

your client is distressed or anxious. Also, do not pepper clients with the kinds of questions we have listed here if they are distressed. Allow time. Now, it is sometimes the case that your client is prepared for change, has a specific problem in mind, and may need neither a lot of time to talk nor a lengthy assessment. In such cases you would be well advised to meet clients on their problem-solving ground. In allowing clients time to talk (say, in most of the first session or sessions) you are learning their style of presentation and dynamics, and you are formulating a working hypothesis. But you may need to do little of this if the client comes with a specific goal and wants to get on with it!

Let's return to the client who rambles. If you are afraid that to interrupt is to break the client's momentum or to impose your own frame of reference, do disabuse yourself of this notion. When a client persistently talks without any focus or affect we advocate that you do indeed interrupt. Let's look at a possible dialogue:

Client: Well I was at my mother's last Wednesday – or was it Thursday? – and I said to her (she's always doing something else when you talk to her) that I was thinking of moving away. I don't know if I want to move too far into the country or not – I might feel isolated, but I'm fed up with the city, the muggings and pollution, you know – and maybe I'll just look for somewhere a bit quieter. The thing about my mother is that she's always put me down. I know I can't blame her, that's wrong, isn't it? She says she hates the city too.

You: I just need to see if I'm understanding you. You've told me rather a lot. I gather that you're not altogether happy with your mother or with where you live. Is that right?

Client: Yes. Well, only last week a man was burgled in my street and had his whole sound system taken. It's terrible. I was just saying to my sister…

You: If I may, I'd like to try and focus on one or two things a little more closely. Can you remind me what it was that made you want counselling?

Client: Well, the doctor says I'm depressed and I need to talk about it.

You: The doctor thinks you're depressed. Your mother, you say, has always put you down. I'd like to know how you feel yourself?

This client may have a certain conversational style that is sprawling, or she may be anxiously defensive. But unless stopped and guided into some focused concerns she may ramble on indefinitely. If you allow her to, she may well waste her time and money. She may also get quite the wrong impression of counselling and may need to have someone help her to focus. This kind of interruption isn't rudeness and it isn't against the rules of counselling! On the contrary, it is sensitive to the underlying feelings of the client and it firmly establishes the idea that counselling is not just an everyday chit-chat but a purposeful and sometimes confrontational exercise.

All that we have said here about letting the client talk, while empathizing and structuring, implies that you respond to the client from her frame of reference. You may have a particular theory of counselling and a hypothesis about this client, but your task, especially in early sessions, is to communicate to the client your understanding of her frame of reference. This means that you need to be able to relax enough to be truly with the client. Some beginning counsellors, naturally enough, are anxious about how they are performing. You may be acutely aware of all your trainers' admonitions, which can lead to self-consciousness. You may be tape-recording your work and anticipate a supervisor hearing it. This can get you into a frame of mind called 'spectatoring' in which you are anxiously watching your own counselling performance. This can easily remove you from your client's frame of reference. Accept that this can happen; it's quite common and it's only human. Don't beat yourself up over it. If you catch yourself at it during a session, just be aware of it and let it go in a meditative style. Bring yourself back into the frame of reference of your client. If necessary, ask the client to repeat something, rather than risk making yourself even more anxious about missing some vital piece of information!

The point about knowing and responding to the client's frame of reference is that you need to be attuned to the content and feeling so that you can initiate movement forward. You listen for the 'leading edge' in what the client conveys. What is most important or urgent in what she says? To which themes does she most often return? What makes her excited, breathless or flat? At which moments does she blush, sigh, become silent or loud? Be immersed in the client's world and respond as far as you can from her viewpoint. You may note that you have a tendency to want to reflect statements back, a kind of technical, empty reflecting; this may be a sign that you are spectating and don't want to risk getting things wrong. This frequently occurs with beginning counsellors, so don't worry. However, the more that you can let this go and immerse yourself in the client's phenomenal world, the better. But don't demand that you must not spectate, because if you do, you will do it all the more!

Summary

Let your clients unburden themselves, tell their story and benefit from catharsis. Interrupt, if necessary, to prevent rambling. Begin to lend structure to what is happening. Allow yourself to enter and to respond from the client's frame of reference. Find the balance between anxious spectatoring and purposeful interruption.

17 Listen for and respond to the problems, not the story

We have said that the client's story is important. In recent years narrative has assumed greater importance in counselling theory and practice (McLeod, 1997). At the risk of seeming reductionistic about this movement, we suggest that its main strength is in encouraging clients to grasp and change the deterministic elements of their script. Most of us like talking about ourselves, especially to others who seem really interested. Broadly, there is a great deal of agreement that storytelling is helpfully cathartic but there are some dissenters to this view. Bell (2002), in discussing criticisms of South Africa's Truth and Reconciliation process, says plainly that 'not all storytelling heals' (sometimes it stirs up memories that are painful or angering and that cannot be worked through). We need to remind ourselves that in brief counselling it is not an appropriate task to gather exhaustively every biographical detail. You will hear, in each story, certain themes or problems that stand out from the narrative. These may include, for example, losses, interpersonal conflicts, need for approval, or moral crises. From a psychodynamic perspective, Coren (2001: 102) argues that 'the use of narrative is particularly helpful in time-limited therapy because it incorporates aspects of the triangles of therapy and persons'. These aspects and themes may be obvious or not, and they may be centre stage or perhaps they will appear and disappear, but your ear will pick them up. We believe it is more appropriate in this way of working to identify such themes rather than to keep an open agenda or to note slowly the many latent themes in the client's story. Look back at Section 4 ('why now?') to see the significance of dealing with what is presented at this time rather than attempting an omnipotent once-and-for-all cure.

You may want to distinguish between a background biographical matrix and the themes emerging in counselling. Beyond that, you can identify specific problems within themes. For example:

Client: It's always been this way for me; it's always been a struggle. Somehow I knew when I went for this job that I wasn't going to get it.

You: You've had these disappointments before and this is another one – it seems almost inevitable.

Client: Yeah. I mean, I tried. I'm well qualified and I put my case well, but somehow ... I suppose at my age, somehow I'm not on target. There are younger people around.

You: From all you've told me, it seems that you're angry at being left out, left behind. You know you've got what it takes, yet you're also aware that it doesn't come across, and your age is getting to you. Is that it?

Client: Yes. As I said, there's something familiar about this, but at the same time I have changed and I do want things now, but I feel penalized.

You: I'd like you to tell me more about the 'struggle', but also about your present circumstances and why you are putting pressure on yourself to seek promotion. Would it be a good idea, too, to look at exactly how you do present yourself at an interview?

We might infer from this piece of dialogue that the client has an underlying self-sabotaging pattern of behaviour and beliefs. But the counsellor decides not to explore (or re-explore) these in depth. He wants to move into the present day, to what brought the client into counselling now, and he asks for a concrete account of how the client conducts himself. In this way the counsellor tapers the client's concerns into workable material. We do not deny that any client's past influences his present experience, and there is indeed a place for exploring significant personal history. But if you aim to be effective in a relatively short time, and if you believe that counselling (and therapy) tends to be shorter, by design or default, than we might like it to be, then you need to separate meaningful and mobilizing information from other (interesting but not necessarily usable) details. Sometimes this will involve you in intercepting the client when he or she goes off into yet another autobiographical lament, and counsellors often find this difficult. But the reality of fairly brief contact with clients (as well as certain pressures from managers) can mean that you sometimes need to do the uncomfortable, to 'cut the client short'. We are not saying there is no place for autobiography or narrative therapy, or even negative narrative (Feltham, 2004) but in counselling that is likely to be brief, its narrative elements need to be relatively brief and purposeful.

Summary

Pick out prevalent themes in the client's story. In collaboration with the client, identify particular problems emerging from these themes, and focus on examples that can provide therapeutic leverage. Accept the challenge of the need sometimes to intercept clients' unhelpful automatic narrative tendencies.

---

18 Ask for any crucial or helpful information

Depending on your training, orientation and personal preferences you may use a formal assessment procedure or not. Even if you disapprove of formal assessments, as some counsellors do, we consider that there are certain items of information it is crucial to know.

It is widely acknowledged, for example, that if someone has a serious drinking problem it is probably useless to try doing any counselling until that problem has been addressed. Therefore, if you suspect (or even if you do not suspect) that your client might have such a problem, ask about it. There are degrees of addiction to, or occasional abuse of, alcohol and drugs. Ask about the use of substances in detail if necessary, whether these are prescribed or not, legal or not. The point about obtaining such information is that if you proceed with counselling while your client is abusing such substances, time may be wasted, the client's honesty and moods may be affected, and you may suffer as a result. It would be appropriate to refer a client in these circumstances to a specialist form of treatment, although you might offer to see them once they had their primary problem under control.

Another crucial piece of information concerns the risk of suicide. If there is any sign of severe depression, such as hopelessness coupled with agitation, lack of supportive friendships, and so on, then you should definitely find out more about the client's frame of mind and the resources available to him. This is one of those areas in which counsellors are sometimes uncomfortable. 'But if I mention it, it just might put the idea in her head', is one fairly typical worry. The chances are that if you experience a concern for your client's mental stability, both of you will be relieved to have it aired. If there is a discussion about suicidal ideation, make it specific, including questions about previous attempts, precise suicide plans, social support systems, and medical or psychiatric assessments. You may decide on the basis of the replies you get that you do not want to take on certain clients. If so, it is essential that you effect a referral in a way that does not further discourage your already demoralized client. Ensure that the client knows telephone numbers of the Samaritans or Social Services. Stewart (1989) believes strongly in the need to confront these issues and to make contracts in regard to them. His strategy for 'blocking tragic outcomes' involves careful history-taking and analysis of ego states and scripts. Your strategy may be more informal, but you are advised to think about it and to address these subjects with clients without embarrassment, but with due sensitivity.

Apart from the subject of suicide and other forms of self-harm, there are other matters that are important to consider. Since we are aware that different counsellors find different kinds of information crucial or helpful, we include a list of some common questions:

- What are your social circumstances? (Family? Friends?)

- What are your financial circumstances? (Employed? Solvent?)

- What are your living conditions? (Homeless? Poorly housed?)

- Do you have any current illnesses? (Physical or mental?)

- Have you had any major illnesses or accidents?

- Are you currently using any medication or substances?

- Do you drink, smoke or seriously overeat?

- Have you been involved in any criminal activity?

- Are you receiving any help from other professionals?

- Have there been any major losses or separations in your life?

- What are your views on sex and religion? (We do not mean that these are necessarily linked but some have suggested that sex and companionship are so important that they must be raised; and spirituality of both traditional and liberal kinds have assumed greater importance in recent years.)

Some clients are pleased to be asked such questions because they may fit their expectations of a medical model of being helped; they may convey a sense of detailed interest in the client; and they will often elicit information that may not be volunteered by the client otherwise. (One of the strengths of homeopathy is its detailed assessment procedure, which conveys a sense of deep interest and attention to nuance.) What you ask will depend on your model of counselling and also on any requirements of the agency you may work in. If you place great emphasis on support networks you may be concerned to know a lot about these. If you have a particularly psychosomatic orientation, then you may well want to know about previous illnesses. (Some counsellors, as a matter of course, ask clients for the name and address of their GP.) It is up to you whether you elicit this kind of information gradually and tactfully, or formally at the outset, or even not at all. Think about what you need to know and why you need to know it. When you are working quite specifically on a focal concern, then this may dictate what you need to know. If you feel that certain questions are an intrusion on privacy, and not relevant for counselling purposes, don't ask them. If you believe that the more information you have, the better, then explain this to the client before asking. (Bear in mind, however, that it is possible to amass an awful lot of useless information!) If your client arrives in distress, you will probably not ask these kinds of questions at that time unless you work in certain settings that require the information.

Summary

If it is appropriate to the way you work, have pre-prepared the kinds of question you will ask to elicit crucial or helpful information. What in the client's life may be crucial or detrimental to counselling? Decide in particular what your policy is on suicidal ideation, alcoholism and other life-threatening areas.

---

19 Make an appraisal of your own 'clinical reasoning' strategies and biases

A topic that has been gaining ground in certain medical circles but also in areas as diverse as speech therapy, forensic science, psychotherapy, physiotherapy and nursing is that of clinical reasoning. This refers to the manner in which we assess clients, arrive at conclusions about them, the cognitive processes and short cuts we go through to get there, and the mistakes and modifications we make on the way. How do we collect information, hypothesize and make sense of clients' presentations? Clearly, to some extent our training in counselling teaches us how to construct tentative theories about the client according to our theoretical model, and how to test out and operationalize our theories in action, both in a moment-by-moment way and after feedback from supervisors. To some extent we also use intuition and common life experience, but the discipline of rigorous clinical reasoning asks us to consider some of the ways in which we may habitually jump to the wrong conclusions and hence deliver a service that may harm or simply not help the client.

We give here some examples from the general field of clinical reasoning studies:

- *Anchoring on salient features.* This entails locking onto obvious features early on in assessment or counselling and failing to look at alternatives. An example might be that if we hear emotive words like 'abuse', 'depression' or 'suicide' we may have a tendency to become preoccupied with that feature and not question it further.
- *Stereotyping or ascertainment bias.* This happens when you see what you expect to find. If your referrer uses certain diagnostic terms, or if you yourself make early decisions based on what you see or infer, you may not get past this. You might assume that disabled clients want to talk about their disability, for example.
- *Commission bias.* A preference for action over inaction, for example to intervene or to suggest action strategies when more protracted listening and suspended decisions may be called for.
- *Gambler's fallacy.* Seeing links between past and future events when these may be independent. This involves the belief that a pattern is present and going along with it instead of trying to disconfirm it. Seeing someone as necessarily susceptible to relapse might be an example.
- *Outcome bias.* This is a tendency to judge the decision being made by its likely outcome. If we strongly believe in our own assessment because it fits with what our theory says about how to help a depressed person become more positive, for example, we may well ignore other relevant factors.
- *Sunk costs.* The more that has been invested in an assessment or ongoing counselling, the less likely we are to abandon our original views and try something different. This constitutes one of the most salient problems for long-term therapy, in which both client and therapist may persist in hope for years (Bates, 2005; Sands, 2000).

All these ideas have something in common, which is a cognitive inflexibility. Now, we all try to remain aware of our possible biases but constant self-questioning (not doubt engendered by low self-esteem, of course) is likely to help us expose such errors in our reasoning. In our field, especially, there is perhaps an inbuilt danger that partisan theoretical models can sometimes produce an unhelpful bias. Some, to put it very broadly, tend to go for the obvious, while others tend always to go for the putative deeper explanation. Unfortunately, some supervisors may inadvertently reinforce this theoretical correctness, instead of also keeping a part of their mind devoted to disconfirmation in the interests of each unique client.

Within the counselling and psychotherapy world there are various admonitions and texts referring to a similar area of reasoning, hypothesizing and self-correction. Just one of these is Robertiello and Schoenewolf's (1987) *101 Common Therapeutic Blunders*, which makes for entertaining as well as sobering reading, showing many ways in which we can all be seduced by our own personal, emotional and theoretical prejudices. There is a danger that approaches such as relying on supervision (even moment-by-moment in-session, covert self-supervision) and continuing professional development plans may not be as systematic as necessary and may also have their own inbuilt biases. For these reasons we recommend that you read some of the clinical reasoning literature (for example, Higgs and Titchen, 2001). In addition, subjecting yourself to occasional brainstorming exercises like 'what if I've got this completely wrong?' can be useful. 'How else might I see the client and what else might I do?' is another way of putting this. Ask these questions both of yourself (your own unresolved personal issues or areas of sub-optimal functioning) and of your espoused theoretical model. This requires a great deal of personal awareness and humility but also a willingness to break out of the box of your training affiliation. Whether yours is a person-centred affiliation or cognitive-behavioural approach, say, it is always possible that the tendency to see and assess exclusively through the lens of that approach may limit your effectiveness. It is true that person-centred counsellors attempt to track their client, to empathize attentively and not to impose their own meanings, but even this strategy can be wrong if what is called for is a complex assessment or active intervention. And while a CBT counsellor attempts to work systematically at an adult level, it is quite possible to miss cues that the client needs a period of uninterrupted cathartic storytelling.

Summary

Consider the topic of clinical reasoning and the nuances of how we can introduce unintended bias into our assessment and ongoing counselling. Find ways of raising your awareness of possible 'errors' that may emanate from you or your approach.

---

20 Establish the reflection process

We recommend that you establish as a norm from the outset the practice of asking the client for feedback on counselling sessions. You have already prepared the ground for this in some of the previous questions here. Let the client know that you value her comments and that you want to be as helpful as possible. How does she feel about the counselling relationship? How can you encourage her to feel and act like an equal partner (or to feel 'taken care of' if that seems initially more appropriate for a particular client)? The reflection process occurs when both client and counsellor step back from the content of the counselling to look at how well the alliance between them is holding. Bordin (1979) argued that the therapeutic alliance consists of bonds, goals and tasks. We have both found in our work that sensitive but explicit discussion with clients about the therapeutic relationship, agreed goals and mutually understood ways of working towards those goals, helps to raise difficulties before they escalate into irreparable misunderstandings or breakdowns in communication. Furthermore, the practice of encouraging an ongoing reflection on the work helps to keep it on course. Your willingness to hear regularly from the client about her views of the counselling process is likely to increase the bond between you. See Bates (2005), Feltham (1999) and Feltham and Lambert (2006) about clients' and counsellors' views about what can go wrong in the counselling relationship and how these pitfalls might be avoided. Questions you might ask to elicit this kind of feedback include: 'How do you feel about being here?' 'How do you feel about me?' 'How do you feel about what we did today?' 'Is there anything I said today that was confusing?' 'What has been most helpful about the sessions so far?' 'Are we addressing the issues that are important for you?' Such questions give permission to the client to be critical, to speak openly and to reflect on the process. They encourage a working alliance, a sense of you and the client working together in the same direction. They also serve to demythologize counselling. Of course, this doesn't necessarily happen easily for all clients; some are much more reticent than others. But you can help in the process of mutual reflection by non-defensive invitation to reflect.

Summary

Get into the habit of asking for comments on how counselling is going from the client's point of view. Encourage clients to voice any doubts about your relationship, about your way of working and the goals towards which you are working with them. Integrate this into your work.

---

21 Identify the client's stage of change

We now want to look more closely at the idea of identifying stages of change according to the model presented by Prochaska and DiClemente (1984). The four main stages are pre-contemplation, contemplation, action and maintenance. Here we shall focus on those stages involving contemplation and beyond because the pre-contemplation stage can be very problematic. People in the pre-contemplation stage regard themselves as not having a problem, or not having a serious enough problem to worry about, or as being able to cope without changing anything. Often such people have come to a counsellor because they've been sent or coerced. They come grudgingly and are clearly not prepared for actual change. If you do work with them, you will need to build trust and to establish that it is their perception of any problems you are interested in (not their family's, for example) and that you are willing to spend time discussing counselling, and its advantages and disadvantages, in relation to their doubts. If you decide not to work with pre-contemplators (and some counsellors do decide not to) then you might offer to see them at a later stage, should they feel ready for counselling. Don't be judgemental of their hesitancy, mistrust or disowning of problems.

When people are in the contemplation stage they are actively wondering about change, thinking it might be a good thing, vaguely wishing for greater clarity in regard to problems, or imagining that someone will be able to tell them what to do. Now, the important thing to remember is to tailor your interventions so as to join clients in the stage they are at. If people are contemplators, it is inadvisable to treat them as if they are pre-contemplative, doubtful and resistant. Equally, you would not treat them as being 'ready to go', that is in the action stage. The most appropriate counselling mode with contemplators is the exploratory one. Understand the clients' questions and hopes and elicit their expectations. Help them to feel understood. Provide the climate in which their confidence in the counselling (and personal growth) process will grow.

Should your client be in the action stage, you will need to adjust yourself to this. Someone may enter counselling with you having already worked on some problems. They may have already thought things through; they may understand their own dynamics or know clearly what they want to do. They are ready to act and may feel impatient with further exploration. Don't make the mistake of regarding this attitude as clients' defensive refusal to examine themselves in depth! There may be such subtleties involved, but we advocate in brief counselling that you address the client's presented concerns until they (perhaps) turn out to be something else! So if your client says, 'I think what I need to do is find another job', don't immediately see this as escapism or as symbolic of something else. Investigate it. 'I'd like to know something about your present job and what kind of job you'd prefer', perhaps followed by, 'tell me what you've done in the direction of finding another job', is more appropriate in this stage of change than, say, 'Are you sure that's what you want? When people are in turmoil, it's often a better idea not to change things around until we're more settled inside.' Don't deny the client's reality. This is not the same as suppressing all your instincts if you feel that such a client is operating on a fantasy of a better life through a different job. Begin with the client's reality.

We shall not go into the maintenance stage in much depth here. Obviously clients will have done considerable work on self-change if they have already thought through a problem and made changes. Someone may come to you in this stage in order to get some reinforcement. Someone who has overcome an addiction, for example, may at times feel troubled by old cravings and seek a means of expressing this and gaining support. He may also be looking for new strategies. Recognize this and work with these concerns. You certainly should not have to go back to square one with such clients.

This last point is crucial. While recognizing the stages of change takes practice, and may never be 'scientific', we believe it sharpens your skills considerably if you are aware of them. But it does have implications. If you are wedded to a single therapeutic theory and you want to apply it to all clients, difficulties will arise. In practice, most counsellors do adapt their style to each client. But if, for example, you work with a pure model of person-centred counselling, you may well have some trouble with clients who come in for help already in the action stage and want more action than exploration. People who have found the motivation to do something to change their life, perhaps to make specific decisions or to give up an addictive habit, are likely to want action strategies and reinforcement for them. They have been through the contemplative stage. If you insist on further contemplation at this point you may lose the client or delay progress unnecessarily. We are not suggesting that you must master half a dozen theories and many more techniques, but we do advocate flexibility. If you work behaviourally, or cognitive-behaviourally, and you prefer a brisk pace in counselling, you will do a disservice to a client who is hovering nervously between pre-contemplation and contemplation. Such a client needs time and support. Having the stages of change model in mind will help you to make rapid adjustments of style and intervention.

What may not be obvious is that, when presenting two or three problems, clients can be at different stages of change with each of them. Recognizing this requires extra awareness and adaptability.

Let us suppose that your client mentions problems with assertiveness, with trying new activities and with the loss of a boyfriend. You may regard these as all one problem stemming from early experiences of attachment and separation anxiety. Within a brief counselling contract, however, in which you are aiming to be as effective as possible, we think you need to focus. The client mentions three areas she wishes to work on. Don't impose your view, if you have one, that these all relate to early material that needs long-term regressive work to correct. We will come to the prioritizing of concerns in Section 28. Here, the task for you is to decide, with the client, at what stage she is with each problem.

Let's say that she split up from her boyfriend a year ago and that she has cried about it and thought through it, but still misses him. Together you may decide that she has grieved substantially for the loss of her relationship and is in a maintenance stage of accepting the reality of it. An appropriate counselling approach may be to help her to express her feelings about her boyfriend in depth when necessary and encourage her to accept the loss. She wants to fill up some time; this relates to losing her boyfriend but also to realistic wishes for personal development at this stage in her life. Perhaps she is contemplative with regard to moving on substantially in her life, in which case you may help her to do some long-term planning when appropriate. However, she reveals that she specifically wants to join a language class now, and she identifies a need to be assertive in relation to this. Here she is clearly ready for action. You meet her action stage with appropriate, well-defined change strategies, for example assertiveness training techniques and identifying and disputing irrational beliefs about the need to feel comfortable in new situations. Remember that clients may spend a lot of time on one problem and little on another, and that may be entirely appropriate.

To help you identify the stages of change, a questionnaire is included (Appendix 2). This will sharpen your own practice. You may decide to use it with clients. If you do, it can be used generally for assessment, or in a more detailed way to identify the stages of change for each problem a client presents.

Summary

Consider integrating the stages of change model into your work. Learn to discern the stages of change your clients are at with each of their problems. Learn to adapt your style and your interventions accordingly.

22 Encourage the client's involvement in the process

It is well established that counselling works better from the clients' point of view when they feel involved and consulted. We advocate that, from the outset, you encourage this kind of involvement. This means that you need to ensure that clients understand the tasks required of them in counselling. It is easy to misunderstand the word 'tasks'. By 'tasks' we mean those activities in which it is necessary for the client and counsellor to engage, and to understand the purpose of, in order to optimize therapeutic progress. Some counselling approaches see progress as implicit and tasks as an alien (behavioural) concept. This is not the case. Ursano et al. (1991) summarize the tasks of a client in psychodynamic psychotherapy as

- developing a working alliance with the therapist;
- learning free association;
- appreciating the atmosphere of safety;
- recognizing the disappointment of the opening phase;
- developing an understanding of transference, defence and resistance;
- learning how to work with dreams.

It cannot be assumed that clients have read all about a certain method or that they will pick it up by intuition or telepathy. Let them know your therapeutic intentions. Explain the value of your methods. Seek collaboration. This does not have to be a long-winded process and it should not be overly theoretical.

Whatever your preferred way of working, your clients always have tasks. These are more obvious, perhaps, in cognitive-behavioural counselling, where clients are asked to do homework, and in sessions where they are actively encouraged to produce examples of their thinking processes. In Gestalt counselling, the client has the task of getting in touch with the 'boundaries' of her experience. In person-centred counselling, clients have the tasks of engaging in the process of self-exploration, learning to trust themselves and their own thinking and feeling processes. We believe much counselling would be improved if counsellors of different persuasions would explain these matters to their clients and seek their collaboration, instead of assuming that clients will guess what their tasks are or naturally fit in with what is going on. If client participation is as crucial as we suggest, then anything that fails to deal with client passivity invites further problems in counselling. You may object that some clients are characterologically passive, and if this is the case you are advised to consider either referral or negotiating a long-term therapeutic contract with them. But sometimes clients appear passive because they are mystified about counselling, and rightly so if they are expected simply to guess what it's all about.

One of the pitfalls of working with passive clients is the temptation to do the work for them, for example by talking a lot. The problem here is that the more you do this, the more you reinforce their passivity. Refrain from falling into this trap. The opposite trap is to become persecutory, of course – perhaps trying to out-stare or out-silence your client. A better way, we believe, is to explore and gently challenge passivity, for example 'it seems you're finding it extremely difficult to let go enough to talk about what's really upsetting you.' 'It's been found that counselling works best when people are ready to take a few risks, however small. Is there anything you're close to risking?' would be an attempted lever. You can also reinforce what change attempts clients do make, however small, in order to establish a pattern of active involvement. Approaches like Ryle's (1990) cognitive analytic therapy are built around the expectation of 'active participation', employing a variety of self-reporting questionnaires and letter-writing tasks.

Summary

Convey the expectation that counselling requires active involvement on the part of the client. Discourage passivity and avoid the traps of leaving your clients to guess what their tasks are, or performing them for them.

23 Use appropriate language and pacing

Clients, as we have said, as you will know, and as may be obvious, differ enormously. Person-centred counselling underlines the uniqueness of clients.

One of the ways in which uniqueness is expressed is language. Class differences in Britain are still fairly obvious and are betrayed in people's accents. In an ever increasingly multicultural society the use of language becomes even more complex, rich and open to misunderstanding. Let's look at some basics.

Some people prefer formal language. By this we mean that some clients will address you as 'Mr', 'Mrs', 'Ms' or 'Dr' rather than by your first name. They may also talk about themselves or people in their lives in formal terms. This may be simply a preference, a cultural norm or a defensive style. Whatever it is, you will do well to note it and to adapt your own language so that it is not, initially, too dissonant. It would not be helpful for Windy to respond to a new client who calls him Dr Dryden as 'mate', for example. On the other hand, a client who readily and naturally calls you by your first name will probably find you rather stiff if you respond by calling her Mrs Brown throughout sessions. Respect for clients does not mean that you should be overly formal. It is quite in order to ask clients how they prefer to be addressed and to tell them your preference.

There are degrees of formal and informal language. Some people, in their everyday lives, swear a lot, and may swear in their counselling sessions. If you are uncomfortable with swearing (or particular forms of swearing) this is something to think about. You are more likely to form a good working alliance if you can either join them in such language or at least feel comfortable with it. We are not suggesting that you put on a phoney cockney accent or adopt a youthful patois that is not your own, and play a part. You will want to be as true to yourself as possible. But if it is apparent that you are from a very different class or culture, the communication between you and your client may become difficult. One way of dealing with this is to notice the client's non-verbal reactions to you. Another is to incorporate into your reflection process with clients questions about your differing styles. 'People do have different ways of saying things and I wonder if we're always on the same wavelength here or not? How well do you think we're communicating with each other?' or 'Have you found anything that I have said off-putting?'

Some people have a very dry and stiff style of relating and may well bring this manner into counselling. You may adapt to it or question it (if it seems to be part of the client's problem). But you may also find it useful at times to introduce humour and colour into the language used between you. This can give permission to the client to do likewise. Experiment with imagery that may evoke feelings. Do all of this gradually. Does the client respond? Are there particular forms of language that communicate effectively with the client where others don't? This can work the other way too. If a client has a 'hysterical' manner (speaking dramatically, shrilly, speedily, for example) it would not help for you to mirror this for too long! You can influence the client, bring her down, as it were, into a way of talking that is calm enough to initiate effective counselling. What we hope these examples show is that there are no black-and-white prescriptions but there are indications for adjusting your language and manner to strengthen the bond between you and to help the client move subtly from one mood to another. Working congruently, you can infer which kind of language style will be more effective.

A note on jargon. In almost all cases, avoid it. Technical language is appropriate, perhaps, as professional shorthand with colleagues. But when working with clients, use their language. Avoid, on the whole, diagnostic terms and psychological terms. (If you are using certain approaches like transactional analysis, where counselling depends on teaching basic concepts from the model, then you will obviously use technical language, but only after you have carefully explained it.) Another kind of jargon is 'I hear what you're saying'. This can be very jarring. Some clients (Colin has been one of them) can be easily put off if they sense this kind of stylized language use. Attend to the client and you will pick up whether or not you are striking the right notes. The wrong notes can also, of course, yield interesting reactions, but in the beginning aim for an alliance, not a misalliance or negative transference–countertransference kind of battle.

Clients are unique in their pacing too. But so are counsellors. The manner in which we process information, both conceptual and personal (emotional) varies a lot. We all speak and think at different speeds. The most problematic scenario, probably, is one in which a very 'slow' counsellor is working with a very 'fast' client. There are reasons for thinking that it is easier for counsellors to slow themselves down than to speed themselves up. Now, we are not saying that you must anxiously attempt to adapt upwards or downwards to your client's pace. But note it. And go with it rather than against it. Clients will be put off if they feel you're hurrying them, and they may well feel exasperated if it seems they're several steps ahead of you. What we're saying here presupposes that a client's pace is not a pathological manifestation, like a 'hurry up' driver. But even if it is, your first task will be to meet the client acceptantly and skilfully rather than to pathologize her.

So what if a client is, say, very slow in delivering her ideas? How do you respond? Remember the reflection process. 'I notice that you're taking quite a time to think about your answers. Is this the way you usually think and respond, and is it valuable for you?' What you are after is information and leverage. The client may say, 'I don't know. I've never thought about it. I think I am a bit unused to this situation, but yes, I'm generally a bit slow in conversation.' You can then investigate this further, according to the focus in counselling. But at a working level, it may imply that you had better accept it, rather than become impatient and cause the client to become anxious.

Summary

Be sensitive to the client's uniqueness in relation to language use. Adapt your own responses as far as you can, allowing yourself to be more or less formal. Avoid jargon. Be sensitive to the client's pace and adjust to it.

---

24 Use your influence base appropriately

Many counsellors believe that to set out to influence clients in any way is a kind of transgression of the very ethos of counselling. It is still the case that some counsellors bend over backwards in an effort (mistakenly, in our opinion) not to convey any direction to their clients whatsoever. It has been shown that even Carl Rogers delivered his 'hmmms' and 'ahas' in a manner that revealed a subtle pattern of differential reinforcement. You may want to think carefully about this, but we feel that it is an unavoidable fact in counselling that you do wield influence. Indeed, Ivey et al. (1987) define counselling and therapy as 'processes of personal influence'.

One way of looking at this is as follows. Clients are often influenced (depending on their personalities) either by the perceived expertness or the perceived attractiveness of their counsellors. In a similar vein some clients will respond more favourably to the formality of their counsellors, but others to a more informal style. Expertness is evident in professional qualifications, training and knowledge, and the setting or area in which you work. Expertness often, but not invariably, goes together with formality. Attractiveness is evident in the counsellor's personality, warmth and appearance and it often goes together with informality. Windy has given the example of how he adjusted his manner from formal to informal when seeing first, a client wanting a formal counsellor, and second, a client appreciating a much more informal style of counselling (Dryden, 1991: 112). This adjustment included removing his tie and joining his second client in a drink of Coke, while both had their feet up on the table. This was not done mechanically or phonily but by design. Windy could do this genuinely because he is able to range from being formal to becoming informal quite easily.

As a beginning counsellor you are unlikely to be able to use expertise in this way to influence your clients. (You might well, however, have expertise in related fields, which you may emphasize.) Good therapeutic bonds are established with counsellors-in-training, for example, when clients warm to their enthusiasm, alertness and even vulnerability. 'I'm a counsellor-in-training and I'm looking forward to working with you' introduces you better than an apologetic or defensive 'I'm just a trainee counsellor and I have to get some experience'! If you are confronted with clients who clearly prize expertness, you might present them with areas in which you do have some expertise. Or you might consider making a referral. But remember how much clients differ, and that many clients will feel reassured by your accepting manner rather than your official status. It is important not to mislead your client as to your qualifications, but equally it is unnecessary and unhelpful (in our view) to present your lack of experience and qualifications in great detail.

Other ways in which formality and informality are evident include the use of humour and the offering of refreshments. Psychoanalysts may be aghast at both these suggestions, but there are some counsellors (and psychotherapists) who welcome clients with some informal chat or even a cup of tea, and freely engage in humour. We are not denying that offering tea can have its disadvantages and do not recommend it as a general practice, but neither is it actually professionally taboo. What is your preferred style? And perhaps more importantly, how flexible are you in varying your style of relating? You can always try to find out which of these practices are helpful and which are not by asking your clients in the reflection process.

Summary

Consider the fact that you will influence your clients, whether it is conscious or not, and whether you like it or not. How can you use this knowledge to improve your service to individual clients? How comfortable are you in adjusting your style? If you are a beginner, accept this and use it beneficially.

25 Be sensitive to important client differences

Clients have different expectations about how their counsellors will act. Richert (1983) divides clients into 'medical modellers' (who expect a high level of authority); 'revelationists' (who look for a powerful and insightful counsellor); 'problem solvers' (who want, not so much authority as technical application from their counsellors) and 'explorers' (who seek a non-authoritarian, fellow-traveller kind of counsellor). Can you detect such different tastes in your clients? And if you can, what do you do about it?

We have advocated an attitude of flexibility throughout this book, and it applies here very powerfully. If you accept a need to identify counselling styles that will best help your clients, then whether you follow a schema like Richert's, or your own intuition, this has certain implications. If you are someone who, as a counsellor, likes to be a fellow explorer, and you have a client who clearly wants to look up to you and obtain some answers, will you spend weeks trying to break down his 'external frame of reference' before going on to address the problems with which he came in the first place? Certainly some counsellors do work in this way. But if you accept the value of a focal approach, and the likelihood of a relatively brief time with your client, you will want to capitalize on clues your clients give you.

Howard et al. (1987) have their own view of client differences. This attempts to match client readiness for change with appropriate styles of counselling from the counsellor. Supporting, teaching, delegating and telling are the main styles identified by these writers. Without going too much into detail, we want to raise the point that this schema too suggests a need for flexibility from counsellors. We don't want you to think you have to enrol in acting classes to prepare yourself for your next counselling session. But we are saying that having one invariant, relational stance towards your clients is unlikely to be sufficient. Arnold Lazarus uses the term 'authentic chameleon' for this requirement to adjust to each client. Horowitz et al. (1984), using a psychodynamic model, recommend an analysis of different personality styles and correspondingly different approaches from practitioners. Counselling is, after all, not simply a case of being true to yourself, but also of being true to and useful to your client. You may not always be conscious of choices, but throughout your work you are faced with choices of adaptation. It is your task, we suggest, to adjust to your clients, rather than their job to meet you on your ground. There may be times when you can't find the required responses within your repertoire. At these times, supervision is, of course, crucial. And, at the end of the day, referral is always an option.

Summary

Clients differ. They expect different things from their counsellors. You can maximize your effectiveness by recognizing differences and by trying to adjust your style. Don't stay in the same mode all the time.

---

26 Consider using a means of assessing how clients react, learn and heal differently

We make the assumption that everyone is unique and our natural tendency is to treat each person differently. But it is common to hear counsellors falling into stereotypical responses to clients. The most common of these is probably, 'how do you feel about that?' Such a question implies that the person does or should feel something, and it may come across to them as critical if they have no ready emotional response. This kind of emphasis on feeling in some counselling mirrors the emphasis in education on verbal and intellectual intelligence. Gardner (1993) has postulated a theory of multiple intelligences to account for the observation that many of us do not primarily process and create in this traditional way. According to Gardner, we might think in terms of linguistic, musical, logical-mathematical, spatial, bodily-kinesthetic and personal (emotional and interpersonal) intelligences. A little thought may make it obvious that while some of us have excellent logical skills, others do not but are attuned to, say, emotional or spatial modes. The Myers-Briggs personality typology is another way of showing how we differ

(Bayne, 1999). These preferences may even help to explain why the very field of counselling and psychotherapy contains so many different approaches. When we unthinkingly apply one approach to all clients, we run the risk of alienating some of them. Here, we look at Lazarus's (1981) multimodal approach to understanding and working with key differences.

Disenchanted with the uni-dimensional stress on behaviour in behaviour therapy, Lazarus formulated a broad spectrum view of the modalities in which he considered we operate. These are: behaviour, affect, sensation, imagery, cognition, interpersonal factors, and drugs or biological factors. These are readily remembered through the acronym BASIC ID. Figure 2 shows how it works to help understand the modalities in which any client typically reacts.

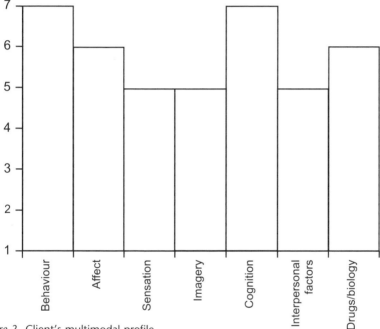

Figure 2. Client's multimodal profile.

Without pretending that this gives a scientific analysis of personality, it nonetheless provides a useful guide to how clients are likely to conceive of their problems, how they may best be met in sessions (with what choice of interventions) and in what ways the client would ideally like to change. You ask your client how much of a 'doer' he is, as opposed to a 'feeling type', for example. How much does he typically think his way through problems, see images of himself in trouble or coping successfully and so on?

Behaviour – what is it that the client does or doesn't do (avoids) that is problematic in his life? Example – drinks too much, spends too much, avoids close relationships.

Affect – what does the client feel or otherwise? Example – often becomes very angry, otherwise shuts down.

Sensation – what bodily sensations are apparent? Example – becomes very tense, experiences palpitations.

Imagery – does the client dream a lot, have nightmares, draw or paint, or visualize himself failing or succeeding?

Cognition – is the client a thinker? To what extent does he try to problem solve, and how? What negative or irrational thoughts does he have?

Interpersonal – what kinds of problems does he have with his partner, friends, parents, colleagues, in the present and past? Does he enjoy company, have good social skills?

Drugs/biology – does he take medication, diet, exercise, attend to his health? Does he gravitate towards medical explanations or is he averse to them?

As well as being a means of gaining useful information, this framework yields ideas about how to proceed therapeutically. For example, if your client is primarily a doer, it may be better initially to offer behaviourally oriented interventions and tasks rather than asking 'How do you feel?' Movement across the modalities can then happen gradually. This approach can be used to address clients' concerns systematically, so that if the main presenting issue is depression, say, you can look together at which behavioural, affective (emotional), sensation, imagery, cognitive, interpersonal and biological/ healthcare tasks to set. Rather than always or mainly eliciting information on the client's childhood, conditions of worth, irrational beliefs or whatever, you are encouraged by this means to elicit information across a range of modes of reacting, learning and healing. The client can be working on improving his health at the same time as he is keeping a diary of his drinking and exploring in-session his feelings about his deceased mother. Working in this broad spectrum way helps to make good use of therapeutic time.

Summary

Consider finding out the predominant modalities of each client and the sequence of these in how they react to everyday situations. Build on the profile you create together to sensitize you to how best to reach your client. Work multi-modally rather than uni-modally.

27 Use an appropriate degree of structure

By structure, here, we mean the kind of framework you give to your work with clients. Once they are engaged in counselling and somewhat familiar with their tasks (with those things you suggest to them as likely to be particularly helpful to focus on), they will need, depending on their personalities and defences, various styles of containment.

Let's look at an example of an 'all over the place', 'hysterical' kind of client:

Client: She just won't stop making that noise with her CDs and I've told her dozens of times, if I have to tell her again . . . Why do I have to put up with this, can you tell me? Oh, I do go on, don't I? It's not as if . . . Why should I have to take it?! It's the same at work with that stupid secretary. Sometimes I think I'd be better off out of it all. Maybe I need a holiday. Do you think I need a holiday? I wish I could just decide something and get on with it!

You: Let me stop you a moment. I'm not sure where you're going. We started off talking about your neighbour. Now, try to tell me again the main problem area for you.

Client: Main problem?! Ha! Sometimes I don't know if I'm coming or going! If it isn't one thing, it's another.

You: There may be a lot of things, but you can only deal with one thing at a time. Now, which of these are you most upset about at this time?

If your client still goes from one topic to another, ask her permission for you to interrupt her. Having obtained this permission, and if the occasion arises again, interrupt politely but firmly. This may be hard work, but it is necessary. This client may be trying hard to keep to the task of looking at a particular problem area, but the task slips away. It is your task to do the reminding, the interrupting, the guiding back into the agreed task. This is what a structure means. It involves an initial agreement, but also main-tenance of that agreement. Sometimes in cases like this it may mean a degree of forcefulness. You may need to drive home a single point. But you may need to initiate a strategy of ordering, of encouraging the client progressively to look at things in an unfamiliar, sequential manner.

Let's consider another kind of client – someone who is rather obsessive or tense:

You: So you agree that you'd like to be able to relax more around the house?

Client: Yes. Relax. I want to. But it isn't easy. I'm sorry. I'm trying. But it isn't easy. I just can't stand to see things untidy. I have to do something about it.

You: I notice, Mary, that you always sit very upright when you're here. Pretty stiff and uncomfortable-looking. Would you like to be able to relax more here?

Client: (Wringing hands) Well . . . well, I, yes, I know I'm not relaxed, but, but that's how I always am, Mrs Jones.

> *You:* I'd like to hear you call me Christine, and maybe sit back in that chair, instead of leaning forward. Will you try that?
>
> *Client:* I . . . you mean now? Call you Christine now? Lean back?

Your task here is to help loosen the client up. This may take some time and you may try various strategies, but they will all be part of a structure in which you have the client's welfare at heart. You won't use the same structure for all clients. In fact, you will always use slightly different kinds and degrees of structure with different clients. By forming ongoing and adjusting 'diagnostic impressions' of clients, you will begin to feel what is required by each one at various times in the counselling process. Referring back to the reflection process, asking the client if what you've done is helpful, will help you to fine-tune the structure.

Summary

Depending on the kind of client, you will decide how highly structured or 'loosely' structured the sessions might be. Get impressions of what your clients require to find a working shape in their counselling.

---

28 Prioritize concerns and select a target concern

While some clients present with a single, clear issue that they wish to address, many begin counselling uncertainly, with a hazy or complex story, and it is one of the counsellor's first tasks to track and 'unpick' the story. You will have become aware of what some of your client's first expressed concerns are, perhaps in a vague or shifting way. What you need to do now is to address concretely the client's concerns in order to prioritize them. We think this is important because, if you don't do it, you run the risk of talking at cross purposes. Your client may be trying to work on one issue while you are well-meaningly and steadfastly, but unhelpfully, referring back to another. So be sure that you arrive at an agreement as to what the concerns are and how they are ranked in the client's mind. Of course, the 'presenting concern' isn't necessarily always the most important or enduring but we believe that in the context of brief counselling it is the best first step.

How can you help the client to decide on priorities? First, consider the severity of problems. Your client may be vaguely discontented with her job, be bulimic, and unassertive. Now, these may or may not be connected. (Some theorists argue that everything is connected, and it may be, but within a brief counselling perspective you are advised not to grope around indiscriminately in the depths of the psyche hoping that eventually everything will fall into place.) Let's suppose that the issue of bulimia is the severest problem at this time. If you and the client agree on this, and you agree that severity is the criterion you will use to decide of priorities, then you can go ahead and work on this concern.

Second, remember the client's choice of concerns. She may be quite clear that what she wants to focus on is her relationship with her father. You may, let's say, not agree with her view (she may show signs of avoiding some anxiety-inducing situation in her present life, for example) but if she wishes to focus on her father you would be well advised to agree to this and work together with her. Suzanne presented with problems in her relationships and excessive drinking. It was agreed that control of alcohol consumption was the first priority and, although the counsellor suspected underlying, unresolved hurts from the past were deeply implicated, Suzanne wanted *only* to control her drinking and left after a few sessions when she felt she had a way forward with this.

Third, there is the criterion of what will effect most change. To return to an example above, suppose that your client has been bulimic for seven years and to some extent it is currently 'manageable'. But she is annoyed with a work colleague and wants to make this clear to him. She wants to tell him to leave her alone. She is poised to do it. With your encouragement, if she goes ahead and states her feelings clearly to him, and he changes his behaviour, she will experience some success. This may then form the first building block toward further changes. It will be a specific change and will offer a taste of success. Rather than making vague attempts to alter the bulimia (which has been very persistent and will not change overnight) you can help your client with small, progressive, concrete changes first. The attitude required to be assertive in this case, for example, may initiate a further process of change that will ultimately help to overcome bulimia.

'You're pretty clear that there are these two or three problem areas. Which of these do you want to start with first?' This is a deliberate, closed-question way of eliciting a necessary agenda. You can, of course, explain why you think it is imperative to set clear priorities, but do this rather than wandering aimlessly through clients' anecdotal accounts with them. This is good practice in providing structure. Client priorities may alter during the course of counselling but by agreeing on what they are at the beginning you have helped the client into a disciplined process of counselling and personal learning. The starting concern does not have to be the most painful or obvious concern. It may be that the client wants to work first on something that will give her hope that is easier or less anxiety-inducing. Mahrer (1989) asks clients to choose a feeling that is at the centre of their attention. He asks, 'Are you ready? Are you willing to start with this now?' At the heart of this is the importance of obtaining your clients' informed consent. What is crucial here is that you and she have agreed what you are working on together.

Summary

Note when your client's narrative includes several problem strands. Help your client to decide on priorities. Discuss the advantages of choosing to start with one in particular. Ensure that you are both committed to work on the same target concern even though this may change later.

29 Agree on a definition and conceptualization of the target concern

You have an agreement on what your client's concerns are and what the priorities are. Now you need to go more deeply into the target concern (the issue you and your client have agreed to address). Let's look at an example:

Client: I just have problems relating to women.

You: Can you tell me a specific problem you have in relating to women?

Client: Well, when I like someone and I think she may like me, I still don't have the confidence to talk. Or I try but I dry up or come across as awkward.

You: So you'd like to be able to approach women you're attracted to and engage them in conversation. Are you saying that you can approach women or that you don't get that far?

Client: In the right kind of situation I can approach them, but then I get awkward.

You: So there are two possible problems here. One concerns the 'right kind of situation' and the other is your 'awkwardness' and how to overcome it. Is that right?

Client: Yes. I suppose I'm saying that I'm awkward around women and I don't want to be.

There are all sorts of possible directions to go in, but here the counsellor wants a mutually understood, focused definition of the problem. This is the 'what it is' and now we turn to the 'why it is', or how the client conceptualizes it. How does this client understand his awkwardness in relation to women? Does he think he has a big nose? Does he think he may actually be gay? Does he think his mother made him anxious? Has he got the idea that everyone else finds it easy? Is he looking for some 'helpful hints for beginning Casanovas'? He may offer his own understanding of it or you may need to probe.

At this point it may help to explain your own view of such a problem. Explain that this is one way of looking at the problem but you are interested to learn if it makes sense to your client. Let's take an example of offering a conceptualization to your client. It is from Windy's work with the client Steve (Dryden, 1990: 47). He has already explained that what he's going to say is only one way of looking at his problem but Windy has also said that he believes it may make sense to him. You don't want to put all your eggs in one basket by explaining that this is *the* way of understanding your client's problem. In what follows Windy explains the model of the role that irrational beliefs play in his problems. Note how he involves the client:

Windy: Right, so to recap, you're anxious about failing your Ph.D. Now we've agreed that it's not failing that makes you anxious but your attitude about it. Now it's important to distinguish between two types of attitude, one that will lead to anxiety and other self-defeating emotions, while the other will lead to concern and other constructive emotions. So if you bear with me, before we focus directly on your anxiety, I want to take you through an example that will help you to understand this important distinction. OK?

Steve: OK.

Windy: Now, I want you to imagine that you have £10 in your pocket and that your attitude is that you prefer to have a minimum of £11 at all times, but that it's not essential. How will you feel about having £10 while you want to have £11?

Steve: Concerned?

Windy: Right, or frustrated, but you wouldn't want to commit suicide. Right?

Steve: That's right.

Windy: Now this time imagine that your attitude is 'I absolutely must have a minimum of £11 at all times, I must, I must, I must', and you look in your pocket and discover that you only have £10. Now how will you feel?

Steve: Anxious.

Windy: Or depressed. Note that it's the same situation but a different attitude or belief. Now the third scenario. Again you have that same dogmatic belief 'I must have a minimum of £11 at all times, I must, I must, I must.' But now you look, in your pocket and you find that you've got £12. Now how will you feel?

Steve: Pleased.

Windy: That's right, or relieved. But with that same belief, 'I must have a minimum of £11 at all times', you would soon have a thought that will lead you to make yourself anxious again. What do you think that would be?

Steve: That I might lose £2?

Windy: Right, I might lose £2, or I might spend it or get robbed. Now the point of all this is that all humans, black or white, rich or poor, male or female, will make themselves emotionally disturbed if they don't get what they believe they must get. And they will also make themselves disturbed when they do, because of their demands, their musts. Because if they have what they think they must have, they could always lose it. But when humans stick to their non-dogmatic desires and don't escalate these into dogmatic musts they will constructively adjust when they don't get what they want or be able to take effective action to try to prevent something undesirable from happening in the future. Now I want you to keep in mind this distinction between non-dogmatic wants and dogmatic musts as we go back to your own situation. OK?

This is an example of a conceptualization from rational emotive behaviour therapy, but you will find ways of explaining your own model concisely so that the client knows how it works. We realize that in certain approaches, for example person-centred and psychodynamic counselling, the 'instructional' style is rarely adopted. The client may be helped by more implicit than explicit means, or at least this is the rationale. But consider these tentative phrases. 'It sounds as if you know you become tense in certain situations and I wonder if I can help you to focus on how and where this happens in your body, so you can understand it better and get some grip on it.' See Gendlin (1996) for copious examples of how to go about this. In some approaches incorporating psychodynamic elements (such as cognitive analytic therapy and cyclical psychodynamics) quite explicit explanations may be given to clients.

Now, conceptualization should be offered tentatively. On hearing your view of why a problem is a problem and how it might be solved, the client may not automatically agree wholeheartedly.

Suppose our client who feels awkward around women doesn't respond favourably to the £11 example, what do we do? This is the point at which you and he need to negotiate your conceptualization of the problem. If he rigidly insists that his problem is because of his mother, and you rigidly insist that it is because of his dogmatic 'musts', then you will get nowhere. But if you both agree that some exploration of his relationship with his mother, coupled with looking hard at how he brings this into his potential relationships with all women, will be of maximum benefit, then you have a more mutual understanding of how you will work. To help you identify your clients' conceptualizations of their problems, we have included a questionnaire on clients' 'opinions about psychological problems' (which was compiled by Chris Barker and colleagues) in Appendix 3.

Summary

Agree together on a definition of the problem to be worked on. Ask clients for their understanding of the problem and the factors that sustain it. Tell them your theory regarding the problem and illustrate it. Then negotiate a common way of looking at this problem.

30 Specify goals related to the target concern

Once target concerns have been identified you need to help the client set specific goals for each of them. In most brief counselling there is an overriding need for direction. This is not the same thing as unhelpful counsellor directiveness, which tends to be based on the counsellor's frame of reference. Set goals collaboratively with the client that are specifically related to each target concern. We refer you to Sutton (1989) for a discussion on the importance of goalsetting. Sutton advocates specific written goals, which are arrived at after some negotiation, which clarify mutual understanding and give clients concrete means of measuring their progress. Ryle (1990) incorporates this kind of ongoing monitoring of goals in his approach to brief therapy. Willer and Miller (1976) established fairly clearly that clients who were consulted in the setting of precise goals were significantly more satisfied with the outcome of therapy than those who were not consulted. Willer and Miller's research also found that a large percentage of clients were not consulted at all. Although this study was conducted in a psychiatric hospital setting many years ago, we believe there is still a strong tendency in many settings not to consult with clients, not to think of goals as important, or covertly to decide on clients' goals for them (for instance, 'this client thinks he wants to conquer his drinking problem but I know that he really needs to uncover a lot of deep pain'). See Bates (2005), Feltham and Lambert (2006) and Sands (2000) for further examples of clients' views.

The more specific goals are, the better. Although it is possible to work with a broad agenda of 'personal development' or 'straightening myself out', these agendas need to be broken down into concrete objectives. We are not saying this happens naturally or easily. It may take some time with certain clients to focus sufficiently to find a clear goal. But that is the direction we suggest you take. 'I just feel I'm not getting anywhere' is the kind of client statement that can mean many things. Goal setting does not imply a facile 'So where would you like to get to?' response to such a client statement. Help the client to spell out what 'not getting anywhere' means, and what 'getting somewhere' would mean. What is really meaningful to the client here? Does the client need to talk about career development, making relationships, or about the possible origins of the 'getting nowhere' feeling, for example? Some approaches (such as reality therapy – Glasser, 1984) home in sharply and quickly on what clients say they want and how their actions often contradict their desires. This style of rapid identification of goals and mobilization towards attaining them is appropriate with some, but not with all clients.

'I don't want to have panic attacks every time I have to dine out, I want to be able to enjoy myself like everyone else' is a reasonably clear goal. The client has a strong motivation. Let's, however, look at variations on this theme. 'I never want to feel anxious again when I eat out or in any other public situation' is an unrealistic goal because of the 'never', and because the goal of total anxiety control is not in keeping with being human! Also, such a goal is not specific enough to work with. Avoid idealized goals. Learn to identify realistic, situational goals. 'I want to persuade my boyfriend that we don't have to eat out' is a goal that contains a wish to control another (the boyfriend) and indicates a wish for evasion. On both counts you will not want to go along with this kind of aim. 'I want to be able to explain to my boyfriend how stressful I find eating out' is an acceptable goal because it is honest and achievable, and points towards better coping. It is within your remit to help clients identify a goal the achievement of which is within their control. It is not, however, your job to talk your client round to your values. 'Yes, eating out is such a fuss, I think you're right to want to avoid it' is not something it is appropriate to say, even if you believe it, because for this client it is normative.

Let's look at how you help a client to operationalize a goal:

You: So your experience of panic recurs, it's acutely uncomfortable, and you want to be able to control or abolish it. Is that it?

Client: Well, I just wish it would go away, yes. But it's getting worse.

You: You wish it would go away, but it doesn't, and you've come to counselling to gain some insight into it and to find a way of overcoming it?

Client: That's right. I can't go on like this. Do you think I can end it?

You: You're clearly keen to end it and I'm keen to help you. I do have some ideas about how to proceed, but first I want to be sure exactly what you want. You tell me you have a dinner appointment next month and you'd like to be able to 'handle' it. Can you tell me what handling it would mean for you? Are you willing to focus and work on that specifically, for a start?

This shows the beginnings of work on a specific problem. Even though the problem is clear enough, agreeing on a concrete goal related to it is crucial. This does not mean that you can talk about nothing else, but it does mean that you have a focal agreement. In this example the client's goal might be made more specific by defining what is meant by 'panic' and what degree of anxiety, if any, is acceptable to the client in that situation, and what handling the anxiety means in specific terms. The client may wander off the subject (and indeed may uncover material of significance in doing so) and you too may be drawn into areas of psychological interest that deviate from this goal. But if the goal has been stated, it is at the very least a marker to which you can refer. The ways in which your client wanders away from the goal will also probably be very revealing. The example we're using here may arouse doubts in the minds of psychodynamic counsellors: may not the anxiety related to eating out be a displacement of some profound unconscious conflict? Of course, it may be. And it may be that in the course of exploring the problem such material will be uncovered. But it may not. In the meantime the client is distressed and clear about the goal of overcoming that distress. Many counsellors set out to be too ambitious. Remember Malan's (1975) findings that therapists are often prone to 'over-determination' (wanting to trace every piece of the underlying dynamics) and to 'therapeutic perfectionism'. What is it that the client has come to counselling for, at this time? Focus on the goals that come from the client and take them seriously. A note of caution, however. Do not collude with unhealthy goals – for example an anorexic client wishing to lose weight.

Does the client have the necessary resources to reach her specified goal within a reasonable time? Is it realistic, for example, for our client who panics when eating out to expect to be able to achieve results by next month? It may well be. Let's say she is highly motivated, she's weary of this disabling anxiety, she's keen to get on with her life, doesn't want to mess things up, has support, and so on. But suppose she's had this problem for five years, she's becoming very depressed about it, she's driven friends away instead of telling them about it, and she's been drinking a lot to try to forget it. The same goal may not be attainable in the same time. It may require longer term counselling, and if so you need to help the client to accept this. But there could be other problems of personal resources. Let's say that she is not used to eating out, she's from a retiring, working-class family, has never learned to eat out, and to be assertive. It will take time for her to learn the skills she needs. She may lack the social skills that are taken for granted in the circles in which she finds herself. Don't make the mistake, then, of ignoring such variables.

Client temperament is an important area, often overlooked or not well understood by counsellors. If we take the subject of humour, for example, you might assume that it's normal and desirable for everyone to want to 'have a good laugh' as often as possible. That assumption can lead to the view that a client who is often very serious may have a pathological problem. This may lead to the prognosis that once the underlying pathology is identified and corrected, all will be well. But this overlooks individual differences and limitations. Do you assume that everyone has it within himself or herself to 'be anything you want to be', for instance? If change, challenge and perfectibility are important values for you, don't assume that they are for all your clients. Your temperament may be such that you strive for ever greater and greater 'self-expression' in an extraverted way; clearly, however, many people are contentedly introverted. In this respect, see Van Deurzen's (2001) critique of counsellors' basic assumptions. Check that your goals and your clients' are aligned. Monitor any tendency in yourself or in your client to set up unattainable goals. Check, too, that your clients' stated goals are their own and not introjected ones. Elicit the clients' aims and help them to distinguish these from your goals, the family's, the boss's, and those of others.

Depending on your approach to counselling, you may take a more formal or informal approach to making contracts for goal setting. Stewart (1989) expresses a clear preference for formalized contracts. He suggests that when you make contracts you consider how feasible, how safe, how observable, how reinforcing of clients' autonomy, and how positively worded they are. 'I want to be able to go out to dinner and enjoy myself' is a positively worded goal, for example. If the counsellor and client agree to work specifically on the client's goal of enjoying himself in a specific situation, this is a formal contract; it may even be written down. You might consider the idea of 'hard' and 'soft' goals, too. 'I want to be able to relax and enjoy myself at that dinner' is a hard goal. 'I just want to know why I have these panic feelings' is a soft goal. Hard goals are specific and carry a high level of client motivation; soft goals are vaguer and often sound less convincing. (You may also be able to see some connection between the specificity of goals and the stages of change at which clients present.) How hard, soft, formal and informal you are in relation to goal setting also depends on your practice, your model and your personality. We suggest that the more you are able to vary your practice according to client needs, the better.

Summary

Set specific goals related to the client's target concerns. Collaborate in making these clear and workable. Check that they are really the client's goals, that it is within the power of the client to achieve them, and that they are not idealized. Respect the modesty of clients' goals. Be prepared to influence clients where it is apparent that their goals are too difficult or too easy. Consider the merits of formal and informal approaches to goal setting.

---

31 Identify the client's past unsuccessful and successful attempts at dealing with the concern

Unsuccessful attempts

We pointed out earlier the importance of discovering whether clients had had previous counselling or other help and what benefits or otherwise they derived from such help. Here, we are looking at past unsuccessful attempts to change a specific problem. Although it is possible that clients arrive for counselling without having made any attempt to deal with the problem themselves, this is highly unlikely. The client may well have made several attempts to deal with the problem. So we encourage you to ask questions like 'What have you done in the past about this problem?' or 'What have you been doing to overcome this problem?' Such questions help the client to identify strategies that have not worked.

Let's take an example of someone who reports that he is 'stressed' and is worried about 'cracking up'. He says that his career has gone out of control. In trying to extend himself, he has taken on too much work. At the same time he is earning too little. He has ensnared himself in a heavy workload and his plan to extend himself has gone wrong. He wants to know what he can do about it before something goes very wrong. You ask him how he has tried to deal with it (he has obviously not been successful) and he replies that he has refused pieces of work, he has talked to his partner about it, he has tried just to 'knuckle down to it' and he has meditated. None of this has worked, he says. 'Was it all hopeless or did some of those attempts work better than others?' you might ask. The point of your enquiry is to identify what has clearly not worked, and perhaps what holds some promise. You also want to avoid what's been tried before that has been unsuccessful, and to build upon past successes. Suppose he tells you that talking to his partner helped a bit, and meditating helped a bit. Find out how these helped, and how his other strategies didn't.

You don't want to offer this client (or any clients) a strategy that has already proved to be ineffective. If clients have never consulted a counsellor before, then this is something new for them, but don't assume that the novelty in itself is sufficiently motivating. The client may have a very supportive partner, but 'just talking about it' may not be enough. The client may be very good at being assertive, so don't unthinkingly suggest further assertiveness exercises. The question of what's been tried without success will yield important clues to how the client is likely to respond to your approach. Note that if the client were to say, 'I don't know what to try, nothing works', then a more global depression may be indicated and, if so, your task will then be to help the client identify specific target concerns. There is a danger in working with clients experiencing depression that your questions about anything unsuccessful might unintentionally worsen their depression, so you need to remain sensitive to this possibility. Generally, no one has a life without some successes and redeeming features (see the next section) and these can be elicited in such cases.

Where a client appears to have tried several strategies energetically but without success, you may consider a more exploratory, unhurried approach, temporarily de-emphasizing effort on his part. Where clients have apparently always become confused when discussing personal difficulties, you may consider new ways of helping them to be specific. Don't offer more of what has proved to be unsuccessful. 'Do something different', as solution-focused therapists say. Capitalize on what you are able to offer that differs from what the client has attempted to date. 'It seems to me you've been tying yourself in knots. How would it be if, when you come here, we focus on one thing at a time, and look at things in a relaxed way?' This may strike the client as sufficiently different from anything she's tried before to warrant hope. We are talking here about a client who has made strenuous attempts to change things. Clients will vary widely. At the other end of the scale you may be confronted by clients who have apparently made little effort to change anything, and there your strategy will be quite different again. You will probably have to help the client to *begin* accepting responsibility for himself. Note, however, that clients' unsuccessful attempts may include a lot of soul searching or ruminating about a problem. Some people read magazines, listen to radio 'phone-ins', consult astrologers, do personal inventories of their strengths and weaknesses, and so on. Why have these not worked? What are you going to do that is significantly different?

Summary

Find out what your client has tried before that hasn't helped to overcome this particular problem. Identify which aspects of such attempts have been unsuccessful so that you can avoid further unsuccessful strategies. Take care not to unintentionally emphasize lack of success but keep the accent on hope.

32 Identify the client's past successful attempts at dealing with the target concern

What we want to advocate is that you aim positively to identify examples of where your client has had any success relating to a target concern. At first sight it may seem contradictory to speak of past successful attempts at problem solution, because if the problem is still there, then haven't previous attempts failed? It may be that some counsellors holding a depth-psychological view of change would argue that past attempts have been only symptomatic successes. Obviously within this brief focal view we are not taking this position. We concur with Prochaska and DiClemente (1984) that change is frequently cyclical (so many steps forward, so many back) and that it is important not to dismiss previous gains. We suggest that you avoid 'all or nothing' thinking in relation to your clients' progress (past and present). Imagine that you have a new client who presents as very worried because after several months of abstinence she has taken a drink. She regards this as total backsliding and condemns herself for it. Now, of course there is a danger here of a serious relapse and you would want to address this accordingly. But will you join the client in her negative focus or instead concentrate on her clearly demonstrated power to be abstinent? This example illustrates that the same event can be viewed instructively or self-defeatingly (Carr, 2004). The potential here is for building on past success or for dramatizing present 'failure'. (We are not dismissing the possibility here that a single drink might signal serious backsliding to come.)

Let's take another example. Your new client reports that she is very anxious about starting a new job after several years of being a full-time mother. You point out that she successfully held a number of jobs before becoming a mother and has successfully taken on the tasks involved in mothering and running a household. She has both past and recent successful experiences to draw on. She may be able to recall vividly the anxiety she felt on starting a new job in the past, or on first being responsible for a baby. Can she recall it and utilize it in her present concern? Clients often dismiss their own positive attributes and skills (for example, 'I'm just a housewife') and you are advised to help them identify and acknowledge these positives when addressing present target concerns.

Referring back to Prochaska and DiClemente's stages of change, you may well have a client who has previously moved through the sequence of precontemplation, contemplation, action and maintenance. She has successfully conquered a problem. But now it reappears. Let's say a woman has previously overcome a self-defeating dependency on violent men. A former lover appears on the scene. She knows he is 'no good' for her but she is agitated, fearful that she will succumb to the old attraction. She is afraid of feeling powerless and helpless. How did she overcome this in the past? Wasn't the attraction just as powerful then? What were the factors leading to her ending the relationship? What were her personal resources? By focusing on how she handled change before, and how she maintained it successfully, you can reinforce her capacity to cope now. It may be that new strategies can be added to old ones, but by investigating old ones and harnessing them, you have a powerful ally.

You will also want to help the client to see precisely at what point she began to lose her resolution. What was different at this time in her life? How did she manage to stay clear of certain men for so long, but now finds herself all but succumbing again? Is it just chance? Is it that she's been unconsciously hankering to repeat bad experiences? Does she often encounter risk situations but usually handle them well? Are there other relevant factors in her life at this time, perhaps weakening her resolve? Look at both her past record of maintaining previous gains and the present threat and ask what the salient current features are. Help your client to put together her past successes and realistic potential for managing the future well. In introducing her to your proposed counselling approach, spell out those elements that will assist her in strengthening the coping skills she already has. Show her how you can help to minimize any tendencies to relapse further. Throughout this process, ensure that you are not dismissing the client's real distress, nor becoming unrealistically Pollyannaish about the good aspects of her or his life and change attempts. Consult the solution-focused literature (for example Milner and O'Byrne, 2002) on this kind of 'solution-talk'.

Summary

Explore with the client past experiences of dealing with the target concern. Investigate patterns of past maintenance and present threat to such maintenance. Build on past successes, remembering to remain sensitive to distress.

33 Identify obstacles to change

It is important not to foster an overly simplistic view of change in counselling. Frequently, change is neither easy for the client nor predictable for the counsellor. While both commit themselves to change attempts, there are various factors that may undermine their strategies. We therefore suggest that you make this clear and discuss explicitly any possible obstacles to progress. As with other material in this book, we are of course presupposing that the client has a reasonably high level of honesty and awareness and that any unconscious factors are not so subversive as to wreck completely conscious change attempts. See Davy and Cross (2004) for examples of barriers to successful counselling. Put the question to your client squarely: 'What kinds of obstacles do you think there may be to your achieving this goal?' Be alert to clients who either want to please you by appearing 100 per cent committed ('nothing's going to stop me') or who may be prey to naivety ('now that I'm in counselling there's nothing I can't achieve').

Having said this, look at what a client of Windy's outlined as her goals and her possible obstacles (see Table 1; reproduced with the client's permission). This is just one person's way of expressing her goals and possible obstacles. The obstacles here are expressed in terms of beliefs, fears and behaviours and are 'owned' as internal processes. The client is articulate and psychologically minded. Your client may be similarly oriented, but perhaps not. You don't have to ask clients to write their goals and obstacles down. With some you may need to offer more examples than with other clients, perhaps by self-disclosing or by referring to others as examples. The task is to elicit connections between goals and internal obstacles, which represents the beginnings of insight. It also provides an agenda for active work on the target problems.

Table 1. Goals and obstacles to change: one client's list

Ultimate goal: to get married and have children	
What I want to achieve	*What I think is stopping me*
To be able to form relationships with people – particularly men.	Inability to share my feelings. Inability to accept warmth/love offered to me. Fear of being 'owned'.
	Hypercritical approach to boyfriends which provides me with carte blanche reasons for not showing my feelings, accepting warmth, being 'owned' and forming close relationships.
	Fear of judgement towards my choice by outsiders: From parents – is he intellectual enough? From friends – is he nice-looking, a drip, etc.?
	Fear of being criticised.
Ability to share my feelings and allow myself to become close.	Shyness. Fear of giving away something of myself. Unaware of what feelings to share. Providing an opening through which others can get close to me and possibly entrap me. Total lack of practice – don't know how. Fear of my feelings being abused → rejection → hurt.
A real willingness to accept warmth offered to me.	Conscious rational thoughts: Is this Mr Right? Do I want to take from him? Do I want him to feel that I am his? Do I want him around a lot? Do I feel anything for him? Do I want to be seen with him? Do I want to share myself with him? Do I want to lose my independence?
	Feelings of insecurity in myself: Why does he want me? What is there in me to like? Does he want me or just the front cover? Is there anything behind the front cover?
	Fear of ultimate rejection → hurt.

Ultimate goal: to get married and have children	
What I want to achieve	*What I think is stopping me*
To be able to express criticism openly (without causing pain), rather than bottling up grievances which allow me to abandon relationships or blurt them out aggressively.	Fear of hurting others. Fear of causing arguments and losing control of myself. Fear of rejection. Inability to find the right words.
Confidence when meeting new people or asking people to do things for me.	Shyness – diffidence. Fear of disdain.
Confidence when talking to people 'senior' to myself in some way, e.g. in school, inspectors, advisers, etc., in politics, party bigwigs; in music, conductors, well-known musicians, brilliant players, etc. You.	Fear of being considered irrelevant or silly. Fear of being criticised. Fear of being disliked. Lack of confidence in my own worth.
The will to contact old friends who have left the area or I haven't seen for some time.	Belief that they don't really want to see me, talk to me, etc. Belief that I am an intrusion and disturbing them.

At this stage we are advocating that you help the client to identify general obstacles. The client may be aware that she is resisting progress. Or the client may attribute obstacles to the environment. 'I can't get on with people because they always snub me. Where I work, they're all stuck-up, they don't want to know you', for example. Keep in mind the possibility that this client's psychological obstacles may include social skill limitations. 'Do you think there's anything at all you could do to improve the situation?' would be an appropriate probe. Or 'I can see that they might be difficult to get on with, but since you say you really do want to get on better, can you think of any ways in which you might do more to improve things?' might help to identify an inner obstacle. How might this dialogue proceed?

Client: I don't know what I can do.

You: What have you tried?

Client: I tried talking to Deborah the other day but she didn't seem interested.

You: Can you tell me what you said to her and in what way you think she showed a lack of interest?

> *Client:* Well, she just carried on typing as if what I'd said was boring.
>
> *You:* She carried on typing. But how can you be sure what she was thinking? How do you know she thought you were boring?
>
> *Client:* Well, why else would she ignore me like that?
>
> *You:* There are several possible explanations of why she carried on typing, but you insist on your own version, with no evidence. I think one obstacle is that perhaps you don't persevere with such conversations as much as you might. Another is that you're very ready to imagine reasons for people not being interested in you. Are you willing to accept that these might be obstacles in you, and not necessarily in others?
>
> *Client:* I know what you mean, yes. Perhaps you've got a point.

With this kind of client you may have to be very persistent, returning to certain points again and again. But there are few people who are not willing to consider that their attitudes may play a part in what apparently 'just happens' to them. Show an interest in the client's world, including possible real, external obstacles. You are unlikely to insist with a black client or a woman, for example, that there are no social obstacles whatsoever to their self-advancement. Take the clients' social context into account, their temperament, and so on. Get to know them; and in doing so, help them to identify blocks to progress and so to anticipate ways in which they might sabotage counselling.

Transactional analysis has looked hard at client sabotage, particularly the kind in which a 'script' may be along the lines of 'don't succeed'. Stewart (1989) gives examples of how people create stale or tragic outcomes for themselves and how counsellors can identify these and contract for a non-sabotaging outcome with the client. Clients have numerous ways of presenting obstacles, excuses, evasions, psychosomatic complaints, and so on. Don't run away with the idea that progress will be or has to be smooth – it is more likely to be an obstacle course – but go over the terrain with the client, mapping out what bumps and ravines you both think could stand in the way.

Summary

Invite the client to spell out possible obstacles to change. Allow for individual differences and accept the probability of setbacks, but bring the likelihood of obstacles explicitly into the picture. Accept the client's way of describing goals and obstacles.

---

34 Heed the special problems of depression and demoralization

Depression is the world's leading mental health problem and set to become the world's leading health problem in the near future. This may relate to the increase in consciousness of global competition and conflict, work stress and breakdown of marriages but possibly also to the exhaustion of the materialist agenda: the realization that we are not necessarily satisfied as we get more. Someone always has more than we do and what we possess is not necessarily secure. Whatever its actual causes, counsellors are well aware that in parallel with the specific events that trigger help-seeking (such as failed relationships, stressful work, health anxieties and trauma-engendering incidents) there is often a depressive undertow. Sometimes this is overtly acknowledged but sometimes not. Furthermore, as time passes and counselling and psychotherapy become more available and tried more, more clients have unfortunate experiences of negative or ineffective counselling. Just as religion, career, relationships and other traditional avenues to happiness do not always 'work', so it would be unrealistic to deny outright that counselling has its limitations and failures. By *not* acknowledging this, we may inadvertently reinforce the sense of guilt that some clients have if they have tried counselling once before and it didn't work or its gains didn't persist. So we have two issues here: (a) those who arrive seeking help but who may be unaware of just how depressed they are and (b) those who have tried various methods (including counselling) before and may be even more depressed at the thought that they are beyond help.

Depression is often treated as just another problem or experience that the client can be helped to overcome by any of a range of therapeutic approaches – and in one way it certainly is. Currently much of the evidence remains strongly in favour of cognitive behavioural therapy (CBT) and antidepressant medication but there is also some evidence for other approaches. In brief counselling there is a great deal of hope that methods of CBT, solution-focused therapy, the 'human givens' approach and also hypnotherapy (Yapko, 1994) can alleviate depressive suffering. The positive psychology movement (Carr, 2004) also offers hope that a new psychology can be forged to combat the epidemic of depressive experience. This movement is implicitly critical of the pathologizing inherent in much psychotherapeutic theory and places its emphasis on 'positive illusions', the engendering of hope, the instilling of expectation. It chimes well with CBT and solution-focused therapy. But, again, there is a danger (especially within time-limited work) that practitioners may well-meaningly swing into such positive strategies without fully appreciating or acknowledging clients' struggles with their depression.

There is a two-way consideration for counsellors here. First, as we have said, too rapid a movement towards hope-engendering and demoralization-combating can leave the client feeling inadequately understood and prone to further guilt. Some clients who have not had good experiences of CBT report this kind of experience. Second, however, too slow an approach risks leaving the client feeling as depressed as before, or more depressed. A criticism sometimes made of person-centred counselling, rightly or wrongly, for instance, is that reflecting back to clients the details and nuances of their depressed story will simply reinforce it. What is called for, then, is sensitivity to each client's personality and stage of change (as we have described in other sections) and a sense of the best balance between empathic understanding and action-engendering. Let's look at this via two different counsellor sentences:

1. It's pretty clear that you're very down right now and I get the impression that it's hard for you to take much in. Is that right?
2. You're well aware of how you feel and how long that's been going on and – if I'm right – it seems you're quite eager to try some new ways of getting on with your life.

Obviously in the first case, the counsellor attempts to resonate with the client's low mood and not overload her with therapeutic expectations. But even the tiny phrase 'right now' marks the impermanent or subtly shifting nature of depression and suggests some hope. In the second case, the counsellor is honouring the client's self-knowledge but catching hold of a glimmer, at least, of readiness to engage with some new therapeutic strategies. Wachtel (1993) gives many excellent examples of how subtly different wording is effective, particularly when you are trying to tease out whether the client needs 'breathing space' or challenge, reflection or action. (This is, incidentally, a reminder of the usefulness of tape-recording some of your work, to focus on such micro-considerations.)

Another feature of working with markedly demoralized clients is that their mood can affect you very powerfully. Supervisees often report that they don't know what to do with certain clients, or even dread seeing them next time, because they seem to ooze hopelessness and the counsellor then also feels hopeless. This is readily understood by psychodynamic counsellors as instances of countertransference and projective identification. The counsellor may feel rejected, just as the client probably does (or once did), or may even have strong physical sensations of sleepiness, dizziness or nausea. Notice these and be sure to discuss them in supervision, because they can be misinterpreted or dismissed, and yet hold important information about the client's state and about the therapeutic relationship.

It is well known that depression can mask other feared feelings, such as guilt, sadness and anger. The saying 'depression is anger without enthusiasm' captures some of this. Instead of uncritically agreeing with the referrer or the client herself that *depression* is the problem, tease out its ingredients and exceptions, but do this skilfully and without suggesting that you disbelieve the person's own account. Rather, you are interested in the nuances of how your client feels and thinks and want to get a full picture. Entering into the inner world of someone who is depressed is difficult. See Solomon's (2002) harrowing personal account of depression for an excellent example of self-understanding and of the vicissitudes of this condition.

Summary

Think about the special challenges of clients who are depressed or for whom depression is an undertow. Gauge carefully the appropriateness of each of your responses in empathic or action-oriented ways, and note how the client registers on your own feelings and sensations. Adapt your overall strategy in the light of your observations and supervisory input.

---

35 Consider specific interventions for specific concerns

We are aware that many counsellors dislike the idea that there are 'treatments of choice' for certain complaints or problems. Common objections are that it is dehumanizing to classify people or to pre-judge them clinically, and that people seeking counselling or psychotherapy should be regarded as whole people (not as isolated, 'medical model' physical complaints). Many counsellors, including those whose approach is psychodynamic and person-centred, claim that their approaches are equally successful with all kinds of clients. Mahrer (1989) regards experiential psychotherapy, for example, as potentially suitable for all (except those who, on trying it, decide it's not for them). Since a certain amount of research has suggested that there is little difference in outcomes from different treatment approaches, this has been taken by some to mean that anything can work with anyone. If this is your position, we suggest you consider, at least, the view that there are preferential therapy methods for certain problems. In fact, increasingly, counsellors are under some degree of pressure to consult and act on evidence-based practice guidelines that indicate which approaches have research evidence to support them.

Frances et al. (1985) reviewed research favouring both sides of the argument. On the one hand, there is ample evidence that relationship or 'non-specific' factors do contribute meaningfully to successful outcome in many cases. On the other hand, there is also ample evidence that certain problems are solved better by using specific interventions. Cognitive therapy has been shown to work very well with depression. Behaviour therapy generally works better than psychoanalysis with alcoholism, smoking and eating disorders. Phobias are more appropriately treated by exposure to the feared object or event in real life than in imagination. The treatment of compulsions is more effective when some form of 'response prevention' is included. Without consulting the research literature, or having a supervisor who does, you are unlikely to know these findings. Common sense often tells you when particular clients are not responsive to your approach to counselling. But an awareness of what others have found can greatly enhance your practice. In being able to conceptualize clients' problems when they call for specific treatment, you can either rapidly adjust your own interventions or refer on.

Striano (1988) interviewed people who had had unsatisfactory experiences in therapy. Many of these reported inappropriate approaches, including physical illness misdiagnosed as psychological, extreme therapist passivity or an over-analytical therapist style and the ill-advised uses of hypnosis and drugs. What this shows is that therapists of all persuasions are capable of error. It is not only the easy-to-condemn medical profession that errs. It is true that the talking treatments are less likely to be dangerous (except in cases where serious illness is overlooked) but you may be able to hasten a client's progress by identifying a specific concern and taking appropriate action.

How do you find out which specific interventions are indicated for certain problems? Obviously you will want to consult your supervisor, who also may or may not be familiar with certain conditions. You will learn to be discerning as you progress in your counselling career. In the short-term, however, the

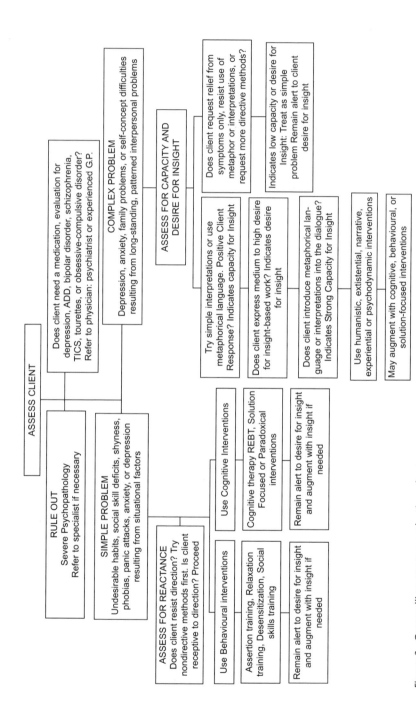

Figure 3. Counselling strategy selection chart.
With kind permission from Mary Lee Nelson & ACA.

best way to find out is by consulting research literature. You might try, for example, Reid et al. (1997), Roth and Fonagy (2005). *Bergin and Garfield's Handbook of Psychotherapy and Behavior Change* (Lambert, 2003), remains, in our opinion, an invaluable aid in familiarizing yourself with research in the counselling field. Also consult the National Institute for Clinical Excellence (NICE) guidelines on mental health online. Another source of precious information is the first-person reports of psychological disturbances written by people like Sutherland (1989) on 'severe mental breakdown'. Sutherland actually gives a consumer's-eye view of choice of treatment (pp. 258–62) which we as counsellors would do well to heed.

Please note that we are not saying that you must become a medically oriented counsellor. In line with the rest of the book we are arguing for putting clients first, even when that might demand extra work on our part or a willingness to re-learn or to refer clients on. If you are in doubt about any particular client, discuss this with your supervisor. Be flexible as to the way ahead. Be especially watchful in cases of prolonged non-improvement or worsening of conditions. As we noted earlier in Section 8 on referral, it is a good idea to become familiar with other allied professionals. In some cases counselling was not the best choice for these clients, or needed to be complemented by appropriate medication. Indeed, the first time Colin ever met someone who had a serious obsessive-compulsive problem (in which the client feared he might have been killing people) he did not at all recognize it for what it was. This client no doubt instinctively noted his lack of experience and dropped out of counselling. Now Colin is much more inclined to note and to act on signs of serious disturbance, rather than to assume that he can contain and aid such a condition in a purely person-centred manner.

Summary

Familiarize yourself with the research literature on specific problems and any indications as to treatment of choice. Be ready to adapt your approach or to make a referral. Always take any doubts to your supervisor.

36 Explain the counselling approach you intend to use

Having obtained a good picture of your client and her goals, you now have a working hypothesis and a strategy in mind. You can now share with her what your intentions are. Together you have discussed conceptualization of the problem and specific goals. While you may in general always be ready to invite the client to reflect on the counselling process, now you put to her your specific proposal. The approach you intend to take will be a distillation of various factors: your own counselling orientation and your ability and will-ingess to go beyond this; your knowledge of the client; your relationship with the client; the client's previous history of the problem and attempts to overcome it; your knowledge of research as it applies (or not) to the client;

and so on. You are ready to offer your understanding of the problem and your explanation of how you intend to help the client solve it.

Whether your preferred approach is person-centred, psychodynamic, cognitive-behavioural, transactional analysis, Gestalt, or whatever, you need to explain how it applies to your client's problem. You and the client need to have a shared understanding of how you are working. In Appendix 4 you will find the second part of the 'Opinions about Psychological Problems' questionnaire, devised by Chris Barker and colleagues. This questionnaire has 47 items covering possible explanations for how people may be helped to overcome their psychological problems. You may find it helpful to use this questionnaire to discover your clients' views of how they may be helped. You are likely to find it useful in pinpointing the approach you use with each client. It can be done systematically, but you must judge the wisdom of that as you work with each client. Bearing in mind the degree to which clients differ, it may or may not be appropriate to use this kind of questionnaire systematically. But however you decide on your counselling approach, decide you must. So how do you put that decision to a client?

In each case the counsellor has to decide on an appropriate way of working with the client. It has been arrived at systematically, perhaps on the basis of the counsellor's experiences with similar clients, with reference to a supervisor, and so on. In each case the important thing is that you begin to explain, briefly, what you think is the core current problem and what you propose to do to deal with it. Each explanation contains a particular way forward which is expressed clearly, without jargon, and non-dogmatically. Depending on need, you might expand on your explanation. We are aware that there is resistance among some counsellors to this explanation process, partly because of lack of confidence sometimes, and partly due to theoretical and clinical reservations. Do consider carefully your reasons for not doing so. But, of course, also remain sensitive to clients' reactions. An obsessive client might ask for a detailed rationale. A client who is very informal might discourage you from offering too clinical an explanation.

Tell your client your overall rationale at the beginning and also explain the therapeutic tasks involved and why you think these will be helpful. If you work somewhat eclectically and you wish to introduce a certain task, for instance the use of a genogram or stones or buttons within sessions – which some counsellors find especially helpful with clients who cannot articulate emotionally charged material relating to complex family patterns, for example – explain it briefly and give it a try. Give the client time, if necessary, to digest the idea between sessions and perhaps to prepare. Ask your client for her reaction to your proposal. Does it make sense? Does it fit with the client's perception? Is your suggested approach something the client feels able and ready to commit herself to? Is it focused enough? Would the client like to make any suggestions? Encourage your client to give honest feedback, and take seriously what she says, noting any non-verbal reservations she may signal. If she gives you a negative or equivocal response, probe for clarification and modify your approach as necessary. A humorous illustration of the possible consequences of not explaining an approach to a client is reproduced from the *Guardian* of 23 June 1987.

Probationer blows a raspberry at apple therapy

Yorkshire's reputation for hard-headedness took a knock yesterday when a young probation defaulter told a court why he had failed to turn up for sessions of social therapy at a day centre. The Crown court, where the realities of the world have traditionally been treated with respect, heard that the course required X to pretend that he was an apple.

Although a fledgling Olivier might enjoy this – nowadays, you could imitate an Apple computer or pretend to mis-hear and be one of West Yorkshire's many Methodist chapels – X was too thin-skinned.

The core of the problem, his counsel, Y, told the court, was that 'he couldn't understand what was being asked of him. He was embarrassed and stopped attending.'

Y explained that the apple was the fruit which broke the back of X who is 19 and unemployed. He had not intended to blow a raspberry at the probation service, but had been baffled by the role played by the fruit in the curriculum.

'He had great difficulty in understanding some of the role-playing exercises he was asked to perform,' she said. 'He was asked to play various fruits, and the last time he went he was asked to pretend to be an apple.'

'I suppose there must be some meaning in these exercises, but he found it difficult to cope with them.'

X, of no fixed address, admitted breach of a two-year probation order imposed on him last December for burglary. He was ordered to do 140 hours' community service.

The probation service could not be contacted last night to give its answer to X's complaint – be it a lemon or otherwise.

(Adapted from the *Guardian*, 23 June 1987, with kind permission.)

Summary

Be prepared to explain to your clients the approach to their problem that you propose to use. Explain this clearly, in concrete terms, and invitingly. Consider any reservations you may have and why. Ask for feedback and accommodate this.

37 Tailor your approach to the client

Remembering our earlier sections on client differences and counsellor influence, be ready to adapt your approach to the individual client. We advocate that you have a working alliance with your clients, that you do not use uncritical jargon and that you offer a specific approach to solving a problem.

Remember that clients have preferences for formality and informality, for expertness and attractiveness, and other counsellor styles. Now, when you are presenting your treatment proposal to a client who is a 'medical modeller' (or who expects psychological treatment from an authority figure – refer back to Section 25 on 'important client differences') and who looks up to you for learned advice, it would not quite be appropriate to give him a loosely worded description of his problems and of your proposed approach. In such a case a rather more 'professional' response might be called for. You might use slightly more professional language, refer to psychological literature and to your own experience of similar cases. If the client appears to want a didactic explanation, you might offer one (provided that it would enhance the client's progress rather than simply bolster your vanity). Conversely, a client who is an 'explorer' (again, see Section 25; see also Richert, 1983) will not want authoritative diagnoses and prognoses, but an openness to experience. With him you will probably adapt your language, drop any suspiciously medical sounding terms and employ colourful and 'experiential' descriptions. (Windy once had the experience, on misreading a client's cues and 'talking research' to her, of being told exactly what to do with his research!) In some cases you may decide to use self disclosure (for example, 'I had much the same problem myself and I found that what worked best of all was . . .'), although generally this should be used sparingly.

Again, remember that these are not facile prescriptions but rough guides and ideas. When you are at this stage with a client and she is looking at you expectantly, and you are nervously wondering whether you've understood, your first attempt may not be quite the gem you'd hoped for. Beginning practitioners frequently become anxiously perfectionistic about each and every intervention and while it is a good learning strategy to examine your interventions in detail, it is counterproductive to become obsessed and self-blaming. But goodwill, good practice and getting into the habit of the reflection process will all serve you well in maturing. Remember that the reflection process is a means of stepping back from the work and reviewing how well you and the client are relating, and how clear you both are about the agreed goals and tasks.

Summary

In explaining to your client what approach you intend to take, bear in mind the importance of how you describe your approach. Ensure that you use appropriate language and that you invite the client's comments. Adapt your style to the client's personality.

PART III
INITIATING CHANGE

38 Begin work

'Begin work' may seem an odd phrase to use at this point because you will have already done a lot of work with your client by now. Think of what has gone up to now as preparatory and inductive. Think of it as the laying of foundations. You might compare it with the large amount of work that goes into some buildings before any structure actually rises from the ground. If the planning, designing and foundation-laying aren't done effectively, the building may collapse.

So you have decided with your client on target problems and specific goals related to them. You have talked about how you will be approaching the first problem. You have received feedback. Now you are ready to implement your plans. Be sure to proceed as discussed and do not succumb to sudden inspiration that will puzzle your client as to what is happening. (Inspiration has its place but probably not here.) If you have agreed that you are going to give the client plenty of space to talk, and that you will mainly listen for some time, then do just that. If you have agreed to help your client to become more aware of his deeper feelings, then proceed to do that. If you have agreed to help the client examine thoroughly his dysfunctional beliefs or early experiences, then systematically do that, at least for the time being. Later there may be a place for some variation of techniques but here be as methodical as you can. Patten and Walker (1990) discovered in a highly revealing piece of research that the people they interviewed (who had had 'marriage guidance counselling') *unanimously* found 'being given explanations about counselling techniques' helpful; 20 per cent found it 'very helpful'. In subsequent research by Walker and Patten, (1990), when counsellors were asked for their views on explaining techniques, only 64 per cent considered this a helpful practice.

When you have covered some ground, enough to let the client get the feeling of your approach, ask for some feedback. 'How is this going for you?' or 'Is there anything you'd like to say at this point?' You are the best judge of when to ask for feedback. If your client is deeply involved in a needed cathartic experience, allow her the time or give her the support she needs. If your approach is person-centred, then close attention to the client's experiencing, including her experiencing of you, will mean that you stay closely in touch with her reactions, verbal and non-verbal. Where your approach is based on a sequence of taught steps, for example in some of the principles of transactional analysis or rational emotive behaviour therapy, then you obviously have to allow sufficient time to do that teaching. But always check that you are explaining the approach clearly, and check that the client understands the approach and its usefulness to her concerns.

Suppose that you have had every reason to feel that your client is happy with the approach you have suggested. She has agreed that to look at her childhood, for example, may well lead to clues as to her present agitation. Yet when she begins to talk about memories, the activity of remembering seems remote from her current troubles. Perhaps she has difficulty recalling much, or remembers scenes but can see no connection between them and the present concerns. Invite this kind of information. It doesn't mean that you have to abandon your plans but it suggests that some modification is called for. Some clients will be readily reassured that a little time will reveal the efficacy of the approach.

Another danger might be that a client will feel rushed. If you are adopting a particularly confrontational or active approach, your client may well offer resistance. He may have liked the sound of what you had to offer in theory, but may find it very difficult in practice. Offer the client plenty of opportunity to give you feedback on any dramatic techniques you may use. Some brief therapies specifically seek to use the client's initial anxieties for therapeutic movement (for example Sifneos, 1972). Davanloo (1985) uses the first one or two sessions for a 'trial therapy' in which vigorous challenging of defences is coupled with the building of an 'unconscious therapeutic alliance'. These highly active forms of psychoanalytically derived technique are, however, specialized. The rapid entry into the client's irrational belief system as practised by Ellis (Yankura and Dryden, 1990) is another example of an active-directive beginning to counselling. We suggest that as a beginner it is appropriate for you to pace yourself, to respect your own developmental needs and limitations as a counsellor as well as the needs of your clients. In general, then, heed the feedback of the client at this stage and be prepared to modify your approach.

Summary

Begin your work with the client as planned. Watch for signs of difficulty or resistance. Ask for feedback on what you are doing and how it is received. Modify your approach if necessary.

---

39 Don't overload the client

We have pointed out in the introduction and need to reiterate here the importance of not bombarding the client with information, questions or demands. In the same way that you would not fire multiple questions at your client within the space of a few minutes, do not attempt to cover too much ground in one session. By all means offer more to clients who readily understand your interventions (for example, those clients who may have read about a particular approach or who have done similar work before) but be aware of what your client is really picking up. You need to be particularly alert to clients who may be afraid to question or confront you and we therefore suggest that you encourage all clients to let you know loudly and clearly if you are going too fast for them.

Remember to refer to the reflection process. 'We seem to have covered quite a bit of ground already. What's your reaction to this?' You might ask specifically, 'How do you feel about the pace we're going at?' Check out what the client has learned, because that's what is important. 'Could you tell me what you've picked up from what we've just been talking about?' is a simple, direct way of checking. Don't assume that a lot of new ideas or a new way of relating to another person will readily be understood. Equally, don't worry clients to death with overly tentative questions when it's apparent that counselling is proceeding fairly well.

We think that one of the implications of being sensitive to individual clients' needs is a willingness to consider different session lengths. The 50-minute hour is not sacrosanct, there's nothing of any intrinsic significance in it at all; it's just a convenience. Now, we are emphatically not saying that you should be undisciplined about timekeeping. Neither are we recommending that you change session lengths willy nilly. But consider that for some clients 50 minutes is a long time. Some people with debilitating physical conditions (like myalgic encephalomyelitis) find it very hard to concentrate or withstand emotional stress for very long. Some clients cannot benefit from long periods of self-examination and your feeling that you must fill out the hour may be taking them past the point of optimal learning. Lacan, for different reasons, often terminated his therapy sessions after a very short time. Balint et al. (1972) refer to 'ten-minute psychotherapy', meaning the critical focus in each session that is experienced by both practitioner and client as a 'flash of understanding'.

The converse of this is being prepared to lengthen sessions. Mahrer (1989) and many other experiential practitioners allow ample time in each session for the experiencing and integration of strong feelings. In practice this usually means not longer than one-and-a-half or two hours. This is explained to clients before the session begins. Other reasons for lengthening session time include crisis and practicality. Although as a general rule it is advisable not to slip over into extra time when your client appears distressed because this may convey the idea that distress (and particularly overt distress shown late in the session) will be rewarded or regarded as 'special'. However, there may be times when extra time is quite valid. There are sometimes dramatic breakthroughs that may be better facilitated by allowing them to run their course rather than cutting them off. It may be that you are working with a particular client, helping her to break through some frozen emotion, and extra time, or the availability of extra time, may take the pressure off her. Practically, there are occasions when clients have to travel some distance to see you, or cannot see you for some weeks, and therefore request extra time in one or two sessions. Provided this is agreed, and suitable negotiations are made for extra fees in private practice, then there is no real reason not to consider this. The obvious caveat is where you have a client who is trying to compromise you or to play games, in which case you will of course consult your supervisor.

Another way in which you can help clients to maximize their learning is to tape-record sessions and offer copies of the tapes to them. This allows them to go over the session as often as they want to in order to ensure that its gains are internalized or that any doubts about the way you are working are aired. Try this and then ask your client to comment. 'Is there anything you weren't clear about, or anything you'd like to suggest?'

Summary

Don't be overambitious within sessions. Listen out for what the client is actually taking in and learning and capitalize on that. Invite feedback on learning and on any problems arising. Be prepared for negotiating session length if appropriate.

40 Vary the level of support and direction

We refer you again to Howard et al. (1987) and the recommendation that you adapt your counselling style according to each client's needs. These authors suggest that two main kinds of counsellor style are supportive and directive. Supportive counselling involves relationship building, empathy and acceptance. Some clients evidently 'thrive' in a climate of counsellor supportiveness, or the same client may at different times require either a predominantly supportive or directive style. A directive counsellor style is characterized by task setting and goal orientation. Although we have dwelt on goals to quite an extent in this book, we advocate an awareness of the needs for degrees of either style.

Remember that this is not a case of adhering to either one style or the other. Indeed, you will fare better if you are able to switch judiciously from one style to another as occasion demands. Let's say that your client has been working hard on a particular problem and has encountered a lot of pain along the way. You may have been very directive in helping him to get to this point. But then it is evident that he has reached a temporary plateau and needs time to digest his learning. You may at this time become much more supportive, perhaps suggesting to the client that he takes his time. You may perhaps acknowledge how much he has accomplished.

Howard et al. suggest that there are variations on this theme. You may, for example, offer a high level of direction and a high level of support at the same time, as in the activity of teaching. If you are using a counselling approach that is based partly on teaching (for example, reality therapy), then you may support and direct simultaneously. Howard et al. suggest as an example of a low support/low direction therapist, the psychoanalyst who is an 'interested observer' offering neither obvious structure nor support. You will learn to adapt your level of support and direction according to each client's needs. To some extent these styles coincide with Heron's (2001) six categories of intervention, and it is worth familiarizing yourself with Heron's model, which includes the prescriptive, informative, confronting, cathartic, catalytic and supportive interventions. The more you are able, in the early sessions, to respond flexibly to your client's shifting needs, the better the grounding you can provide for successful counselling. The more you practise 'changing gears', the better.

Summary

Be aware of how supportive and directive you are at different times and consciously vary the use you make of these styles of counselling. Learn to adapt to the changing needs of clients throughout sessions.

41 Consider initiating between-session work

What we mean by between-session work is any task or assignment deliberately undertaken by your clients to enhance the impact of counselling. Your preferred approach may or may not include the idea of between-session work. We suggest that you consider its advantages in the light of what we said earlier about the importance of client activity in brief counselling. Your session is just one out of 168 hours in the client's week. All sorts of factors impinge on the client during the week. All kinds of opportunities for growthful risk taking present themselves to the client in her everyday life. Budman and Gurman (1988) emphasize that 'being in the world is more important than being in therapy'. This is a point you may want to communicate to clients who show signs of dependency on counselling or of reluctance to extend the gains of counselling into their everyday life. You will not be doing this if you do not believe in it – if, for example, you see the value of counselling as lying primarily in intensive transference cures. However, even psychodynamic counselling has its tasks for clients (Ursano et al., 1991) which include paying attention to dreams. Some psychodynamic counsellors instruct clients on the importance of recalling and if necessary writing down the contents of dreams.

Reinforce the importance of psychological work in everyday life. This means that you may, for example, suggest to clients that they pay extra attention to their relationships, their moods, dreams, instances of avoidance, and so on. Stress from the beginning that counselling is one part of life or a temporary tool for better living, rather than a semi-permanent retreat from life's difficulties. Do this sensitively, according to clients' personalities and stages of change. With a client, for example, who is experiencing a hectic lifestyle, you do not want to add to that by setting a heavy schedule of homework. (In such a case you might begin to try out the idea that your client identifies a possible ten minutes in the day 'just for himself'.)

We will go into greater depth on the subject of homework later. The task for you to consider here is the argument for between-session work, your own attitude to it, and the timing and wording of it. It is easy to get into a pattern early in counselling that is hard to break later. Therefore, we suggest that you prepare your 'case' for between-session work. It might go something like this:

It's clear that you're very committed to achieving your goals here. As you told me, you want to be able to walk into your office and not be overcome with anxiety about people looking at you and your getting the idea that you're inferior in some way. We can look at a lot of the problems here. But counselling works best when there's an active engagement with everyday life. For example, if you were willing to begin to make notes of exactly how you feel and what you think when you walk into the office, that would help a lot. Gradually, I'd like you to be able to take a few risks with people at work, like asking them what they think about you. But for now, I'd just like you to bear in mind the power of practising new things between our meetings.

This kind of explanation paves the way. It gives an idea of what is to come. It helps to mobilize clients. Again, as a reminder, it could cause some clients to feel anxious, so remain aware of individual reactions and adjust accordingly. Do it at an appropriately early stage, showing the relation between the client's initial goals and the achievement of a momentum in counselling. It may be that if your approach is a person-centred or psychodynamic one, you will not want to be this directive at all; or you may prefer to use such ideas later in the process. Adapt your explanation, making it as short or as 'authoritative' as will appeal best to the particular client. And of course refer the issue to the reflection process.

Summary

Since the typical counselling session is a small part of any client's week and the counselling process is a relatively small part of a client's life, think about tasks which can help clients consolidate their learning and extend it in the future.

---

42 Continue with the approach (or modify as appropriate) until clients have reached their goal or are confident of reaching the goal on their own

As you proceed with your approach to the client's problem, you will inevitably notice her reactions. Whether your particular approach is person-centred or more active-directive, the client will have reactions to it from the very beginning. Although you will have explained how and why you are working in the way you are, your explanation may differ from the reality experienced by the client. We suggest that you adhere to the approach you have taken and have agreed with the client, giving it a fair chance to take effect, while observing your client's reactions to it.

Imagine that you and your client have agreed that it is important for her to recall instances in which she has felt 'let down', for example. She has agreed to scan her mind for memories and to give details of when she has felt that friends have not supported her. She has agreed that vague statements like 'people are always letting me down' are not very helpful in locating the core of her problem. So she sets out to identify specific instances of this concern, and you give her plenty of time and gentle encouragement. But she becomes frustrated. Perhaps she has consciously complied with your suggestion, but less consciously she may be feeling angry that you cannot instantly appreciate and agree with her view of how people let her down. Because of this mismatch between her reactive feelings and your attention to the chosen approach, progress is awkward. You notice that she is restless, sighs a lot, kicks at the carpet and claims that she can't remember much. What will you do in this case?

In being persistent and sensitive to your client's reactions, you may well be confronted with a decision. In the extreme, you might push for an outcome to your approach ('come on, there are obviously times you can remember when you've felt specifically disappointed with friends') or abandon it altogether ('well, this doesn't seem to be working, so don't worry about it, forget it').

Avoid these extremes. You might elicit her reaction – 'I notice how hard you're finding it to concentrate. Can you tell me what you're actually thinking now?' If she is angry with you or the 'chore' of being specific, she may either then tell you so or deny it. Another avenue might be, 'If this isn't working too well we can leave it for now and take a different approach.' Whichever way you decide to elicit her reactions, leave her with options. If you and she agree that the chosen approach is not working out, ask 'How do you think we need to change tack? Can you think of anything you or I need to be doing to help things forward?' This kind of question helps to consolidate the working alliance. When you notice signs that the client is withdrawing, or getting distracted or frustrated, do not ignore them or consign them to pathological categories. Even if there may be, for example, passive-aggressive features involved in the client not being able to remember, respect her apparent difficulty. Refer to the reflection process (for example 'Perhaps the task of finding these specific memories is not quite right for you at the moment. I wonder whether you have another idea as to how we can get at this problem?'). This will reinforce your client's commitment to her targets in coming to counselling and it will reinforce your position as a flexible helper.

Clients don't, of course, always give obvious signals that something is amiss. They may not be aware that there is, or they may be too polite, compliant or unassertive to say so. It is good practice to invite clients to raise any doubts they may have. Do this sometimes even when there are no signs of doubt. This practice helps to create a climate of freedom and enquiry. It prevents the unhealthy accumulation of grievances and thus aids therapeutic momentum: when the client and you can quickly identify strategies that are unhelpful and then discard or modify them, then energy can be devoted to problem solving. We recognize that not all counsellors find it easy to elicit immediate reactions in this way, perhaps especially when they might be negative, but doing this sometimes, practising it, is better than avoiding it altogether. Difficulties of this kind – wanting to invite feedback but finding yourself avoiding it – should certainly be taken to supervision.

As you and your client continue to work, both of you may become aware of real progress. Let's say that your client begins to recall instances of being 'let down' by a friend and describes them in some detail. You then encourage her to distinguish between her own interpretations of being let down and other possible interpretations of events. She begins to realize with mixed emotions that she has indeed, in many cases, misinterpreted events, even if not dramatically. Gradually, with your persistent help, she comes to see that what has happened to her was perhaps not the awful trauma that she thought it was. This takes subtlety on your part and may include small verbal nudges, humour or other microstrategies. Her mood may lift as she realizes what part she has played in creating this recent cloud of 'depression'. You help her to prepare for her next meeting with her friend, and she can look forward to it with some relief and hope. Her first goal is in sight. When you and she are confident that this first piece of progress is consolidated, you can begin to reconsider whether that particular approach has any further use.

Summary

Proceed with your chosen approach to this problem, giving it every chance to work. Be aware of your clients' reactions to it and invite their feedback. Raise any doubts clients may have about your approach and be prepared to change accordingly. Monitor the process until the particular goal is in sight.

---

43 Consider the range of your techniques and build on them

The old adage that if you only have a hammer, you treat everything as a nail, is pertinent here. Sometimes one main approach – and possibly one main technique within that – may be enough, but rarely. Banging away isn't very subtle. But neither is unwavering gentleness optimal. The subtlety of your counselling, and your ability to work effectively in a brief time, is likely to be enhanced by building on your range of available techniques. Now, depending on your training and affiliation, you may be resistant to wandering outside your usual approach. To some extent, the bad name given to eclecticism has discouraged practitioners from using (or openly declaring that they use) a range of techniques drawn from different therapies. Increasingly, however, counsellors working in time-limited contracts in primary care and elsewhere find they naturally have to adapt what they offer. Reflecting back on Section 26 on a multimodal framework, let's consider something of the range of techniques – above and beyond core conditions and common counselling skills – that are available for responding to clients.

Behavioural techniques

Anything that calls on the client to *do* something may be thought of as behavioural. Homework is a good example, because it is an encouragement of the client to be active in their own betterment in some way. Teaching assertiveness skills (or modelling them) to clients is behavioural in the sense that it involves action in the real world. Rehearsal of interview skills, of how to make friends, how to ask people out, can all lend themselves to in-session work. Roleplay can be used to demonstrate simply how to go about being assertive in certain situations. It can be done playfully to move the client towards greater assertiveness if that is helpful. The point is that such exercises instigate action, experiment, risk taking and the lessons that can be drawn from it and explored. The rise of coaching, mentoring and personal training in recent years testifies to the desire for and usefulness of direct micro-teaching. We do not think of this as directiveness in the negative sense but as a technical supplement to the brief counsellor's skills, to be used judiciously.

Emotion-oriented techniques

Focusing, chair work, and emotive visualization (Mahrer, 1989a, 1996) are examples of working purposefully to increase feelings and/or enhance or understand them. These are indicated when the client wants to try them (say, in order to convert anger or numbness into appropriate sadness) or when a breakthrough may well be achieved by an emotive experiment. In our increasingly cognitivized age, the use of such humanistic methods may have declined somewhat (and counselling offices are not always designed to contain noisy and demonstrative work) but there is still a place for them. Most affective or emotional techniques involve asking clients to notice their current levels of feeling, even if these are low, in order to identify where they happen in the body, how they are suppressed, and what it feels like to begin even minimally to increase them (Greenberg et al., 1993). Awareness, followed by encouragement to speak more loudly, with due emotion, *to* the imagined other person instead of *about* them, completing expressions of emotion instead of aborting them – these are some typical ways of increasing feeling.

Sensation-oriented techniques

Like emotion-focused techniques, sensation-oriented work addresses the client's physical tension, stress, butterflies, knots, and somatized problems generally. On identifying any of these areas, you can then consider what is in your repertoire that you can competently offer. Massage may help but unless you are trained and able to arrive at a satisfactorily ethical agreement this should usually not be undertaken (Embleton Tudor, 1997). In principle the sensory modalities of sound, smell and taste can also be worked with, perhaps via music therapy and imaginal olfactory exercises. Relaxation and mindfulness exercises, on the other hand, are more commonly used, are not necessarily contentious and can be easily conducted in-session. The eyes-closed, calm breathing, gradual muscular relaxation from head to toes is probably the most common kind, along with restful images and resolutions where helpful. Mindfulness, associated with Zen Buddhism in particular, has become quite widely practised, for example in approaches like dialectical behaviour therapy and cognitive therapy (Hayes et al., 2004). This can involve concentration exercises (teaching the client how to focus calmly on an object) or simple stillness instructions (awareness of breathing, watching one's thoughts without controlling them, appreciating the experience of timelessness). Obviously sufficient time must be available and you need to be alert to any possible contraindications. Some people, while in need of relaxation, nevertheless react badly to imposed or sudden changes to their usual stressed lifestyle. And others may dislike closing their eyes and relaxing in another's presence if, for example, they have been abused.

Imagery-oriented techniques

Those clients who are artistic, who have rich dream lives or who show great interest in visual work, who spontaneously employ metaphors, are good candidates for imagery work. Asking them to report their dreams or to bring in artwork or create it during the session is likely to be productive. But there are also simple ways of tuning into clients' preferences and working visually. For example, a question like 'Can you see yourself doing that?' elicits a sense of the client's mastery in visual form. ('Close your eyes and imagine. ...' is a directive form of such an enquiry. Many hypnotherapeutic and neuro-linguistic programming exercises are directive visualizations.) These small interventions can be followed through and elaborated into exploratory visual narratives. The solution-focused miracle question is visually oriented, encouraging clients to see (and also feel) motivating images and their accompanying sense of positive outlook. Mahrer's (1989) preference for working (literally) alongside the client, with closed eyes, maximizes the focus on emotive imagery work. You might consider developing your own blend of person-centred (taking up the client's cue) and counsellor-offered imagery technical foci.

Cognitively-oriented techniques

Cognitive therapy, rational emotive behaviour therapy and other forms of cognitive behavioural therapy (CBT) take the client's thinking patterns as central to therapeutic work and have intricately developed techniques to offer. But most counsellors, whatever their orientation, are familiar with the concepts of injunctions, scripts, shoulds, musts and oughts. In other words, identifying the way in which the client habitually thinks, and how these thinking patterns are implicated in self-perpetuated problems, is common enough territory. 'What are this person's automatic assumptions about life?' is a natural partner to the counsellor's wondering 'What are this client's painful or suppressed feelings?' But some people habitually say, 'I think' rather than 'I feel' and this may be an indication of a better modality in which to work with such clients. Denial of feelings, rationalization and intellec-tualization are not, contrary to some views, the invariable manifestations of defence mechanisms but are sometimes a personal style. Relatively straight-forward enquiries like, 'What were you thinking just before x happened?' can be used as information-gathering exercises and lead-ins to further cognitive work. More formally, explanation of the REBT model of ABC (actualizing event, mediating belief and emotional consequences) can often help to challenge the view that one must helplessly react emotionally to every eventuality. Daily diaries are quite commonly used to help clients identify their mood and behaviour changes and to utilize in counselling sessions for further exploration. Explicit problem-solving techniques (for example, brainstorming, force field analysis, balance sheets) are also cognitive in nature, as is much narrative therapy that elicits the client's cognitive constructs and suggest alternatives.

Interpersonally oriented techniques

The person-centred and psychodynamic approaches have different rationales but they both focus strongly on what happens in-session between client and practitioner, one using core conditions and aiming for relation depth (Mearns and Cooper, 2005) and the other fostering and working through transference. Both work partly on corrective emotional experiences: if you can learn new ways of relating to your counsellor, you may be able to relate better to your partner, family, friends and colleagues, as well as putting to rest unfinished business from your past. Gestalt therapy draws partly from the 'I-Thou' of Buber (1947), encouraging direct, open and honest communication. Blanton (1994) extends these ideas to a concept of radical honesty and existentialist therapists aim for authenticity. But other interpersonally oriented techniques focus on social skills and assertiveness training beyond the counselling session. Clients who live isolated lives may sometimes benefit more from the concerted practice of new skills than from protracted analysis. Consider, too, the wisdom of referring some clients to groups where they learn more, or more quickly, from others with similar needs. Similarly, the rationale for counselling couples as opposed to individual counselling is often that the people concerned mainly need to communicate with their partner about their relationship.

Drugs/biological, health and lifestyle-oriented techniques

To a degree, this modality represents a critique of the psychologizing of individual distress. We do suffer from illness (detected or otherwise), from poor health habits, excesses and insufficiencies. One of the most common examples of the benefits of attending to this modality is that depression is often helped by moderate exercise. But consider other common problems: drinking too much alcohol and caffeine; overeating or eating an imbalanced diet; sleeping too much or too little; excessive inactivity or hyperactivity; abuse of illegal drugs, legal drugs (such as cigarettes) and prescribed drugs, as well as ignorance about or resistance to needed medication; hypochrondria, somatization and morbid fear of doctors and hospitals are also causes for concern. Disabilities, chronic pain and limited life chances stemming from oppression or unavoidable realities feature here. Excessive work stress and local environmental damage should also be considered in this modality. Counsellors cannot always do much about these issues. Often referral to health professionals or knowledge of health psychology is needed. But awareness of them, consciousness-raising for clients and encouragement to seek appropriate help or initiate and maintain better health habits are within the counsellor's power. See Daines et al. (1997) and Stout (1991).

Since we all tend to have preferred modalities or learning styles, it is unrealistic to insist that counsellors master the entire range of techniques. It will also come across as incongruent if you strain to work in a modality with which you are obviously uncomfortable. Equally, guard against the over-enthusiastic use of new techniques that you may have learned recently. Certain approaches are prolific with techniques that appear dazzling and compelling and, on the face of it, even ideal for brief therapeutic work. But we advocate the considered and timely use of techniques that commend themselves as useful for some clients at some points in their counselling. For further ideas on techniques, consult Jinks (2006), Neenan and Dryden (2004), Rosenthal (1998) and Thompson (1996).

Summary

Look for ways of expanding your repertoire of techniques and consider how you might use them in a tailored and timely fashion with those clients most likely to benefit from them. Consider referral when you cannot directly offer needed help.

44 Deal with any actual obstacles that emerge

Obstacles can emerge at any stage of counselling, and can take many forms. We have looked at the possibility of obstacles arising in the beginning stage of an approach to clients' problems. We have suggested that you be sensitive to signs that your approach is not quite appropriate or is not well received by your client. But there can also be obstacles in the way that you and your client communicate with each other. The hesitancies, doubts and instances of ambivalence that make themselves apparent non-verbally and paraverbally are important to look for. These are signs of possible 'ruptures to the therapeutic alliance'. It is important constantly to monitor the nature and strength of the therapeutic alliance and threats to it (Dryden, 1989), so we recommend that you focus on immediate experiences of such threats as appropriate. For example, when your client responds to one of your suggestions with faint enthusiasm or passive aggressive silence and you see by her eye movements that her mind has wandered off, you might say directly, 'I sense that you're in two minds about what we're talking about here. Perhaps part of you is unconvinced by what I've said?'

Allowing for the complexity of human beings and therefore of the counselling process, you will understand that obstacles range from clients' defensive withdrawal or transference, to reasonable and conscious objections to particular interventions reflecting different aspects of Clarkson's (1990) framework of therapeutic relationships. Be alert to this complexity and avoid viewing every obstacle as necessarily either an unconscious conflict or a commonsense and pragmatic problem. To put this differently, both transference reactions and direct interpersonal problems in communication can and do occur in counselling. While you cannot guarantee always to eliminate transference, you can keep it in perspective by constantly encouraging clients to express their reservations overtly. In order to help clients do this with some comfort, indicate to them in various ways, from the beginning of counselling, that your 'ego' is not on the line. Let clients know that counsellors expect them to engage in interactions that are often more testing than normal social intercourse. Let clients know that their comments are welcome. Assure them that you take them seriously. Part of your job is to empower them and this is achieved by validating their struggle to articulate what feels 'right' and 'wrong' to them.

Now we need to modify these statements. Because transference reactions do occur, it is not appropriate to overlook them and to take everything at face value. Maintain a certain degree of scepticism. Watkins (1989) establishes how crucial it is not to overlook transference phenomena. Sometimes you notice certain refrains (for example, the client may use a phrase like 'well, you would know, wouldn't you?') which are directed at you but which clearly derive from another relationship or expectation in the client's life. Often these can be dealt with by responding, 'You often tell me that I know certain things which I may or may not know. You sound as if you know me, or imagine you know me, very well. I wonder if I remind you of anyone?' Sometimes there is a fairly simple transference of identities of this kind and the client may readily realize and admit to the original identity. But often, too, the client may not be fully conscious of, or able to verbalize, how you remind her of someone important in her past, or how you evoke strong and significant feelings in her.

Casement (1985, 2002) is a leading exponent of the concept of unconscious supervision of the counsellor by the client. Casement advocates close attention to what clients say that may reflect something they feel about you. When clients do not feel understood or safe, for example, they may communicate this implicitly to their counsellor by using symbols from dreams or by talking about other people who have not understood them or kept them safe. It is a useful practice to listen for any such clues to clients' perceptions of obstacles. While some clients may say openly, 'you just don't understand me', others will let you know symbolically or obliquely (for instance 'my doctor just didn't seem to have his mind on things when I saw him the other day'). We advocate that in brief counselling you do not want to encourage transference, but you also cannot overlook it. Cultivate the art, then, of being aware of your clients' unconscious communications. Ryle (1990) considers that work with transference is a key part of his brief therapy model, as do all other psycho-dynamically oriented therapists (Coren, 2001; Flegenheimer, 1982). If you do work in this way, you may positively welcome the 'obstacle of transference' as an invitation into the client's inner world. By all means accept such an invitation, but within brief counselling you are advised to concentrate hard and to make overt any transference reactions as quickly as possible.

Sometimes an obstacle will be in the form of an obvious block. The client may stall every time a certain subject comes up. She may change the subject whenever you touch on something painful. When there is something of this sort, that is clear to you but not to the client, help her to disclose whatever is hidden or suppressed. Find ways of helping her to probe and explore. Feed back to her how difficult it appears to be for her to talk about her sex life, for example. Respect these difficulties but do not ignore them. At the very least make it known that you have noticed. If necessary agree to postpone exploration of such difficult subjects until later. Often clients need time to process and articulate thoughts that touch on painful or confusing experiences. But do voice your observations sensitively when they occur.

Returning to the more everyday obstacles, there may be something going on in the client's family, for example, that is a distraction for them. Perhaps they keep telling themselves that this is not the place to discuss it, but even so it is nagging at them and impeding progress in counselling. There may be something in the client's domestic or occupational life that has no obvious bearing on the problems they have brought to counselling, yet which preoccupies them. Or there may be worrying practical problems connected with counselling. Your client may be finding it very difficult to find time off work to come to counselling; she may be having difficulty paying for counselling. Such matters are not necessarily pathological, and sometimes there may be no short-term solutions for them, yet if they are not addressed they can seriously affect the quality of the counselling. Use your common sense and sensitivity in eliciting such concerns. It is not necessary or helpful in each and every session to search for possible obstacles to counselling, but you need to be attuned to signs of such problems arising.

Summary

Look out for any non-verbal signs that your clients are having difficulties with the way you interact with them; their transference reactions to you; painful or distracting issues; or practical problems. Encourage clients to voice any doubts or concerns.

---

45 Be aware of, and respond to, possible threats to the therapeutic alliance from missed or cancelled appointments

It is possible at any stage of the counselling process to have the experience of a client simply not turning up for a session, without prior warning, or telephoning to cancel or postpone at short notice. Most counsellors will experience the frustration of waiting for clients who do not turn up for a first or second session. Obviously some people find themselves in crisis and just able to make an appointment for counselling but subsequently feel too anxious to follow through, or, having taken some action, either feel better or persuade themselves that they do not now need counselling. Too often, perhaps, the counsellor is unable to ascertain the reasons for clients not showing up for first or second or third sessions. With the increase in counselling practice in primary care, most of which is short term and time limited, counsellors sometimes find that people are being referred to them by a GP when they, the clients, are not fully committed to or accepting of the idea of counselling. This can be especially frustrating when waiting lists build up alongside missed appointments and there are no opportunities for quickly refilling vacant session slots.

We address in Part VI the subject of clients failing to turn up and how you may deal with this. But how should you respond in the earlier stages? We suggest that you (or an administrator) routinely write to any client who does not turn up, letting them know that they are welcome to make another appointment, if that is the case, and clarifying any implications for payment or waiting lists. Such letters are better kept brief and, although warm, to the point. Don't make people feel uncomfortable but do be clear about what is and what is not on offer from you following a missed appointment. You do, of course, need to be quite sure that you communicated unambiguously to your client the terms of your appointments in the first place.

We think it is unlikely within the course of brief counselling that clients will choose to miss a session and suddenly turn up to the subsequent session. We have known, for example, of clients in long-term psychoanalytic therapy choosing to miss an appointment (but having to pay for it) just to know what it feels like, or to test the therapist, consciously or unconsciously. But what does happen in brief counselling is that certain clients telephone to say they are ill; they may leave you a message or they may tell you directly. Sometimes they will say such things in a tone of voice that conveys ambivalence about continuing in counselling at all. Sometimes white lies are given because the client is not sufficiently assertive to tell you directly that she is disillusioned or afraid. Do not expect clients who are new to counselling to address you assertively and do not respond impatiently to people telephoning with 'excuses'. Politely state your readiness or otherwise to see them again at another time.

When clients cancel a session it can be viewed as a message to you. Whereas clients who disappear altogether before seeing you or after seeing you once may not be accessible for discussion, clients who miss or cancel but return need to be sensitively listened to for reasons and nuances. See Casement's (1985, 2002) method of learning from clients' indirect messages to you. Some clients may know that actions speak louder than words, and their absence may be conveying something important to you. Perhaps it is 'Do you really want to see me?' or 'I'm not going to make this easy for you' or 'I don't know if I want to be here'. Absences can convey direct messages to you. They may also convey 'messages' from the client's unconscious about aspects of past abandonments, losses, and so on. Some clients come from chaotic family backgrounds in which unreliability is the norm, and they may repeat this behaviour with you. You don't have to be a psychodynamic counsellor to want to address the issue of a cancelled appointment, its possible meanings, and the threat it may pose for the therapeutic alliance (Dryden, 1989). You do need to explore the idiosyncratic meanings of client absences, lack of punctuality and other signs of ambivalence or indiscipline.

Sherman and Anderson (1987) suggest several antidotes to the likelihood of clients' premature termination. Their review of literature on premature termination revealed, for example, that the sending of reminders after a missed appointment reduced first month drop-out rates from 51 per cent to 28 per cent. They also found that the use of 'imagination-explanation procedures' further helped to reduce drop-out rates. Such procedures may include having clients imagine themselves completing at least four counselling sessions successfully. You may experiment with this idea by simply asking clients about their general experiences of seeing through and completing tasks when they initially seem difficult. If you have reason to believe that clients may be wary of coming to several counselling sessions, or may need to have the 'culture' of counselling explained carefully to them, then it is worth considering such anticipatory exercises. Whether you anticipate the possibility of clients missing sessions, or you have to deal with it when it arises, consider what the client may be telling you non-verbally and how you can best respond in order to cement the therapeutic alliance.

Summary

Follow up by letter clients who drop out, but accept their decision. Consider possible reasons for missed or cancelled appointments, including cultural, idiosyncratic and psychodynamic factors. When the opportunity presents itself, address the issue appropriately.

---

46 Begin work on a new target concern

Having helped the client to achieve her goal or to move substantially and fairly reliably towards it, be prepared to move on to her next target concern. There is a temptation, perhaps, at this and later stages, to become sidetracked into client narrative that may not aid the change process. Help your client to recall the agreement between you as to prioritized concerns. Do not briskly move off from the first concern without checking that your client has, in fact, digested her learning and has achieved her goal or is in sight of doing so. But when you are sure that it is appropriate, address the next concern.

In raising the next concern, be sure that you do not assume that there is a connection between these concerns. There may be, or there may appear to be, but ask the client about this. Let us suppose that an initial goal of standing up to her boss has been reached, and another goal is set that has to do with controlling overeating. Your client may consider that there is no connection between them, yet in learning that she has greater ability to withstand difficulties than she thought she had (in standing up to her boss) she realizes that this improved sense of her abilities will also help her in addressing her overeating. In this case, you might proceed to work on the second concern using the same approach that you used on the first concern. The client, in this example, has understood how she can generalize her new learning from one concern to another. When you are faced with a client who is close to realizing such a connection, you might say, 'I wonder if you can see any way of putting into practice what we talked about in relation to your boss with this concern with overeating.' You may be able to ease her into finding the connection.

However, progress is not always so smooth. She may successfully confront her boss, but see no connection between this achievement and her concern with overeating. Explain as well as you can any possible connection between these two concerns. Do so tentatively and ask your client for feedback. But if there are clear signs that your client perceives them as two quite separate matters, begin your negotiations on the second concern from a fresh perspective. Go back as far into the process of defining the problem as is necessary, letting the client talk and renegotiating an approach that makes sense to her. Show that you are open to understanding how she views this concern as separate from the first.

The process of moving from one target concern to another is a demanding one for the counsellor. Because you want to make the best use of your time together, you realize the value of generalizing learning from one problem to another. Obviously some learning is at an emotional level and may not always be easy to articulate. But because it is necessary to maintain a good working alliance, you will be constantly referring to the client's frame of reference and the nuances of her verbal and non-verbal expression. It is a fact of counselling practice that clients often experience confusion or distress as they confront stubborn personal problems. You may see clearly a connection between one concern and another and you may be impatient to demonstrate that connection. With some clients this will be easy to achieve but with many it will not. Help each of your clients to explore their new issues as fully as necessary.

Summary

Be ready to move on to a new target concern. Where possible, help clients to generalize their learning from one concern to another, and take this process of generalization as far as it will go. Where this is not immediately possible, help clients to trace the salient factors in their new concern.

---

47 Identify and work on themes rather than concerns

You can move from working at the level of isolated, concrete concerns by listening for themes. By themes we mean those basic assumptions, scripts or refrains that you become sensitive to as your work with a client proceeds. Themes straddle the various concerns. There may be a connection between two concerns, but a theme is a 'higher level' understanding of what is involved. For example, your client may report that she feels criticized by her father, her husband and her best friend. She may not at first regard these as anything but separate instances of people causing her some discomfort. As you listen, you form the hypothesis that this client is very sensitive to criticism, which may in fact be one of her themes.

> *You:* Let me give you my reaction here. I wonder if, in a sense, the link here is a difficulty you have in coping with being criticized. We've talked about how your father, your husband and your best friend appear overly critical of you. Do you think you might be overly sensitive to criticism? If you do, we can look at why this might be or what you're telling yourself at those times when you feel particularly criticized.

This kind of identification of a theme is offered to the client as a hypothesis. You put it clearly enough for the client to understand how you arrived at such a hypothesis but you also leave the way open for disagreement or clarification. What you are doing here is bringing together elements from the client's story, and showing a possible linking theme. 'We've talked about situations x, y and z. Can you see a common connection here?' The client may, of course, reply that she cannot, in which case you will need either to rephrase your hypothesis or perhaps return to it later. Listen carefully for such themes and highlight them for the client. Even when she cannot see an immediate connection between concerns, she may well think over your hypothesis and gradually come to agree. As you work together, you have the opportunity to show her what theme is behind her many concerns: it may be, for example, that when she feels criticized she interprets this to mean that she is worthless.

In the example above, you might follow through with:

> *You:* Let's see if, the next time you get upset, you can ask yourself, 'Am I getting upset at the criticism? If so, what am I telling myself in each case where it happens?' I'd like you to note these thoughts down and tell me about them next time we meet.

This statement effectively takes up a theme and shows how it can be observed and tested. The purpose of learning to identify connections in this way is to economize on time and to help the client to maximize her progress. The alternative procedure of taking each concern up as a discrete problem is time consuming and risks some loss of momentum.

We have spoken here of a theme that neatly links concerns, but there can be several themes running through clients' concerns. Don't assume there is only one, then, but listen for the two or three that may well be involved. Some approaches to counselling, like transactional analysis, 'specialize' in identifying scripts, mini-scripts, drivers, and other instances of important themes in clients' lives. In fact in transactional analysis it is thought that most people have one main driver and possibly one or two others. Stewart and Joines (1987) talk about the practice of 'driver detection', which is the art of listening for and observing signs of recurring themes. Even if you do not practise TA specifically, you will probably be aware of ways in which your client repeats certain patterns of behaviour and thought. In cognitive therapy (Blackburn and Davidson, 1990) a major task for counsellors is to listen for clients' schemas, or ways in which they typically construe the world and act accordingly. Blackburn and Davidson advocate a process of helping the client to identify 'themes and words which recur' over the weeks of counselling. However you work, you will develop an awareness of how clients focus on and repeat certain themes.

Summary

Listen for themes in what clients tell you, and raise these for discussion. Identify themes that link individual concerns, and help the client to understand how these predominate. Show clients how to focus on themes so that they can see how they operate in their everyday life and how they might work to change them.

PART IV
ENCOURAGING
CHANGE THROUGH
HOMEWORK

48 Explain your rationale for clients doing homework in general

We realize that some counsellors and counselling orientations are not in favour of employing homework assignments. The more relationship-based approaches are generally disinclined to introduce such between-session work. Macaskill (1985) differentiates between the 'being with' and the 'doing to' approaches, but shows that some psychodynamic practitioners (who are in the 'being with' group), including Wolberg (1980) and Ryle (1990), advocate the use of homework; and that Davanloo (1985) recognizes the advantage gained by clients who work on problems between sessions. In person-centred therapy, Rice (1984) suggests that clients may be encouraged in certain cases to identify emotive situations between sessions as 'a very productive kind of "homework"'. In cognitive behavioural therapy and counselling, homework is an integral part of the process. Blackburn and Davidson (1990) consider homework-setting one of the basic skills for cognitive therapists. Our own view is that the explicit use of homework assignments enhances therapeutic progress and should be thought of as a basic skill for clients as well as counsellors.

What are the reasons for advocating that clients engage in between-session work? As we have pointed out previously, the typical counselling session is one hour out of 168 in the client's week. The course of counselling itself may consist of a few weeks or months in the client's life. Unless we are considering success in counselling to result mainly from fortuitous factors (for example the 'non-specific' relationship factors) we are forced to ask how the process of change actually occurs. Some research into brief psychotherapy (see Koss and Butcher 1986) suggests that a variety of factors contribute to successful outcomes, and clients' levels of activity rank among these. By learning to implement new behaviour themselves, clients reinforce their commitment to change. The interaction between the counselling session and the everyday world is important in confirming for clients that they are the agents of change and that they have the power to change. This interaction can be made explicit, and we believe it is wise to make it so in brief counselling. Unless clients are told about the benefits of putting what is learned in counselling into ongoing practice, there is a risk that they will learn by default to be rather passive in effecting change in their lives.

Explain to your clients, then, that it is usually helpful to engage in some activity related to counselling between one session and another. You do not have to call this activity homework. 'Homework' to many people conjures up an unpleasant image of difficult and undesirable schoolwork. You may decide to try other terms, like 'assignment', 'task', 'practice' or 'between-session work'. Indeed, for some clients with a preference for activity, any such ideas may be welcomed. The growth of cognitive behavioural therapy (CBT) has made many aware that it is an integral part of counselling, and in addition some clients themselves now ask for such tasks. But you may also describe the nature and desirability of homework without using specific terms. 'Perhaps you can consider what it might be helpful to do between now and our next meeting in order to focus better on your concerns' is the kind of statement that invites clients to take up homework without actually calling it by that name. You might illustrate the purpose of therapeutic homework by referring, for example, to learning to play the piano: the lesson is important, but practice during the week is essential. Or, obtaining advice from your doctor about exercise and diet is important but you still have to *do* something yourself. Homework does not have to be obviously 'behavioural': any activity relating to counselling and change can be useful, including thinking about what to discuss, making lists of items to discuss, and putting aside time in the week to reflect on counselling issues. Encourage clients to view themselves as active investigators of their cognitive processes, feelings, behaviour and psyches, in the counselling room and in their living-rooms and offices.

In cognitive analytic therapy, homework 'represents the enlistment of the patient as her own co-therapist and serves to promote self-awareness and self-control and to minimise regression' (Ryle, 1990: 30). If you and your client are committed, together, to a goal-directed approach to counselling, there is likely to be little difficulty in communicating your rationale for homework. If you have reservations about homework, you are likely to communicate them to your client. We suggest that you acquaint yourself with the arguments for homework being an integral part of the counselling process, before you discuss the subject with your clients. When you do discuss it, notice your client's non-verbal reactions and invite her to put these into words. Deal with any reservations and correct any possible misunderstandings in a respectful manner.

Summary

Consider your own views on homework and what evidence there is for or against it. Explain its usefulness to your clients in whatever terms are most acceptable to them. Convey the idea that homework accelerates progress and helps clients to become their own counsellors. Invite feedback.

49 Think broadly about different types of assignments

As we have said, homework can cover many different tasks. We give you a sample here: reading, writing, questionnaires, monitoring, behavioural tasks and imagery.

Reading

You may wish to ask your client to read some specific text relating to the kind of counselling you practise. Models that rely on teaching certain schemas, like transactional analysis and rational emotive behaviour therapy, are often well-explained by relevant literature. When clients agree to do such reading, they are helping to accelerate the counselling process, they are saving session time, and they are becoming an active participant in change. Some counsellors (for example Scott, 1989) give specific reading material to clients with certain problems. Scott uses, for example, a short 'handout' called *There's Hope* with people who are depressed. Often such short texts are very useful with people who have specific addictive problems. In some areas of Britain schemes have been set up whereby GPs can prescribe certain self-help books for their patients, who then collect them from the library that has them specifically for this purpose. Fennell's (1999) *Overcoming Low Self-Esteem* is one such text. Self-help manuals related closely to certain approaches are also widely used (for example, Greenberger and Padesky, 1995). Some counsellors advocate large 'doses' of reading, which constitutes a kind of bibliotherapy in itself. Therapeutic reading can include novels and poetry if what is suggested has some specific likelihood of raising themes that are pertinent for the client. You would do well to discriminate between clients who may and may not benefit from such reading assignments. Those with literacy problems or who are already overloaded with other reading commitments (for example, students) may not take kindly to the idea. Also, aim to match the level of reading assignment to what the client will feel comfortable with; otherwise you may risk demoralizing the client.

Writing

It is often useful to ask clients to write something about themselves. This can be done in various ways. The simplest is a brief, first-person account of salient material. 'What I want from counselling' is one way of constructing such an exercise. In some settings, clients are asked to complete full 'life stories' for presentation within a session. Personal construct counsellors (Fransella and Dalton, 2000) often ask clients to write a self-characterization, which is a short description as if from the point of view of someone who knows the client as well as anybody could possibly know her. This exercise, and many others, are used in cognitive analytic therapy (CAT). In CAT, clients are engaged in many writing assignments, including letters addressed to the counsellor. Ryle (1983) suggests that writing assignments fit well into a psychodynamic framework. It is sometimes helpful to ask clients to write a letter to a father or mother, or anyone who is significant to them. Such letters need not be sent, because the very writing of them can be cathartic or instructive. The field of therapeutic writing has grown within the past decade, with some claiming that it can either supplement face to face counselling or, in some cases, substitute for it (see Bolton et al., 2004, for examples).

Questionnaires

We have referred earlier to the questionnaires of Chris Barker and colleagues, which can be used to elicit clients' views on counselling (Appendices 3 and 4). There are, of course, many questionnaires designed to elicit psychological information. Common examples are the Beck Depression Inventory, used in cognitive therapy; the Psychotherapy File, used in cognitive analytic therapy; and the Structural Profile of multi-modal therapy. All these questionnaires elicit information directly from the client and provide the basis for focused work in sessions. Clinical and counselling psychologists, community psychiatric nurses and some counsellors working in the NHS are more likely to use these than others. Needless to say, some people (many counsellors as well as clients) dislike questionnaires, so you need to be sensitive to their use, as well as trained in their application, and explain their rationale carefully.

Monitoring

It is a good idea, and one commonly practised by cognitive-behavioural counsellors, to ask clients to spend some time between sessions looking at their own behaviour and noting, in particular, times of stress or difficulty and accompanying thoughts and reactions. This exercise can be done by simply keeping a diary. It can also be done formally by completing, for example, a 'daily record of dysfunctional thoughts' or a 'weekly activity schedule' (see Blackburn and Davidson, 1990). Existing models can be taken as they are, adapted, or new ones easily created. Structured exercises of this kind can be particularly helpful for clients who are depressed and who have difficulty focusing on specific situations.

Behavioural tasks

You may care to suggest simple behavioural tasks or more systematic behavioural strategies. Asking your client to get up a little earlier in the morning, to spend more time looking for a job or to spend ten minutes each day tidying his room, for example, are all tasks that may help a client incrementally towards greater self-efficacy and coping. You may teach your client assertiveness techniques, such as rehearsing clear statements, saying 'no' without qualifying it, and so on. Or you may, at an appropriate time, suggest to your client, for example, that he takes the risk of asking out a woman or man, asks for a raise at work or tells his brother that he loves him. Self-control desensitization and flooding are examples of formal behavioural exercises (see Bellack and Hersen, 1987). It is difficult for most counsellors to take the time out for *in vivo* exercises, in other words accompanying the client in a live situation and helping them, and normally rigorous prior training for this is required. But in principle it is occasionally more effective to either have the client practise new skills in real situations or to help them directly.

Imagery

Some clients are particularly responsive to the use of imagery. In psycho-analysis dream reports and interpretations are common and in Jungian therapy guided imagery is used. In brief counselling you are less likely to have time for extensive reflection on dream material, particularly on a week after week basis. But therapists like Mahrer (1989b) argue that therapeutic dreamwork can be attempted in even a single (if perhaps longer) session by actively working through a dream's images and making its attendant feelings present and vivid, with time for understanding and any resolutions stemming from it. You might teach a client relaxation exercises, for example, which incorporate the use of visualization: 'You are walking through your favourite peaceful setting, it is a beautiful day, warm and bright, and your worries have evaporated, you can forget them.' Clients who readily engage in such imagery can often use similar imagery in their own everyday lives. This process can be enhanced by making a tape-recording of your instructions and offering it to the client. Imagery can also be used, of course, by asking your client to draw or paint images of special significance, and to bring them to a session for exploration. Imagery often helps clients to express feelings that are hard to verbalize. A qualification in art therapy is not necessary for such an exercise but care should be taken about allowing sufficient time for the exercise, for exploring its meaning and any catharsis it engenders, as well as being sensitive to whether the client wants to keep the picture, leave it and return it, and so on.

This is not an exhaustive list, but it is intended to remind you of what is available and to stimulate you into considering creating your own exercises. Since each of your clients is unique and has a different learning orientation, different homework assignments will be appropriate in each case. We are aware that the negative connotations of the term eclecticism are sometimes aimed at such practices but there is no reason why a purposefully selected, creative task should not be implemented from time to time provided, like any other intervention, it is done with due skill and ethical awareness. Ask yourself questions like: could a particular piece of homework jog this client out of his impasse? Is it time now to get this client to take some risks in her life? What is the best way to help this client get in touch with these difficult feelings between sessions? Is there a way of overcoming the amount of stress my client experiences in certain situations? How can I construct appropriately helpful tasks for my client? Such questions are ones that you may well want to take to supervision.

Summary

Familiarize yourself with the variety of homework assignments it is possible to use. Consider what uses your clients can make of various kinds of homework. Ask yourself how well you can integrate particular kinds of homework into your own approach in a way that will best help your clients.

50 Allow adequate time for negotiating homework in the session

When you are first introducing the idea of homework, you need to allow sufficient time to do this. You also need to introduce it sensitively, not being so anxious to 'get it in' that you cut into something important that your client is already working on. Once the idea of homework is established and genuinely agreed by your client as acceptable and helpful, it is good practice to get into a habit of setting time aside for negotiating homework. We suggest that you allow five minutes at the very least, before the end of the session, to talk about and set up a homework assignment. If you do not do this, your client may feel rushed, you may convey the feeling that homework is not an integral part of counselling and that your client is not, after all, an equal partner in homework negotiations. Anticipate, then, the need for time at the end of the session. If you should find yourself without sufficient time to discuss homework, it is probably better to omit it altogether rather than to rush it.

It is sometimes the case that an obvious or likely assignment is suggested by something the client is discussing in the middle of the session. If so, note this and return to it at the end of the session in order to formalize it. Whether it is the case that you get an idea or the client comes up with one half-way through the session, don't be tempted to dwell on it there and then, because it may well be superseded by other material and then get forgotten. Your client may say, for example, 'I know I want to say something to her, but I'm not sure how to put it.' Noting this, you might suggest, 'That seems like a worthwhile idea to follow-up. Shall we discuss at the end exactly how you might prepare to say what you want to say to her?' You are both then free to continue with other work, and you have a useful item for homework.

Interestingly, Albert Ellis, pioneer of rational emotive behaviour therapy, which places a high premium on homework assignments, confesses to not always remembering explicitly to set or check it (Yankura and Dryden, 1990: x). While he regularly suggests to his clients that they read one of his books and listen to recordings on REBT, he says, 'I sometimes neglect to check up on clients' specific agreed-upon homework . . . because I get too absorbed in some of the things they are telling themselves and in disputing their irrational beliefs. My forgetfulness in this respect is my problem – perhaps stemming from my own low frustration tolerance.' This is a reminder that we will not always get things right in our counselling, but it is a good idea usually to prepare ourselves for negotiating homework.

Summary

Leave sufficient time to negotiate homework. Allow at the very least five minutes at the end of the session. Don't be tempted casually to set homework in the middle of a session. Be sensitive to your client's need for time.

51 Explain your rationale for specific homework assignments

While you may have given a broad outline of the usefulness of homework, when it comes to specific applications you need to think again. Clients may readily agree with you that homework 'sounds like a good idea' in principle. Such agreement may be too readily offered, for example, by compliant clients. The concrete task of discussing homework and preparing to carry it out, however, is a test of commitment and understanding.

Suppose that you are at the end of the second session with a new client. He has been telling you that he gets very 'wound up' at work when people put pressure on him. His goal is to 'feel relaxed' and 'not to get defensive' in these situations. Together you and he have started looking closely at what he is telling himself about such daily events and his reactions to them. Now you suggest to him that he notes his thoughts and reactions at work. You ask him to write down the thoughts he has before, during and after an occasion at work when people 'put pressure' on him. You might explain that we frequently misinterpret events according to our previous learning experiences; we often expect things to go wrong, for example, even when they are going well. Suggest to him, in this example, that people may or may not actually be putting pressure on him. Ask him to monitor carefully any similar event, along with his thoughts, to check on how he construes 'pressure' and how he makes himself tense and defensive. Suggest that he writes his observations down. Tell him that by establishing the links between events at work, his own thoughts and feelings at the time, and his being 'wound up', he may be able to discover the root of this particular problem in himself, and resolve it.

Summary

Carefully explain to your clients your reasons for suggesting a particular piece of homework. Show clients the thinking behind it and show them how it relates to their goal in counselling.

---

52 Negotiate, don't set

There may be an assignment for your client that appears to you as if it will be obviously necessary or clearly helpful but your client may not at all agree with you, or may appear to agree but silently resent your assumption that you know what is right. There is certainly nothing wrong in your having good ideas about homework assignments but always check with clients whether they regard them as appropriate ideas. Some clients are especially sensitive to authority issues, and if they sense that you are beginning to impose ideas on them they will be likely to react adversely. The ethos of counselling is built around respect for clients' autonomy, so it would be counterproductive to ignore your client's autonomy unwittingly.

Describe the assignment you consider suitable for your client. But then invite his reaction. At the same time, watch for his non-verbal responses. If he half-heartedly agrees with your idea, put to him your observation that he doesn't seem very enthusiastic. Encourage him to voice his doubts. Ask him if there is any way he would like to modify the assignment, and be genuinely keen to meet his ideas. If he still seems equivocal about it, ask 'can you think of anything you could do between now and next week that would be more helpful to you?' Allow him to construct his own assignment or challenge. Reinforce the proposition that homework helps clients to change, but de-emphasize any idea that you are 'in charge' of it. Stress that it is a colla-borative endeavour.

There is a subtle danger that in avoiding the setting of homework, and placing emphasis on negotiation, you may be tempted to abandon or ser-iously dilute the idea of homework. Your client, for example, may be a better negotiator than you are, and a better game player! Indeed, if there is any struggle going on between you and your client then it may surface in the issue of homework. If this is the case, refer to the reflection process. Ask your client how, in view of his reservations, he feels about homework and the way you discuss it. If such a discussion becomes an obstacle, consider the possible transference issues involved. Macaskill (1985) and other psychodynamic practitioners are fairly confident that homework negotiations will raise transference issues, which should then become an appropriate focus for work. But another perspective on this is that the more you place responsibility with the client, the fewer such problems between you are likely to arise. By encouraging your client to suggest his own homework, for example, you show him respect. 'How might you put what we've discussed into practice between now and next week?' is one way of negotiating rather than setting homework. Of course, also consider that there will be some clients for whom homework is not indicated at all – that is, those who primarily need accep-tance, time to tell their story, to grieve perhaps. Remain sensitive to this.

Summary

Don't present homework in the form of an order. Respect the client's autonomy and invite comments on your ideas. Modify assignments or allow the client to suggest alternative assign-ments. Focus on obstacles which may arise at this stage.

---

53 Ensure that homework arises out of the session's focus

You may well be tempted, in reflecting on what your client has told you, to think of an 'ideal' piece of homework that you can suggest to her or him at the next session. Or you may hear of a particular exercise and wish to put it into effect. We suggest that you do not do this. Rather, note the idea but save it for an appropriate occasion.

It is advisable that any homework assignments relate to what has been discussed in the particular session. This means that you are called on to be creative. This is why we advocate that you familiarize yourself with the range of possible homework assignments so that you can adapt as necessary to each client at each stage of their counselling. Spend the time in sessions listening to your clients, and allow assignments to formulate themselves in your mind without distracting from the discussion in hand. An assignment will be much more powerful if it follows naturally from the material that has been discussed in the session. It should act as a bridge between the session, the client's target concern, and the goal at any particular stage of counselling.

In the earliest stages of counselling you will probably not want to suggest challenging homework tasks that risk scaring clients off. You will allow clients time to understand the approach being used, and time to unravel the elements of their concern. The homework used, then, should reflect the client's stage of learning. Sensitively judge assignments to match the client's ability to carry them out. But also match them with the immediate concern. If your client is aiming to overcome a social anxiety problem, for example, and you are in the early stages of counselling, it may be appropriate for her to monitor her thoughts and recall scenes from her past when she felt such anxiety. If, in a particular session, she talks about a certain place she used to visit, which she associates with 'funny feelings', you might suggest that she writes down her thoughts and memories about this place. This would provide a link between the 'there and then' and the 'here and now' and between her in-session concerns and her target concern. This would fit in with her wish to understand why she feels anxious in certain situations. At a later stage, you might suggest to her that she deliberately puts herself in certain situations in order to confront the anxiety, but at an early stage such a task could well be quite inappropriate.

Summary

Link a homework assignment to what is discussed in the session, suspending any temptation to try interesting but inappropriate exercises. Be mindful of the stage of counselling your client is at, and link homework with target concerns appropriate to this stage.

54 Agree to the content of the task, being mindful of the client's abilities, circumstances, learning style and past history of doing homework

When you come to formulating the precise piece of homework with your clients, it is important to take into account their ability to perform it. You may have in mind a very promising idea for homework that, however, simply may not match what the client can do. Writing tasks are an example. Writing may come very easily to you but perhaps not to your client. Or it may come easily to some clients but not to others. At the extreme, your client may be illiterate, dyslexic, or have psychological resistances to writing. The client may or may not have told you and may be willing or not to let you know. If you have reason for doubt about this, elicit such information sensitively and if necessary find another way that your client can do the homework assignment. Tape-recording can easily substitute for writing. You also need to take any disabilities into account. Again, some disabilities may be obvious but others not. If your client has trouble concentrating or thinking systematically, then don't set any complicated thought-monitoring exercises, for example. Don't ask clients to perform any exercises requiring mobility that is beyond their ability. A subtle example of this is myalgic encephalomyelitis, a debilitating condition that often makes sustained physical or emotional effort very difficult. When it is apparent that there are such obstacles, look for other ways of presenting assignments.

Another kind of possible obstacle is sometimes found in the client's circumstances. Consider, for example, the issue of your client's personal finances. She may have discussed this subject with you or it may not have come up at all. Suppose that you discuss together your client's wish to meet more men, and you suggest that one way to do this is through the small ads in certain magazines or Internet sites. Some clients will readily agree that this is an appropriate and practical course of action to take, but it does cost money. It is possible that your client is paying you whatever disposable income she has; she may have other commitments, or she may be receiving state benefits. Don't, then, assume that what is possible for you is equally possible for your client. We suggest, too, that you don't assume, as some therapists do, that 'if you want it badly enough, you can always find a way to afford it'; some clients do live on very limited incomes and may not have the skills required cleverly to juggle finances. The growth of counselling in primary care means inevitably that a proportion of clients, who receive medical help free, may have little if any extra income for therapeutic exercises. Consider your client's home or living environment and how this may impinge on her ability to carry out tasks. You might suggest that she meditates, without realizing that she lives in a crowded and noisy flat, for example. (She may be able to modify this after practising assertive skills, but there may still be difficulties.) You might suggest that your client listens to a tape of your session together, without realizing that the only tape-recorder she has access to is in a shared living space. You may tell your client how important it is that she goes out, joins classes, and has fun, without realizing that she lives in a small village, has no car and experiences severe practical difficulties in getting to places.

In addition, take into account your client's values. It might seem relatively easy for you to confront your father, for example, but it may be very hard for clients from particular cultures to question the authority of their fathers or other authority figures. Your client may have sincere religious, political or other affiliations that preclude certain kinds of behaviour. Of course, these may need to be questioned as part of counselling, but don't assume that all such positions are pathological or secondary to, say, white middle-class therapeutic values. We know that many trainees, in their placements, sometimes have difficulty noting and accepting that for certain clients the typical Western goal of personal autonomy at all costs is not shared by their clients from cultures where more value is placed on family integrity and authority, as well as divine authority (Palmer, 2002).

Consider, and ask about, your client's learning style. Is she someone who learns best from reading and reflecting, or rather from direct action and risk taking? Is she more likely to respond to an assignment using imagery? Will she respond better to highly structured work or to homework that leaves her room for her own creativity? This information may become apparent from counselling sessions, but you may have to make it explicit by asking, 'How do you think you best learn?' Give her some examples of learning experiences. Ask her how she has learned best in the past. Which learning experiences has she found most exciting, enjoyable or challenging? Which experiences has she found most unrewarding or frightening?

An important principle to bear in mind is what Windy (Dryden, 1991) has called 'challenging but not overwhelming'. When you are constructing appropriate homework, remember to pitch it at a level that maximizes motivation and learning without paralysing the client with fear. Describe your ideas for an assignment and then negotiate an appropriate level of risk or effort. It is important to involve the client fully in the fine-tuning of setting the task. The task has to be not only sufficiently unlike the client's everyday routine to involve new learning, but also sufficiently palatable and performable to avoid the client sabotaging it. Look for non-verbal reactions to your suggestions. Suppose that your client expresses a fear of driving, even after having passed her driving test. You suggest that she takes a drive around the block next Tuesday; she looks unmoved. You suggest that she drives up the M1 in the rush-hour; she looks terrified. Perhaps she will be more responsive to the idea of driving to a place on a Sunday afternoon where she will be greeted by friends who will give her dinner. Find the appropriately motivating task by talking it over with your client. Remember that clients have expectations regarding tasks. Efficacy expectations are expressed in the forms: 'Can I do it? Do I have the capability for this task?' Outcome expectations are expressed in the questions: 'Will it help? Will this task help to lead me to my goal?'

Consider the client's history of doing homework. She may have done assignments with you before, or with another counsellor or helper. If not, she will probably have executed homework tasks at school or college, or perhaps as part of a job. The usefulness of discovering such past attempts lies in the clues they may give to her attitude to different tasks and the manner in which they are set. By taking into account the above factors, you are more likely to be successful in arriving at suitable tasks for each occasion. Finally, don't forget that indicative tasks are often embedded in the client's very narrative. The client who keeps returning to the need for a difficult but necessary talk with her partner about the problems in their relationship isn't so very far away from doing it and may require only empathic reflection of this, and support.

Summary

When presenting your idea of what kind of task will be helpful, consider whether the clients will be able to do it; whether clients' environment and resources will permit them to do it; whether their learning style matches the kind of task suggested; whether the task represents challenge rather than being overwhelming; whether their past experiences of homework are relevant.

55 Check that the client understands the assignment and its purposes

Clients may agree to your propositions regarding homework without fully understanding them. There is a lot for clients to think over in most counselling sessions, and sometimes they are still turning over information in their minds from earlier in the session when you are discussing an assignment. So keep this in mind. The chances are that if you work through the stages of explaining and negotiating homework, then you and your client will be tuned in to each other at this point. But do check that this is the case. Does your client understand why you are suggesting this piece of work? Does he truly understand it, or is he merely nodding an empty assent?

One recommended practice is to write assignments down. It has been found in the field of health psychology that written reminders of behaviour to be practised are very important in enhancing change attempts. Some counsellors use purpose-designed stationery for such written records of assignments. You can get, for example, a no-carbon-required pad which will record the agreed assignment for both you and the client. Omer (1990), in discussing the concept of 'promoting expectancy', suggests that announcements in appropriately expectant tones of voice can help to reinforce messages of importance. 'Now I am going to give you your homework for the coming week', he suggests as a useful formal announcement, for example. Against this approach, we would argue that it minimizes the client's input into the homework setting. Of course we recognize that some counsellors would be uncomfortable with some of what we suggest here. However, don't underestimate the importance of the part your client has to play in discussing and designing homework.

Summary

Allow for the possibility that your clients may not immediately understand what you are asking them to do, and why. Consider reinforcing homework messages by committing them to paper and underlining their importance.

56 Agree when and where

Again, although the client may appear to have understood and approved the assignment, she may still leave the session without a clear idea of exactly how she will carry it out. It might seem like 'a good idea at the time' (during the session) but in the cold light of day, at home, without support, it may lose some of its clarity or attractiveness. It is also quite possible for counsellors themselves not to follow through, either because they do not really believe in the value of homework or because they sometimes lack the confidence to be specific, to set aside the 'dogma of non-directiveness' and to be appropriately assertive.

It helps to concretize the assignment if you talk about when and where it is to be carried out. 'When do you think you might be able to do this?' may elicit some clear commitment. But the client may respond with 'oh, sometime in the week, I suppose, when I have the time.' This is clearly a vague, ambivalent response. 'It's often helpful to consider a specific time' is a possible rejoinder. Similarly, 'where do you think would be a good place to do it?' will encourage the client to picture herself in an appropriate situation. Gently move your client into as specific an agreement as possible. Negotiate with her any obstacles to choice of time and place. If she does live in a noisy flat, for example, ask her where else she might go to carry out the assignment or how she can enlist support. By going through it in this way you reinforce the importance of homework, helping the client to visualize herself doing it and putting it firmly into time and place. This makes it far less easy to forget or sabotage.

Summary

Negotiate and agree on the best time and place for your client to carry out the homework assignment.

57 Distinguish between 'try' and 'do'

Stewart (1989) gives several examples of how clients protect themselves from real commitment to change. A primary device for avoiding commitment is that which is worded as 'I'll try'. When you ask your client if he is ready to go ahead and complete a particular assignment and he tells you that he will try, it is a good idea to pick him up on it. 'I'll try to do it' is such a commonplace phrase that it is easy to accept it at face value, yet if you look at what it means it becomes apparent that it represents an escape clause. When you ask someone 'will you do this?' the most direct replies are 'yes, I will' or 'no, I won't'. When someone replies, 'I'll try to do it', this frequently means 'I'm not really committed to this idea and I doubt if I'll do it'. It can contain the nuance, 'I may do it but if I fail to, then I can always say that I only said I would try.'

Listen for this, or similar ambivalent phrases. (Stewart suggests that 'I want to', 'I can do it', and 'I think I will' are comparable.) If you sense that your client is speaking ambivalently, confront this. 'You've said you'll try, but will you?' is an obvious counter; or 'I didn't ask you if you would try, but if you will do it – will you?' Of course, you do not want this to sound authoritarian, so you may need to 'soften' it with your tone of voice or humour, but without lessening its importance. Because 'trying' smacks of half-heartedness, it is advisable to elicit commitment. If you allow the client to 'try', then you may well be giving them the message that you do not regard their efforts as serious. Confronting people with this issue need not be accusatory. Delivered in a straightforward, even humorous, way, it conveys your concern for the client's progress. It sometimes helps to demonstrate to the client what the difference between trying and doing is. A simple and vivid example is to ask the client to 'try' to click his fingers without actually clicking them. Then ask him to 'do' it. As he immediately clicks his fingers he can vividly appreciate the difference between trying and doing.

Stewart advises, too, that you listen for even more subtly hidden ambivalence. A client may say 'I will do it' in a tone of voice or with accompanying bodily gestures that say, 'but don't be surprised if I don't do it'. So be alert to non-verbal reservations and share your perceptions with the client. 'Are you sure you will? You sound a little hesitant to me' might be your response to such ambivalence. Elicit your client's commitment but avoid being persecutory! Particularly avoid coming across as demanding or bossy with clients who are depressed or highly sensitive to perceived criticism.

Summary

In general, be wary of allowing your client to leave you with an 'I'll try' response. Point out the ambivalence in this phrase and seek your client's commitment to carrying out the assignment being discussed.

58 Identify potential obstacles to homework completion

The ambivalence towards homework embodied in the phrase 'I'll try' is just one example of the obstacles that can arise in relation to homework. We suggest that you actively help the client to identify any present or embryonic obstacles to completing assignments.

Ask your client if she is aware of any factors in herself, in others, or in the environment that may stop her from carrying out her homework. She may be aware of some resistance, for example, as you are discussing the assignment. Some clients may say, 'I realize that as we're talking I'm actually thinking that there's no way I'm going to do this homework' or 'I'm catching myself planning how I'm going to tell you next week that I was too busy to do it'. Not all clients will so readily disclose such ambivalent thoughts, however. You may need to probe a little. If the assignment involves others then how will your client use these other people as a pretext for not completing her assignment? If there are environmental constraints, these need to be discussed before the session ends so that alternative assignments free of such constraints can be discussed or steps to overcome the environmental obstacles can be taken by the client. Here, as elsewhere, collaborate with your client in finding realistic ways to reduce or eliminate all such obstacles.

You may notice various signs of resistance to homework as you talk with the client. Perhaps she quickly changes the subject, or looks blank, or sullen. Perhaps she has told you how often she gets into battles with 'authority figures' in her life. 'Do you think that might crop up here?' is a question that might help her to confront a potential pattern of sabotage. Such questions can be put in a lighthearted manner without losing their importance. What you are trying to do at this stage is to minimize self-defeating obstacles and maximize commitment.

Summary

Ask your clients what possible obstacles exist between them and the successful completion of homework assignments. Explore such potential barriers to progress as fully as necessary.

---

59 Initiate mental rehearsal

Clients are often helped to prepare for homework assignments, particularly those that involve some degree of risk, or behavioural challenge, by engaging in mental rehearsal. You will often hear people retorting, 'Oh, I just couldn't see myself ever doing that!' You can demonstrate to them that they probably can see themselves doing it, even if the image is accompanied by apprehension.

Mahrer (1988), working humanistically, put forward the idea that an ideal experiential therapy session consisted of four steps, the last being the rehearsal of 'new ways of behaving in prospective scenes'. The client pictures and experiences herself acting as she would like to, and this mental rehearsal is aided by having her eyes closed. For example, she may say that she cannot picture herself asking a man out. So you guide her through a brief visualization of just such an occurrence. She may become self-conscious and laugh. Ask her what is happening; ask her to continue with the picture: at what point does she begin to find it difficult? Help her to follow through the rehearsal as far as possible, identifying any snags along the way, and then imagining ways to overcome them.

Mental imagery can also be externalised creatively using Gestalt-like exercises. For example, the woman who wants to work on her anxiety about confronting her partner might use the counsellor as a stand-in for the partner, and be encouraged to try out different phrases, with different levels and kinds of emotion, even playfully, to see how it feels and what the especially difficult parts of it are. Mental rehearsal can be taken as a tentative stage on the way to actualization, so that if this particular task is simply not within the client's current zone of emotional and behavioural ability (that is, it is too high on her hierarchy of anxieties), return to its application in the real world later if appropriate. The solution-focused technique of asking the miracle question (Milner and O'Byrne, 2002) – having the client imagine a tomorrow in which the problem has gone – engenders a kind of mental and sensory rehearsal, a reminder of how much better life could be, followed by eliciting the client's idea of what possible small steps could be taken towards it.

Encouraging your client to anticipate and rehearse such scenes reinforces the efficacy of homework. She can see that it is indeed possible that this task will achieve something important for her. Note that you are not conveying any guarantee that what she envisages will 'come true'. She may not get the reaction she hopes for. What you are reinforcing is the idea that the steps leading up to such risk taking are within her control. You are also encouraging her to foresee obstacles and to engage in problem solving in relation to them.

Summary

Have your clients picture themselves carrying out the homework assignment, including any problems that arise along the way. Use the mental rehearsal to reinforce the client's power to carry out the task and to solve problems.

---

60 Establish criteria for success

It is advisable to establish with the client how she will know that the homework has succeeded. What will constitute success? Take the example of the woman preparing to ask a man or woman out. She has never done it before and always considered it as being beyond her range of possible behaviours. Now she can see that it is possible for her to do it. Nothing can stop her from asking a man or woman out. But at what point will she have succeeded? If she interprets the assignment as asking a man or woman out and having him or her accept the invitation she may well be disappointed because she cannot predict or control the response: he or she may well say 'no'. In this case, seek her agreement that success lies in her bringing herself to ask the person out, and nothing more. If the person agrees, this is a bonus but if not she has still succeeded in completing her assignment.

Assignments that involve other people may prove particularly problematic. In these cases you need to establish clearly that the criterion for success lies within what the client can achieve for herself. If she has always wanted to sing in public, and does so, this is success, even if she does not get the applause she would like, because that is outside her control. The environment and other people are outside her control. Ensure that she understands this and that she truly accepts that when she has discharged her task, she has succeeded – whatever may follow. A predictable problem for some clients is the projection of perfect success. In the example of the public singer, she may wish to sing 'perfectly', or like another singer. Your task then is to help her to accept a realistic baseline for measuring her performance. This may be that if she finishes the song, success is hers. It may be that if she sings in tune she will have succeeded. These tasks are probably within her control. 'To bring the house down', however, is not a realistic goal. With clients who are perfectionistic you need to spell out the terms of success with special care: it is the doing of the assignment, not brilliant execution, which is success. You may even have your perfectionistic client deliberately perform in a mediocre fashion, in order for her to learn, for example, that she can accept herself when she does less than perfectly. And of course it is important not to inadvertently suggest that the client rates *herself* as a success or failure but as someone who has had success or otherwise in specific instances.

Summary

Ensure that your clients will be able to measure whether they have succeeded in carrying out their assignment. It should be within their personal control and should not involve perfect performance or self-rating.

61 Explain the 'no-lose' nature of homework assignments

You will strive to set meaningful and testing pieces of homework but you also need to remember the non-judgemental nature of counselling. You do not want to create a new set of 'conditions of worth' for your client, so that she will feel good if she succeeds and bad if she fails. The objective of homework is to accelerate and consolidate learning but not at the risk of inadvertently reinforcing your clients' sense of failure. It is not a condition of their worth as people that they complete a task.

Accordingly, explain to clients the following possible outcomes from homework:

- They will do it well, and as a consequence will probably feel good, and all will be well, at least for a time.
- They will do it badly, and as a consequence may feel bad. In this case the opportunity presents itself for them to give and receive feedback on what happened.
- Whether they do it well or badly, they may prove to themselves that they are capable – perhaps more capable than they had imagined.
- They will not do it at all, and as a consequence will, again, have the opportunity to give and receive feedback on how and why they did not do it.

Whatever the result of the nature of the assignment, something will be learned. This is what we mean by a 'no-lose' assignment. In describing this idea to your clients, they will probably feel considerable relief. We do not suggest, however, that you present the no-lose explanation in such a way as to commend the poor-performance and non-performance options. Convey the desirability of success but avoid conveying any insistence on it. Paradoxically, many people perform better knowing that they do not have to do well. In particular, anxious clients may benefit from hearing this no-lose clause.

Summary

Let your clients know that no matter what outcome there is to their homework assignment, something will always be gained.

---

62 Check homework

Having carefully negotiated a homework assignment, if you fail to follow through and you ignore the subject the next time you meet, you convey the idea that homework (and indeed perhaps the working alliance itself) is not important after all. Even more damagingly, you may undermine the client's respect for you and for the counselling process. So, if homework is worth setting, it is worth checking. 'Checking' may not be the best word if it suggests suspicion and distrust; we mean it, rather, in the sense of reviewing and showing genuine interest.

At the beginning of the session following an agreed assignment, say to your client, 'Let's first of all talk about what you and I agreed that you would do. Tell me how it went.' This is a straightforward invitation to discuss the outcome (whatever it is) of the homework. Do not be afraid to enquire. Your client will be expecting you to ask. Your enquiry does not have to be (of course, *should not be*) persecutory, in the sense of 'checking up on' him. It is, rather, respectful of his efforts. 'How it went' also includes your interest in the kinds of thoughts and feelings the client had that may have prevented her from carrying out the agreed task.

It is usually good practice to begin the session with this enquiry but there may be instances in which your client arrives in distress. In such cases you will naturally allow appropriate space for ventilation of distress. But don't let this throw you off the subject of homework. Return to discuss and check the homework before the end of the session. Use common sense in regard to this; obviously if your client has undergone a major unforeseen misfortune do not pursue the subject of homework. On the other hand, be alert to the possibility that some clients may wish to divert your attention from the agreement regarding homework.

Summary

Do not overlook homework. Check on what progress clients have made with their assignment. Initiate open discussion of what was learned from it. Be sensitive to the timing of your enquiry.

---

63 Check whether or not the client did the homework successfully

First, check what the client learned from the experience. Take, again, our client who was to ask a man or woman out. She returns and tells you, 'Yes, I did it, and he said he'd love to go out with me. I was amazed!' She learned that to ask assertively for what she would like actually paid off – she got it (on this occasion). Alternatively, she might say, 'Yes, I asked him out and he was quite pleasant but said he already has a relationship.' What did she learn? Perhaps that she had the ability and courage to do something new and risky, that she didn't feel as anxious as she thought she would feel; she felt, in fact, only mildly awkward when he told her he was already in a relationship.

Did the client learn what was intended (that she was capable of asking someone out and that regardless of the response she could come out of the assignment with self-respect), or something else? It is quite possible that there will be an unexpected outcome. Suppose she asked the person out, he said he would like to go out with her, and she realized that she was not so interested in him after all. This may lead you to a further chain of enquiry. Or suppose that he said he would like to go out with her and he had been trying to summon the courage to ask her out; she might learn from this something about the near-universality of social anxiety, or about how much time can be wasted by such anxiety. This client might, on succeeding in this assignment, suddenly realize that she had spent her whole life putting things off; or, more mundanely, she may learn that this man really isn't her type.

When you respond to the client's account of success, avoid giving approval to her as a person. Rather than saying, 'you did really well, you're fantastic', for example, try something more like, 'that was really good'. This latter statement praises the deed, not the client. It introduces or reinforces the idea that actions are more or less desirable but people are not to be rated on the basis of their performances. From a person-centred perspective you might say 'it sounds as if you're really pleased with yourself and I know I'm feeling excited for you too'.

Summary

Discover what the client learned from doing the homework, whether the learning was that intended or not. Capitalize on this progress, but direct your enthusiasm at the accomplishment rather than the person.

64 Check whether the client attempted the homework but did not succeed; discover the reasons for this

If the client says that she failed to do the homework, explore what she means. Ascertain whether or not the client actually began to do the homework. An attempt is different from an 'I'll try' in that the former is an approach to doing it (which fails somewhere along the line) whereas the latter has an element of ambivalence about it from the very beginning. When it is apparent that she did make a serious effort, praise that effort (for example, 'it was good that you started to do it') rather than the client as a person.

Find out what happened. Probe for the details. How far did she get with the assignment? What ran through her mind as she approached it? Was she aware of a specific point at which she realized she wouldn't follow through to the end? Was there, after all, something in the environment, or not within her control, which prevented her from succeeding? To return to our client who was about to ask someone out: she may report that she got as far as talking to him but lost her nerve when it came to proposing a date. Her effort can be applauded and something can be learned from the precise factors that prevented further success, which you need to discover. She may say that she went out to a place where she knew she would meet someone she liked, but panicked and returned home; this could present quite a different picture of her level of functioning. By pursuing this further, you might learn, for example, that she panics in other situations too, and this may indicate that you need to adjust your approach with her. It could be that she got as far as asking the person out, but sabotaged it subtly by asking in a rather negative way. Be encouraging about the degree of success achieved, no matter how small, and use the details to discover what the problems are and how they might be resolved.

Remind the client that the assignment was a no-lose one. Tell her that it is helpful that her attempt has yielded useful information on which to proceed to work. Then consider the way forward. Depending on the circumstances, you might suggest that she simply repeats the assignment again next week. Or you may suggest some modifications to it. What you can also do is to show how this partial success has within it certain links with her other obstacles to change, thus reinforcing the importance of the homework. It also gives important clues to what you need to work on together with the client in terms of the nature of the block. It is really acceptable to fail, but advisable to persevere if you choose to effect long-term change.

Summary

Find out how the assignment did not succeed, including the details. Praise the client's effort, and not the client personally. Elicit from the details factors that can serve as data for problem solving.

---

65 Discover reasons for the client not attempting the homework

Dryden (1990) shows many of the reasons for clients not attempting their assignments after they have been set (see Appendix 5). These include misunderstandings over the nature of the task; 'excuses'; rationalizations for not doing homework in general; objections to the stress or difficulty involved in the task; forgetfulness; depression; reassessing the assignment as inappropriate. You may well give clients such a list to prompt a discussion about how they blocked themselves from doing the homework assignment if they really don't know why they didn't do it.

Again, elicit the details of the client's thinking in relation to the homework, and identify the obstacle so that you can work to overcome it with the client. At what point did she decide not to do it? How did she convince herself not to do it? How does she feel about not doing it? How does she feel about the counsellor having set it? Was it truly negotiated, rather than set? Emphasize again that, within a no-lose arrangement, it is good that this information can come to light and lead to further discoveries. Refusal to complete the homework might represent the client's hatred of having things imposed on her, for example; she may have realized that she didn't want to do it but she was too afraid to tell the counsellor, and therefore showed her feelings indirectly by not doing it. This discovery can lead to new insights and directions in counselling. Consider ways to design new or modified assignments.

Summary

Find out why your client did not attempt the homework and work with the client to explore the obstacle. Discover possible reasons by initiating discussion on the client's feelings and attitudes regarding homework. Renegotiate or modify the assignment in the light of what you and your client have discussed.

66 Encourage the client to take increasing responsibility in setting homework assignments

Having negotiated homework assignments with your clients, you have given them a taste for discovering what homework works best for them and how to design it. Clients will learn some of the skill of designing suitable assignments from you. Their commitment to homework will hopefully grow as they discover the impact it can make on their learning. But it may not automatically follow that the client takes over the responsibility for setting assignments from you.

As you have shown your clients how you design and negotiate homework they may realize that they can do this for themselves. The value of doing homework may be clear to them, but you may need to make a direct suggestion. 'How would you like to think of an assignment for yourself this week?' might be a simple way of putting this. Or, suppose that the client is facing a particularly momentous challenge in her life; you might suggest that she considers what piece of homework will be sufficiently potent to help her face this challenge. Let's say that she has to address a large audience and is feeling very anxious; you might ask her to construct an assignment that will help her to desensitize herself – she might, for example, force herself to speak up in front of a meeting of senior managers at her office, or to rehearse her speech in an empty theatre. You may give her ideas, but gradually withdraw your initiative and encourage hers.

If she claims not to have the imagination to think of assignments, you might ask her, in a given case, what sort of assignment she imagines you might set her. Alternatively, you can encourage her to brainstorm: 'What are all the possible ways you might rehearse this forthcoming speech? Just list them without too much thought, however bizarre they are.' Ask her to write them down. Having listed various realistic and unrealistic possibilities she can then proceed to look at the advantages and disadvantages of each one, and to choose one that is suitable and efficacious. Using humour and imagination can stimulate a sense of learning by fun. Alongside the fun, however, you need to convey the message that the goal of brief counselling is to help your client towards autonomy; therefore, the more she takes responsibility for devising and executing homework assignments, the better the prospects for her future. Again, as with other matters, this needs to be communicated non-judgementally and with a readiness to explore obstacles.

Summary

Gradually encourage your clients to take over the setting of homework assignments and everyday challenges. Help them to do this by demonstrating how it is done. If appropriate, initiate a climate of humorous exploration of possibilities. Reinforce the rationale for autonomous task setting.

67 Set homework assignments for yourself in order to enhance empathy with and help the client more effectively

In generaly, counsellors are advised to have some experience of being in counselling or therapy, in part to learn what it is like to be a client. We advise you, too, to experience homework assignments yourself. First, by setting yourself homework assignments you will appreciate the technical issues involved. Second, you will experience some of the thoughts and feelings that clients experience in undertaking homework. Third, you will be able more authentically to negotiate and follow through on homework assignments with your clients if you have undertaken similar assignments yourself. Fourth, you may also come to appreciate the problems and benefits involved in self-generated homework and self-change generally. Fifth and finally, you can set yourself homework directly related to your counselling with particular clients (for example, consulting relevant research literature or devising a form to elicit certain information).

How do you go about all this? If you are still in counselling you can ask your counsellor for help with homework assignments. However, if you are not in counselling, you can still effectively undertake homework. What current or chronic obstacles or discomforts are there in your life? You may be relatively free of crises, but most people always have areas in their lives which can benefit from attention and change. Do you, for example, procrastinate, avoid certain situations or people, chronically underrate your abilities, or experience mild anxiety or depression? Is your life stuck in a rut? If so, use your own insights and learning to focus on specific concerns and to arrive at goals that can be operationalized. Then use the same procedure we have outlined in the previous sections to set appropriate assignments for yourself; adjust your ideas as necessary to find a good fit between your focal concern and the precise assignment.

It can be an instructive exercise to do homework in parallel with your client. Take, for example, a problem that is about as difficult for you as the client's is for him, and try to mirror his efforts in real concerns in your own life. This kind of exercise keeps you in touch with what clients are facing and helps you to remain inventive. In some cases it can be useful to self-disclose to clients the kinds of difficulties, successes and failures you encounter. We refer you to Section 49 on different kinds of homework for suggestions on what you might undertake yourself.

Summary

There are various benefits of doing homework assignments yourself. By setting assignments for yourself not only will you achieve personal learning, but also you will strengthen the bond between you and your client.

PART V
COUNSELLING IN THE
MIDDLE PHASE

68 Follow through on themes and consolidate gains

It is not possible to state exactly when the middle phase begins because the length of counselling relationships, even in brief focal work, varies. Even in a relatively few sessions there is likely to be a period of characteristic engagement and depth between the 'hello' and 'goodbye'. Clearly, there are certain characteristics of a beginning phase, as there are of the ending phase. The middle phase tends to be a time of deepening trust and intimacy between counsellor and client; a working pattern has been established. At the same time, difficulties may arise: impasses between client and counsellor may appear; and the client may encounter deeper material.

Keep your client's focal concerns in mind. When you are well established in the counselling process, a good deal may have been learned. (It is also possible that this might not be the case – we refer to the problem of lack of progress in Section 79.) Build on any early gains by gradually introducing your client to wider applications of what she has learned. We have already discussed the idea of identifying themes (by which we mean scripts or overarching dysfunctional beliefs and attitudes) rather than individual concerns (or problem situations in clients' lives). By the time you are working in the middle phase of a counselling relationship you will probably have many opportunities to work thematically. By this we mean that you can increasingly draw out themes from the examples of everyday concerns that clients give you, and work more intensively on these. Remember not to treat each session as if it is the beginning session: capitalize on what you have both learned and move forward.

If your client has reported several instances of fearing the disapproval of others, for example, you may work on how her thinking contributes towards those fears. Perhaps she gradually learns in counselling, and by homework assignments, that she can have an argument with someone and discover for herself that she does not have the dire need for approval that she thought she had. Extend this thematic learning by helping her to look at other situations in her life where she imagines that she has a great need for approval. What you are then doing is to provide your client with a method, a philosophy or technique for dealing directly with her life and its future problems. This is where, although the counselling may be brief, you have the chance to practise 'seeding' for future client changes. Seeding is the act of offering and reinforcing change goals that may not be realized until some time after counselling ends (see Zeig, 1990). We believe it is crucial for counsellors to take this into account because otherwise it can be counterproductive and frustrating to demand to see change within the period of counselling itself.

You may have held firmly and successfully to your original approach with the client, but at this stage you are still in a position to extend the learning that is possible from that approach. Dryden (1990) demonstrates how the counselling process in rational emotive behaviour therapy adapts according to the stage of counselling. But as well as adapting your approach from stage to stage, and from each of your client's concerns, you may come to realize that certain aspects of your approach work better with particular clients. Remaining within an REBT approach, for example, it may become apparent that your client responds consistently to rational emotive behavioural imagery, rather than to strictly verbal and logical examinations of her thoughts. In other approaches, it may emerge that your client has an obvious preference for linking insights in her life now with events from her past. She may respond very favourably when you try an exercise based on psychodramatic techniques. By the middle phase you may well identify a particular modality (such as imagery or behaviour, among others) which suits your client best (see Lazarus, 1981). If this is the case, capitalize on this by reinforcing lessons learned through this modality and by introducing any further exercises belonging within it.

Summary

Continue work on your clients' focal concern and gradually help them to extend what they have learned from specific situations to more general applications. Work thematically and identify any particular modality in which your client learns better.

69 Keep on track with respect to original concerns

The other side of generalizing from specific concerns to thematic learning is that original concerns may be forgotten or put aside prematurely. There is a danger that your client will wander from one subject to another rather superficially. This danger is one that the critics of brief counselling often level against counsellors: that by encouraging 'superficial' problem solving and 'flight into health' you encourage the client to gloss over deeper, more painful and subtle, well-defended material. Return to the original concern as often as seems necessary to ensure that your client is not running away from it and is not 'problem hopping' or 'solution shopping'. In other words, although brief counsellors deliberately practise selective attention, they do not advocate avoidance.

Do not allow your client to lure you into lengthy casual conversation, or into long discussions about red herrings. You need to be as alert to the defensive or symbolic use of conversational decoys as any psychoanalyst, and we suggest you draw your clients' attention in such instances to what they are doing. Ask them if they are aware of how they are changing tack in the conversation. Ask them if they are anxious. This is easier to detect when they are obviously going off at a tangent from the therapeutic task at hand. A subtler form of escape from threatening inner anxieties is often shown through compliance. The client may welcome your demonstration, for example, of how to generalize from one concern to another and how to work thematically. He may be only too keen to get away from certain raw bad feelings associated with his presenting problem. You need to be on the lookout, therefore, for any such manoeuvres. This can and should be done not in a spirit of 'catching the client out' but from a respectful attentional attitude.

Summary

Keep the original concern in mind and return to it until you are both sure that it has been fully addressed; do not be drawn away from it for defensive reasons.

---

70 Balance the gains of being goal-directed against the gains of relationship factors

We have stressed throughout this book the need to maintain a central focus or foci. Relationship building is often seen as a primary concern in the beginning phase of counselling. However, it may be that you will risk what Rowan (1989) calls 'aim attachment' (that is, being overly concerned to produce results), thus minimizing the power of relationship factors in the middle phase. Clarkson (1990, 2003) draws attention to the importance of 'the multiplicity of psychotherapeutic relationships'. These include the 'I-You' or person-to-person relationship; 'the working alliance' or adult-to-adult rational relationship; 'the transferential relationship'; the 'developmentally needed' or reparative relationship; and the transpersonal, highly intimate and spiritually informed relationship. We have alluded previously to the working alliance and to transference factors. Reference has been made to Buber's (1947) emphasis on the significance of two human beings (you and I) meeting at a particular time. A central plank in our argument for brief counselling has been the use of the reflection process, which is based on respect for the client and for the need for mutual understanding. We have also discussed the way in which counsellors can become aware of and use their influence base with each client. It is important that you notice and deal appropriately with any signs that your client may benefit more from her direct relationship with you than from goals and techniques.

The developmentally needed relationship, says Clarkson (1990: 153), 'refers to those aspects of relationship which may have been absent or traumatic for the client at particular periods of his or her childhood and which are supplied or repaired by the psychotherapist usually in a contracted form during the psychotherapy.' Although such therapeutic work is often undertaken with more seriously damaged clients over a long timespan, it can also become apparent during brief work that clients are deriving benefits from their relationship with you that are of the 'corrective emotional experience' kind. For example, clients who have had particularly poor relationships with their parents may find in you someone who for the first time really takes them seriously, or who shows them ordinary human concern and respect. While the presenting concerns may have been 'focal' (for example, bulimia) the client may realize during counselling that she is sensing something she has previously missed out on – understanding and concern. Some clients, for example, will ask for hugs, or will want to engage in a certain amount of 'small talk', perhaps because they had very little of these when they were children. Be sensitive to the possibility that such requests sometimes represent new discoveries to some clients; they may never have been able to ask for these things before.

Should aspects of the 'transpersonal relationship' become apparent during counselling, recognize these and respect them. Sometimes you may be aware of an additional, spiritual dimension in your work with some clients. Don't ignore this or consign it to the category of pathology (although some clients, and some counsellors, sometimes try to cover up their personal suffering by involvement in this area of interest). If spirituality manifests as an issue, decide together on whether you can profitably work with it within your present, brief contract, and be prepared to renegotiate if necessary. If you have such an interest, for example if you are familiar with analytical psychology, psychosynthesis or other spiritually oriented approaches, you may decide that it is appropriate to work in this area. Or you may decide to refer your client on to practitioners who do work in this way, or to a priest or other suitable helper. Heron (2001) refers to the 'transpersonal process cue', which may alert you to the breakthrough of an 'altered state of consciousness'. (The client may suddenly look very different, sit differently, or use spontaneous new imagery, for example.) Most clients do not seek brief counselling in order to explore such states, but it is possible that some clients, having benefited from a certain amount of groundwork in counselling, will spontaneously enter such states. Be aware then, that the counselling relationship can in some cases engender various needs and experiences which were not 'bargained for' at the outset. It is well worth consulting Mearns and Cooper (2005) on 'working at relational depth' and Rowan (2005) on the variety of therapeutic attitudes towards clients (instrumental, authentic and transpersonal), as well as West (2004).

Summary

Be mindful of how your relationship affects clients. While some may be very goal directed, others may benefit from the respect and concern you give them. Some clients may experience new states of being following initial counselling. Decide on whether you will work with these, renegotiate your contract, or refer on.

71 Explore possible areas of mutual unawareness; refer to supervision

You may become conscious during the middle phase not only that your client avoids certain subjects but that you, too, draw away from some subjects. Or you may be vaguely, uneasily half-aware that something is not being addressed. There can be a variety of reasons for such an occurrence. It may be that you have allowed a certain culture of cosiness to develop between you, for example, which is hard to change. Sometimes you may have clients you particularly like, or who remind you of close friends. These occurrences are aspects of countertransference, which can be anything the counsellor feels strongly towards or about the client – see Maroda (1991); Rowan (1989); Watkins (1989). In such cases you do not always immediately realize that something is amiss. You seem to get on well with the client and the client gets on well with you; both of you are gratified and view this as self-evident progress in counselling.

One way to probe such occurrences is to ask your client directly, 'do you think there is anything that we haven't discussed and that might be of importance?' If you are aware that the relationship has become cosy, you might try saying 'we seem to get on very well here, and that may be fine, but sometimes it can be a sign of things becoming too easy. Do you have any thoughts on that?' Notice whether, in considering asking such questions, you tend to shy away from them, preferring to leave things as they are. If you do, ask yourself what need you may have to keep things cosy. Have you let the counselling slide into a non-therapeutic, comforting relationship instead of a working one? If so, what might you be afraid of if you do confront the client with some difficult issues?

If you have been tape-recording sessions you can listen to your tapes with such questions in mind. Better still, you can play them to your supervisor and ask for feedback on the tone of your interventions. Are there signs that you are backing away from challenging the client and making life (in counselling) easy for yourself and your client? It is easier for you to ask yourself this question if you are at least dimly aware of something of the kind seeping into your counselling. However, this phenomenon can be made all the harder to detect if you are unconsciously presenting your work with certain clients as non-problematic. Trainee counsellors often say in supervision, for example, 'oh, I haven't got much to say this week; there are no problems with my client.' Or you may not present a certain client for supervision. This selectivity may well be unconscious but it is sometimes an indicator of a degree of unawareness. For this reason (among others) Windy often asks trainees to bring all their tapes to supervision for him to make a 'lucky dip'. A willingness to expose any and all of your work is a good way to avoid this kind of problem from taking root. Even without using such tactics, your supervisor is there as another set of eyes and ears and can offer fresh perspectives on work, which you are missing.

Summary

Look out for any signs of overly comfortable or cosy relationships with any of your clients. Watch for any reluctance on your part to be challenging. Monitor all your work for such instances and take all cases to supervision.

72 Encourage clients, when appropriate, to see themselves as others see them

An area of unawareness that many practitioners report finding it difficult to tackle concerns clients who complain copiously about their lot, often about how unfairly treated they are by others, without considering that they themselves – or their own behaviour – may actually be problematic for others. Let us spell out what we mean. You will probably encounter some clients who have a tendency to arrive at the session late, who seem to want something magical from you (rather than working hard themselves) and who complain about conflict with partners, peers or colleagues, and perhaps life generally. We might say they are pre-contemplative, that is, not ready for serious therapeutic work, but we think there is more to it. Such people (and there may be some struggle not to label them as 'difficult' or as acting out) have the characteristics of presenting in some degree of crisis and having little insight into their own contribution to the problems they are running into. The difficulties in working with this kind of client may be compounded by the norms of counselling training, which emphasize the importance of empathically viewing things from the client's frame of reference. More mundanely, it can be compounded by the fact that we almost always hear only the client's side of the story, unless we are couple counsellors.

An example is Carole, a middle-aged woman who comes to counselling following some years of low-level conflict with work colleagues. She appears hurt and mystified ('how could they treat me like this?'), she has been talking to a union representative, has had time off work, and feels stressed and victimized. The first appointment had been carefully arranged to fit in with her childcare arrangements and yet she was still quite late. Carole asks you what you can suggest to help her deal with this situation and to feel less stressed. You probably respond accordingly, showing an understanding of her plight and beginning to offer tentative strategies, perhaps some exploration of her automatic thoughts about other people's views about her. Yet your honest feelings, which we can refer to as countertransference or congruence clues, tell you that you are not hearing the whole story. Of course you can try to work constructively with her on the basis of what she tells you. But you cannot help but suspect that she may come across to others somewhat as she is coming across to you, which is as rather 'difficult', lacking in insight and an objective sense of how her behaviour may impact on others. There is a dissonance between her reported story and what you discern for yourself, and a further gap between Carole's ostensible request for help and her underlying resistance to hearing anything challenging. In brief counselling in particular, if you are to work with such clients, you need to think how you can avoid colluding and help the client to hear some things that may seem unpalatable. One of the main tasks called for in this kind of scenario is that of helping the client to entertain and learn from significant information. How can this be effected? Consider the following possibilities:

- There are certain tactful phrases and probes you can use. 'If there's anything about you that others might find difficult, and your best friend in a spirit of honesty were to tell you, what might she say?' is one such example. Or, perhaps 'Would you be willing to try this? Can you tell me about three of your interpersonal strengths and three areas of interpersonal weakness?'
- Judicious self-disclosure can be useful. Try something like this: 'We all have our blind spots. Take me. I think I'm a fairly well-rounded and considerate person, yet my partner tells me that sometimes I get irrational and moody about certain things. I don't like hearing this, but when I think about it, I have to admit he's often right. How about you? Does this ring any bells?' (Remember to balance the strategy of self-disclosure with an awareness of the risk of alienating the client, undermining her confidence in you, and so on.)
- Ready-made exercise such as the Johari window can also be useful. Although this is mainly used in groups, there is no reason why you can't adapt it to some individual clients and its visual nature may be additionally helpful. One version of the Johari window explains the quadrants of the window in these terms: *public arena* (what is shared knowledge, such as biographical facts); the *blind spot* (information about which we are unaware or unconscious but others may see in us); *façade* or *hidden area* (those things we know about ourselves but self-protectively deny or hide); and the *unknown area* (anything yet to be discovered, for example in counselling). (See Tosey and Gregory, 2002.) This objective-looking instrument may help clients to see that others have benefited from viewing matters in this way and, used skilfully, should open up subtle aspects of the client's inner world.

The public arena:	**The blind spot:**
e.g. 'I know I'm quite shy'	e.g. 'I don't notice how sarcastic I can be until it's pointed out to me'
The façade or hidden arena:	**The unknown arena:**
e.g. 'I act tough sometimes because I don't want to reveal, even to myself, how much I was abused in childhood'	e.g. 'I don't know what I might find out about myself if I give counselling a chance'

Figure 4. The Johari window.

Let's not pretend that there are no potential problems in trying new strategies with such clients. If they sense that you are prematurely marginalizing their view of factual oppression from people and situations in their lives and presenting your own more probing view, they may quit counselling and/or complain about you. We also want to underline the need for sensitivity here. Where a client has been made to feel bad about herself as a child by demanding and demeaning parents, it is obviously not appropriate for you to repeat this scenario in counselling; you need to avoid even unintentionally conveying the impression of non-acceptance. So hard work may be required to ensure that your client does feel genuinely accepted by you, even as you collaboratively work at challenging and changing some of her more problematic traits. Do not reinforce the sense of rejection felt by those, for example, experiencing low self-esteem or labelled as having a borderline personality disorder. Distinguish between acceptance of the person and questioning of their blind spots and façades. Careful thought about taking on or referring such clients is necessary, especially with limited time, and supervision is of course crucial.

Summary

Recognize those clients who may need to develop a fuller view of how they impact on others. Help them to take more responsibility and gain insight by choosing from a variety of subtle probes, exercises and self-disclosure. Remain sensitive to the impression you are making on the client.

---

73 Remain open to the possibility of in-depth therapeutic work

A common criticism of brief counselling, and certainly of short-term time-limited work, is that it necessarily tends towards the cognitive and away from the affective, emotional or psychologically deep. To some extent we have probably conveyed that view in this book. But even within very short-term counselling it is sometimes possible or even necessary to engage the client at some depth. This is the view of Ecker and Hulley (1996) and Mahrer (1989a) among others.

- *Scenario 1.* The client, a woman in her mid-thirties, has been recently bereaved. Her partner died in an accident. Although a strong person with her own career, financially secure and with good friends, she had been planning to try for a baby with her partner and now these plans have been brutally ended. She is not irrational about the death, nor cut off from the natural grieving process. She does, however, have a lot to talk through and while doing so cries deeply. She says she wants to be able to do this now and feels that the time available (eight sessions) will be sufficient. Although the counsellor is concerned about the time factor, her gut instinct is that her client does indeed have a realistic sense of what she needs to do and how long will be sufficient. The promptness of counselling is more important to her than the length. Much of the counsellor's work is about listening respectfully, occasionally prompting or 'giving permission', and verifying that she is safe to leave, has support and a means of continuing with her life without undue traumatic effects.

- *Scenario 2.* Andy, a man in his late forties, arrives in turmoil. He works in public relations and hates it. He is in a second marriage and is convinced it is all going wrong. He says he married in good faith but in haste and he is realizing painfully that he is stuck, terrified of ending it and causing great distress to his wife. He is deeply stressed about his lifestyle (besides the job he hates), having a 'huge' mortgage and various commitments he no longer values; he drinks far too much at times. For some years he has been reading about Buddhism and alternative lifestyles and he is on the point of deciding on a major life overhaul. His turmoil is profound; he cries at times and wrings his hands. The counsellor considers cognitive strategies for helping him re-examine his views but it seems obvious that he has already done so much soul-searching and knows what is right for him. They both agree that the six sessions can be used to look at some the practicalities of how he will make the changes he wants to, as well as preparing for the inevitable emotional upheaval ahead with mindfulness and distress tolerance skills (Kabat-Zinn, 1990).
- *Scenario 3.* Suzanne recently watched a television programme that featured some scenes of childhood sexual abuse. For many years she had been aware of her own abuse but had managed to persuade herself that it was in the past and no longer important. Now, she is suddenly overwhelmed with feelings of nausea and dread and has started taking time off work sick. She sees you in a GP's surgery and takes two or three of her available ten sessions to begin to speak directly about her experiences. She says that during the week she had been having strange, scary feelings of standing outside herself. She trusts you and you feel reasonably competent to work with her, but you are so concerned at the depth of her distress that you agree to see her for support only while you arrange long-term therapy with a local low-cost psychotherapy service.
- *Scenario 4.* You have seen Steve for two sessions and an intense relationship has developed. He has been through a number of drug experiences in the past, as well as being involved in petty crime and some cult activity. He has a great deal of insight into himself and is struggling to get himself back on course. There is something very likeable about him, about his sincerity, humour and courage. You have had some similar experiences, which, after some reflection and discussion in supervision, you share with him. This helps him to explore more deeply and the relationship between you intensifies. Even during some fairly long, anguished silences you both have a sense of purposefulness and hope. Alongside this is an awareness of risk but it is a risk that you both feel ready to go through. By the end of your eight sessions you both agree that invaluable work has been done.

These different scenarios demonstrate some of the material that expresses itself in emotional depth and some of the key issues counsellors must deliberate on. Is there sufficient time to address such issues effectively? Is there a danger of getting too deep within the time available, and of matters becoming worse? Is referral the better course? Is there a danger of collusion or countertransferential enmeshment? Issues of emotional depth do not always make themselves obvious at the time of presenting and assessment. The counsellor may or may not have the competency or confidence in particular cases to stay with the client's distress and work at the necessary depth. Equally, depending on your experience, training, maturity and self-awareness, you may sometimes feel intuitively able to respond to the client just as he or she needs you to. It is sometimes a fine judgement to make, whether to proceed at depth, to offer a different way of working (for example, supportively), or to refer. In some cases it is possible for counsellors to argue strongly with managers for extra time for such clients. Supervision is always vital. Resiliency, integrity and personal awareness are crucial.

Summary

Allow for the occurrence of states of deep feeling and turmoil that may be worked with even within short-term counselling. Always consider the advantages and disadvantages of becoming engaged in such cases, including possibilities of referral if necessary.

74 Balance the head and heart aspects of counselling

Undeniably, the cognitive behavioural therapy (CBT) approaches emphasize the cognitive and rational faculties, although their critics often unfairly suggest that they omit or suppress emotional elements altogether. Likewise, humanistic and transpersonal approaches are sometimes caricatured as neglecting cognition and overemphasizing feelings when they simply value the latter highly. There is no getting away from the fact that each approach has its theoretical and probably practice bias too. This is all the more reason for all of us to pay attention to any possible over-emphasis that may be less than helpful to the client. Colin, for example, originally embraced primal therapy, in which a very high premium is placed on strong feelings, but has adapted his views and practice over the years. Windy, while remaining an advocate of REBT, places more emphasis on the importance of the subtleties of the therapeutic relationship than Albert Ellis does. Within primal therapy is the practice of what is in effect a cognitive debriefing and behavioural resolution-making following deep feelings. Within REBT is a belief that shame and guilt are unhelpful and one is free to be emotive and enter emotive situations without judging or rating oneself for doing so. Guinagh (1987) attempts to bring these two facets of personality and therapy together in his text focusing on catharsis and cognition. Lazarus (1981) includes affect and cognition in his scheme of modalities, just as Heron (2001) includes conceptual and affective modes in his. We believe that any good counsellor will be concerned to (a) be realistic and self-aware about her inclinations towards 'heart' or 'head' theories and practices and (b) adapt her style and responses as necessary with each client. Of course, there are limits to how much any of us can congruently and convincingly do this. As two male authors and academics, we also realize that there may be gender-specific limitations involved here too!

The heart aspects include open-heartedness, warmth, love, simplicity, untutored innocence and defencelessness. Brian Thorne has focused on the significance of tenderness and Paul Gilbert (2005) on compassion. Certain humanistic and transpersonal training courses outside of universities and colleges emphasize the heart and soul in counselling and there is a danger that the university – traditionally concerned with assessment, evaluation, evidence and critical thinking – inadvertently *over*values the head. The increasing weight placed on the professionalization of counselling may also unintentionally have the effect of playing down the role of simple fellow feeling. Although most of us, even the 'non-person-centred', are trained to be as congruent and authentic as possible, it is quite possible that the professional role might erode some of this in time. The heart aspect is more likely to be evident in a peaceful, meditative setting where the pace is as relaxed as it needs to be. It involves an unforced reaching out to the client, an I-Thou encounter that can potentially risk the counsellor's 'position' as helper rather than helped. While we have said that this heart aspect is suited more to a relaxed setting, it is quite possible to heed it in brief work too.

The head aspect is about judgement, discernment, analysis, rationality, calculation and caution. Without this, counselling risks becoming an undisciplined, sentimental and unaccountable activity. It is probably no accident that the counselling field has swung from the pre-eminence of humanistic approaches in the 1970s to the ascendancy of CBT in the 2000s. The thinking counsellor weighs up evidence, keeps a part of her mind critical in the sense of questioning assumptions and plans ahead. This approach is more likely to set goals and work through cognitive obstacles. It may well lend itself to a brisk pace. It may inadvertently become impatient with unnecessarily circuitous methods or woolly hypotheses. Colin has a particular negative reaction to the unthinking use of words and phrases like 'I'm on a journey', 'it's the process' and 'it's the relationship' and has found that, when asked exactly what these mean, many counsellors are unable to give a clear reply. Likewise, the concept of intuition has some dangers about it, especially when counsellors unthinkingly insist that their intuition or gut feeling reigns supreme and needs no explanation.

So, the head and heart aspects often pull against each other and there is sometimes a real danger of an unhelpful bias in one direction. Each of us probably has an inevitable bias. But paying attention to this, slowing down or sharpening our pace, being unguardedly open to our own feelings towards the client or judiciously weighing up what the client is saying, as necessary, offers a good check against extreme bias creeping in (Bayne, 1999; Bryant-Jeffries, 2005).

Summary

Get a sense of how the head and heart aspects operate within you. Consider the merits of each and find a balance within and across sessions according to clients' needs.

75 Consider how best to use supervision of brief counselling

We have made various references to use of supervision. Here, we consider the specific needs and problems associated with the supervision of brief work. First, let's acknowledge that with the increase in counselling contracts of six weeks (particularly in primary care but also elsewhere), it may be the case that you barely discuss certain clients in any usefully proactive way (Feltham, 1997). This is especially true of counsellors who receive monthly supervision. Hence, unless you alter your pattern of supervision, you are likely to rely quite heavily on self-supervision for short-term cases much of the time. We recommend for trainee or beginner counsellors in this position that you consider more intensive supervision, perhaps weekly. This need not mean weekly sessions of one hour; sessions could be shorter. But alternative and imaginative kinds of supervision are also possible. It is quite in order to contract with a supervisor to engage in telephone or email supervision (provided confidentiality safeguards are in position – see BACP, 2005) to help shed extra light on the contents and dynamics of short-term counselling contracts.

Here, we will assume that you have access to supervision that is sufficient to discuss your work with quite short-term clients. What then are the salient considerations and what is the best use of such supervision? The following list contains some suggestions:

- Is your supervisor familiar with the challenges of brief counselling? If their own background is in long-term, open-ended work, they may not quite appreciate what is involved and there could be an unintentional and unhelpful mismatch between you.
- Have you and/or your supervisor had any specific training in the kind of brief or time-limited counselling you practise? If not, your professional development needs should be discussed.
- Explain to your supervisor what the particular challenges for you are of the context in which you work (for example, you may *have* to practise non-negotiable time-limited counselling; you may not always feel happy about all the referrals you receive).
- Consider whether there are any special ethical issues requiring attention. For example, have you been referred a client by someone who has promised something you cannot deliver? Or is your client vulnerable and might short-term counselling leave him stranded with no follow-up? Is it acceptable or not to see a client in your own private practice after you have initially seen him in primary care?

- Examine what the advantages and disadvantages of brief counselling are for your clients and for you and your preferred way of working. Some counsellors definitely prefer long-term work and feel frustrated by short-term contracts, for instance, and this can lead to resistance to working focally and ending in a planned way.
- Discuss any specific difficulties presented to you in brief counselling. For example, many trainees report difficulty in encouraging their clients to find and maintain a focus.
- Where a client has multiple presenting or emerging issues, how can you realistically focus on one or two of these and help the client to find his own way forward with others?
- How will you respond when your client brings up unexpected and possibly very difficult material (such as childhood sexual abuse) in the fifth session of a six session contract?
- How will you manage counselling logistically when a client misses a session or requests extra time?
- What are the challenges involved in helping the client to anticipate relapse after counselling and how best can you prepare her or him for the ending of counselling?

While not a comprehensive list of what may come up, this should provide you with some thoughts about specific connections between brief counselling and supervision needs. You may need to be quite discerning in a search for a suitable supervisor and assertive in ensuring that your supervisor understands the challenges you face. There is the particular challenge of arranging supervision times so that you can meaningfully discuss your clients rather than finding yourself having only token check-in discussions about clients with whom you have almost finished.

Summary

Take time to consider what your specific needs are for supervision of your brief work. In particular think about the suitability of your supervisor, the timing of your sessions and the content of what you need to discuss.

---

76 Be alert to your client's dependency on counselling and on you as a counsellor; help clients to orientate themselves towards personal confidence and autonomous growth

Although you will have discussed with your client the nature of brief counselling, and you may have already discussed termination, she may nevertheless show signs of clinging to the counselling relationship or to you. There is a difference between a certain level of intimacy and liking and a more dysfunctional level of dependence. We also recognize that some clients need to learn to become intimate and not to remain aloof from their counsellor or terminate prematurely. But here we are focusing on the kind of client who you will recognize as wanting to make counselling and the counsellor the centre of her world. We fully acknowledge that psychodynamic counsellors will focus on transference issues here but remind you that many such counsellors work successfully in short-term contracts either by making transference a secondary consideration (ego support may be thought more constructive) or by making it a central feature from the outset and working vigorously with it (Molnos, 1995; Coren, 2001).

Sometimes this is a sign that there is little between-session work going on. If your client turns up for sessions saying, 'I've been thinking about this problem and wondering what you'll think about it', this can be an indication that you are becoming her guru, or a substitute for her making her own efforts to change. In such a case, you might respond, 'What do you think I would've said if I'd been there?' or 'Insofar as you have your own "little voice" about such problems, I'd like to know what that was telling you.' Encourage the client to own the learning she has done and to practise it in her everyday life. Do not be drawn again and again into the role of the wise consultant. As Sheldon Kopp (1974) advised clients, 'If you meet the Buddha on the road, kill him.' By this he meant that it is dangerous to invest too much faith in apparently omniscient others because it erodes your own personal learning potential. You don't have to respond to such questions with a wooden and unimaginative, 'you'd like me to tell you what to do'. Remind the client of the work you have done together and the themes you have been working on; encourage her to do her own work. Ask the client 'What would I have said or done in that situation?' But then ask the client to consult her own 'inner counsellor' (by which we mean her own decision-making processes). Encourage her to recreate a scene in which a problem presented itself, and in which she relied on some idea of what you or other 'wise' people in her life would have done or said, and ask her to create a different solution of her own.

Reinforce the agreement that counselling is to be brief. Let your client know that she is capable. When your client conveys the idea that she is too weak to cope on her own, or hasn't yet learned sufficient skills or garnered enough emotional strength to entertain the idea of ending counselling, consider changing the pattern of sessions. 'Well, let's see if that's true. Shall we test it out? I suggest we might schedule a break of two weeks, say, and see how you get on.' In this way, clients can empirically test the idea that they cannot cope without you or counselling. (We are assuming here that there is no genuine crisis involved.) It may even come to the point, towards termination, that your client claims not to be able to continue without you, or insists that she have more sessions. Simon Budman demonstrates (in Budman and Gurman, 1988: 362) that it is sometimes necessary to argue your case for not offering further sessions with some degree of force. Should you encounter such resistance, it is useful to be able to state clearly why you consider time-limited counselling to be appropriate. Part of your statement should reinforce the client's coping abilities and the idea that gains in counselling continue to operate afterwards. Remind the client that counselling is a tool to help with better living. In doing this, it is necessary that you believe what you are saying! It may be that in some cases you will decide to refer the client on for long-term therapy.

Summary

Look for signs that clients are becoming overly dependent on the counselling process or on you as a counsellor. Check that they are putting what they learn into everyday practice. Suggest breaks in schedule to allow clients to test out whether or not they use what they have learned from counselling in their lives.

77 Be alert to any deterioration in your client's condition and respond appropriately

A small percentage of clients may, as counselling progresses into the middle phase, show signs of worsening. There can be a temptation, for example, when a previously tense and expressionless client starts to break down and cry, to regard some forms of distress as indications of therapeutic progress; sometimes that is the case. But there is also a danger that some people get into a pattern of regression, crying, writhing, 'somatizing' (for example, experiencing many headaches) and so on, that should not be regarded as routine signs of 'getting in touch with feelings'. It is true that for some, counselling can be painful before it gets better, but this is not always true. Equally, be mindful of consumer feedback suggesting that clients sometimes do not recognize their own sense of distress or dissatisfaction with counselling, or do not always receive helpful responses from their counsellors when they question why things are not going well (Bates, 2005; Sands, 2000).

Mays and Franks' (1985) study of 'negative outcomes' in therapy listed many signs of deterioration as a result of therapist errors. These signs included depressive breakdown; destructive acting out; increased anxiety; exaggeration of somatic difficulties; increased guilt or confusion; lower self-esteem. Colson et al. (1985: 72) suggested that 'therapists or analysts were often slow to recognize the negative-outcome patients' actual personal and treatment needs and to shift treatment approach accordingly, from tactics suitable for an expressive psychotherapy to a more highly structured and supportive approach'. If your way of working particularly uses challenging and uncovering interventions, you need to take extra care at the assessment stage, to monitor the reactions of all clients, and to be well supervised. Look out for any tendency you may have to want to push clients overly hard. Don't let the excitement of eliciting dramatic abreactions, for example, blind you to the possibility that your client (and you) may be getting too deeply, too early, into chaotic and painful material. If this happens inadvertently, respond by offering more structure (more talking through of problems and feelings, more specific monitoring of daily moods).

Whereas some clients fail to make due progress because their counsellors are not skilful or effective enough, others deteriorate because their counsellors are too therapeutically ambitious. Learn to recognize your own limitations and those of your clients. When clients become rapidly distressed, or frequently distressed, or often confused, take this to supervision but also consider making use of other resources. In the case of severely depressed clients, for example, it may not be enough to ask them to 'close the escape hatches' (Stewart, 1989). Consider getting psychiatric advice; advise the client to consult a GP; consider making a referral to another counsellor or therapist. Although some counsellors have an anti-medication stance, some clients are helped by antidepressants, for example, and such medication can often be used in conjunction with counselling. Familiarize yourself with local and specialist resources. Learn to identify which clients show signs of deterioration under which conditions. Overcome any anxieties you may have regarding your own professional status: if you have doubts about your ability to deal with particular clients, discuss these with your supervisor and do not hesitate to make a referral.

Summary

Heed any signs from clients that they are getting worse in counselling. Do not confound exhibitions of deep feelings with obvious progress. Monitor such cases carefully, taking them to supervision and if necessary referring them on.

---

78 Deal with any crises that may arise

If you are counselling someone over a period of months, it may well be that life events will arise which distress or preoccupy your client. They may very well cut across the work you are doing. Suppose that you are working with a client on an eating disorder, and a friend of hers is suddenly involved in a fatal accident. Your client will probably want to spend time grieving, and integrating the impact of this event into her life. It is highly likely that such an event will temporarily become more important to your client than her previous concerns. (This is assuming that your client is not in such a critical state herself that her own welfare should take precedence over an accidental event concerning someone else.)

Significant life events during the course of counselling can dramatically alter its outcome (for better or for worse). Respond sensitively and appropriately to such events. You may need to check with your client that she wishes to alter the contract at such a time. 'It seems that you need time to talk about this. Shall we put aside what we had planned, and return to it when you feel the time is right?' Do not make assumptions about how upset or not the client will be but watch for non-verbal signals of denied grief or other reactions.

Some fortuitous events may represent crises for counselling but not, apparently, for the client. Suppose that your client suddenly wins or inherits quite a lot of money, is elated, and feels that her problems have evaporated –

what will you do? It may well be appropriate to agree with the client that she seems relieved, happily preoccupied and not in need of any further counselling at present. But you would be wise to suggest that the present elation may not last and that you will be available should she wish to return at a later time.

Another category of crisis is sometimes seen in clients who are accident-prone or histrionic. In such cases the crisis may not be 'real', or it may be unconsciously 'created' by the client. You may not meet such clients very often, but some, who have what has come to be known as a personality disorder, for example, will create crises in order to get attention (Norton and McGauley, 1998). Often these clients are better served by therapists with specific training in cognitive analytic therapy or dialectical behaviour therapy. Or some clients may 'hit bottom' during counselling and inflict harm on themselves. At times like these you will need to consider seriously whether you can continue with your contract, or if there is a need for referral. But what you cannot do is ignore such events. In the case of clients who regularly present with 'crises', you need to feed this back to them and to consider if brief counselling can proceed if clients have little or no insight into their behaviour. See also Leiper (2001).

Summary

Pay attention to genuine crises and check that your clients receive from you, or get elsewhere, the support they need to deal with them. Be aware of the varieties of crisis that can occur and of how they may require quite different handling.

---

79 Evaluate progress and deal with any disappointment that the client has regarding the rate of progress

You may become conscious of the client's (or your own) enthusiasm flagging during the middle phase. It may feel as if counselling sessions are becoming something of a ritual. Take such signs seriously and instigate a review of progress. Some counsellors suggest formal review sessions as a matter of course, and this is a practice to be commended, provided that it is not allowed to become an empty ritual of uncritical mutual congratulation. But what do you look for in either formal or informal evaluation discussions?

Check on actual progress regarding agreed goals. Have they been reached partially or fully? What obstacles remain to achieving them? Beyond individual goals, to what extent has progress been made with the client's underlying constructs? For example, if the client's goals related to becoming less anxious, how has she achieved this? Has she learned to identify, say, her irrational beliefs and how to challenge them? Where has she come to at this stage in counselling and what remains for her to achieve? In what ways does she find you helpful and unhelpful? How can you offer more appropriate help?

Evaluation is both quantitative and qualitative. It may be ongoing, if you have developed the habit of constantly referring to the reflection process, or it may be scheduled in as a formal procedure. Sutton (1989) is a proponent of precise client measurements of change in counselling and simple progress charts or verbally reported numerical scaling methods are used in cognitive analytic therapy and solution-focused therapy respectively. Such measurements cannot be taken unless you and your client agreed clear and unmistakable goals at the outset, which include what she wished to achieve and how she would know when she had achieved it. Simple graphs can be used for this purpose (see Figure 5). Ryle (1990) has built into his model a variety of evaluation procedures for both client and counsellor.

Completing a progress chart: instructions for your client

Having agreed which goal or goals you are working on with your counsellor, use this progress chart to record your own view of progress towards goals. Write on it a specific goal. Consider each week whether you are moving towards or away from your goal (or not moving at all). Enter what scores seem appropriate to you: +5 means that you have attained your goal (or that your original symptom or problem is gone); −5 means that matters (in relation to this specific goal) have got much worse. Scores in between indicate degrees of improvement or deterioration, as judged by you. Each week, mark your score on the chart with an x and discuss it with your counsellor. Remember that you are not scoring *yourself* but how much change there is in relation to your goal for change.

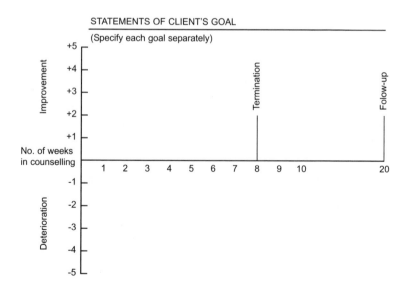

Figure 5. Client progress chart

We are aware that many counsellors dislike the notion of evaluation, or at least of formal evaluation of progress. In the humanistic camp, Rowan (1989: 171) gives a 'list of criteria for doing good therapy', which some counsellors may find compatible with their approach and useful as a means of evaluating their work. Person-centred counsellors are unlikely to engage in formal evaluation unless the client requests it, yet may be very aware of the progress their clients have made (or not made) according to Rogers's (1990) 'seven stages of process'. Rogers's process continuum begins with clients perceiving themselves and events in fixed terms and ends with clients appreciating the nuances of their own feelings and the choices before them. Rogers's view was that these stages could be evidenced in time-limited therapy (he cites Lewis et al., 1959) and it seems, therefore, that even person-centred evaluation of counselling progress is quite practical. To some extent, how you structure evaluation of client progress is a matter of taste. You might also measure results against Prochaska and DiClemente's (1984) stages of change. If your client has moved from contemplation to action or maintenance on certain target concerns, then progress is clear. When evaluating, be sure to involve your client as fully as possible and to clarify which points you agree and do not agree on.

At this stage you may learn that your client is disappointed with the rate of progress. This can either signify that change has indeed been slow and very modest (and that it relates to client motivation or counsellor interventions) or that the client has harboured unrealistic fantasies of change. Indeed some psychoanalysts have argued that disappointment is a necessary stage of maturing – realizing that life is not as we would ideally like it, that we did not receive perfect parenting and will not get everything we want in life, including an ideal therapist or counsellor. You need to ponder on and check these possibilities carefully. Garfield (1989) advocates explicit discussion of such disappointment. It is often the case, he argues, that the way in which clients deal with (or even set up) disappointments, reflects other similar phenomena in their lives. This is not a licence to dismiss valid criticisms of your counselling, however: do heed what clients tell you about your counselling style. Garfield (1989: 100) also suggests that 'if the therapist is seeing a client who meets the general criteria of being a suitable candidate for brief psychotherapy and there is no discernible progress after five or six interviews, the therapist should attempt some evaluation of the case'. Caution needs to be taken that you neither try to hurry inappropriately in such cases, nor overlook possible causes of non-improvement.

Summary

Either look for signs that an evaluation of counselling progress is called for, or initiate a formal review session. Consider ways in which you and the client can evaluate progress, including ongoing reflection and formal written assessments. Use baseline measurements that suit your approach and your client's needs. Deal with client disappointment.

80 Be prepared to renegotiate goals where it becomes apparent that presenting concerns concealed other problems

In counselling and psychotherapy the client's material can often, of course, be other than what it seems. We do not think that brief counsellors are, or should be, any less aware of this than long-term practitioners. However, in working focally there is a concentration on certain material and a risk, therefore, of overlooking other concerns. Both consciously and unconsciously, clients sometimes conceal or de-emphasize certain matters, which may surface later in the counselling process.

At a conscious level clients may occasionally decide 'not to bother you' with certain matters; they may be aware of something painful that they cannot bring themselves to discuss immediately; or they may even, in embarrassment or defensiveness, lie to you. This 'not bothering' or withholding may happen more in time-limited work (Regan and Hill, 1992). In cases where a client discloses to you that there is something on their mind which they have not discussed before, listen carefully to this new material and help the client to decide what priority to give it in counselling. In cases where clients tell you that they have concealed something, show your interest and concern non-judgmentally. Ask whether there is anything in your manner that has made it difficult for them to tell you before. Be ready to set new goals with the client if the new material is critical, and discuss whether it fits in with the approach you have been using.

An example of a fortuitous discovery of concealed problems is given by John Marzillier (in Dryden, 1992). Marzillier was using behavioural methods with a client whose problem was a difficulty in urinating in public conveniences. In order to help the client, Marzillier purposefully accompanied him to a pub where the client had to drink enough to be able to urinate in the public toilet. While he and Marzillier were drinking and waiting for the drink to pass through the client's system, they talked informally (and without design) about the client's life, his family difficulties and career dilemma. Marzillier reports that progress with the urination problem was slow and the client left treatment to travel abroad. By chance they met two years later, and Marzillier was surprised to discover that the client first failed to remember the (urination) problem, and then admitted that it was still in evidence but of no great consequence. The lessons of this reflection are that our intentions and methods are not always appropriate and that clients sometimes have more important underlying problems or preoccupations. Some psychodynamic practitioners insist that problems invariably have deeper, underlying dynamics that must be addressed. While this is obviously not our position in this book, we suggest that you remain aware of unexpressed undercurrents in your client's material.

What may happen when previously undisclosed matters are brought out at this stage is that the client will ask for more time. What was apparently a straightforward and even somewhat reasonable fear of going on underground trains, for example, turns out to relate to sexual abuse in childhood. In such an instance, what will you do? Unless there is a very good reason, don't change your original brief contract into a completely open-ended arrangement. If appropriate, agree to lengthen the work with your client, but first discuss this issue in supervision. Sometimes there is a compelling case for such extended work, as in this example. But sometimes clients will resist the termination of counselling and create dependency by producing urgent new reasons for being given more time. Discuss all such cases in supervision to ensure that you are not being drawn into a collusive relationship with your client. To take the same case of sexual abuse, your decision to continue to work with this client may include questioning your knowledge and ability in working in this area. It may be appropriate to refer the client on. In various examples of clients discovering hidden material and getting into deeper areas of distress than they and you had anticipated, consider the appropriateness of referring on to counsellors or psychotherapists who work more at this level.

Summary

Be aware of new material surfacing in counselling and of any necessity to negotiate new goals accordingly. Question whether you can offer what your client needs, whether you can change your approach, or if there is a need to refer on. Do not automatically slip into open-ended work.

---

81 Help the client to understand the non-linear nature of change

Change in counselling is rarely, if ever, smooth and uni-directional. If we have inadvertently given this impression in this book, please forgive us! The therapeutic change process can commonly include elements of hesitancy, enthusiasm, sustained commitment, 'conversion', stuckness, 'peak experiences', disappointments, incidental learning, crises, relapses and stable maintenance. Relatively little has been written about the implications of chaos and complexity theory for counselling (but see Chamberlain and Butz, 1998). Clients quite often hope for or expect dramatic, rapid and irreversible changes. The degree of fantasy involved may be directly related to the amount of suffering in the client's past. The reality is that counselling can be a rough ride, with ups, downs, moments of uncertainty and doubt, and times of backsliding. Explain this to your client at an appropriate time, and explain that this is a universal experience rather than only true of them.

A model of non-linear change that may be useful to consider is that given by Windy (Dryden, 1990). This includes the three dimensions of frequency, duration and intensity. Ask your client if he experiences his distress or difficulty more or less often than previously (frequency). Likewise, when the distress occurs, does it last as long as it used to do or a shorter time (duration)? When it occurs, is the distress as intense as before, less so or more so (intensity)? Help the client to be specific in identifying these factors. Often it is useful to have her record these items on paper, especially if she is anxious about progress. Such recording is a systematic feature in cognitive analytic therapy, where clients are encouraged to rate their progress on target problems on a weekly or similarly regular basis.

Prochaska and DiClemente (1984) view the change process as circular rather than linear. Particularly in relation to clients with addictive problems, but also in relation to clients broadly, they speak of a 'revolving door' model of change. Depending on the stage of change at which they enter counselling and at which they terminate or drop out, clients will often proceed in circles of change, re-entering the sequence of contemplation, action and maintenance, for example, until stability is progressively achieved. Even without dropping out of counselling, clients may 'go in circles' of contemplation and action from session to session.

Summary

Explain to your clients that progress is rarely the smooth affair that they would wish it to be. Encourage them to monitor their own progress on each target concern. Convey across the message that non-linear change is the norm.

---

82 Recognize and deal with any impasses

Impasses (stubborn obstacles) can occur at any stage of counselling but often occur most frequently in the middle stage. It has been noted of organizations as well as individuals that there is an inbuilt conservatism. People wish to change but simultaneously experience a wish to remain the same; what is familiar is reassuring and what is unknown often evokes fear or wariness. When your clients reach a certain stage in their counselling, the easier goals may have been reached and more challenging goals may present themselves and invoke anxiety or resistance. Such impasses as may result from this resistance can relate to the client-counsellor relationship or to clients' relationship with their tasks and everyday life (Davy and Cross, 2004; Leiper, 2001). Impasses can also come from, or be exacerbated by, your unheeded countertransference or incongruence (the attitudes you have towards your clients, of which you may not be fully aware). Some counsellors believe in staying with impasses and in using the core conditions of counselling gradually to erode them; others find it more helpful to employ deliberate strategies. Consider various examples of impasses.

The client will not work actively or confront feared obstacles

Ask the client if he understands the tasks required of him in counselling. Does he think he can perform them and that they will be effective in achieving his aims? He may have appeared to understand and agree with you but is not really convinced, and hence seems stubborn. Does he, perhaps, believe that progress should come easily, that counselling is a passive and primarily receptive exercise? Confronted with a need to make effort and experience some discomfort, does he have an attitude of low frustration tolerance (meaning that he believes that he cannot tolerate the discomfort)? Are you pushing him too quickly or too soon? Remember the 'supporting but not overwhelming' principle. Look at the possibilities of obstacles on both your side and his. Consider, too, using an 'advantages and disadvantages of maintaining/changing the present behaviour' inventory (Appendix 6). This kind of exercise can help to demonstrate to the client his perceptions and beliefs regarding the good aspects of not changing and the bad aspects of changing, in both the short and longer term.

The client is overly concerned about his relationship with you

Sometimes clients will draw you into social conversation, wanting to know all about your week, your thoughts, your own experiences, and so on. Many clients experience their counsellors as 'the only person who ever really listened to me' or 'the only person who really knows me'. This can lead to an idealizing and mistaken focus on the counsellor. Skilful psychodynamic counsellors will interpret such instances of transference in a timely manner. But there is often the possibility that clients secretly regard you as their salvation and consequently do not stretch themselves in their everyday life. Remind clients that the purpose of counselling is personal understanding and change, which involves dealing with their own concerns inside and outside the counselling room. Find your own way of keeping your client focused on his tasks. This can conclude work with the transference. It can also entail a practice of discouraging social niceties. Mahrer (1989a), for example, discourages what he sees as the dysfunctional 'role relationship' of counsellor and client by getting straight into the work; by sitting parallel with the client, with closed eyes; and by focusing entirely on the client's inner experiencing.

The client focuses on others and on circumstances

Some clients talk rather a lot about their partners, their jobs, the weather, their holidays, and so on; some clients tell you how awful their partners or bosses are; or how terrible their childhood was (see Section 72). There is often a lot of truth in these accounts, but not necessarily truth that can be useful. The clients are in counselling to effect changes for themselves. Remind them of that. The people in their life cannot be changed. Sometimes clients blame circumstances rather than accepting personal responsibility because then they might believe that they have to blame themselves. In some cases you have clients who experience great difficulty in not talking incessantly about other people and circumstances: it is probably their habitual style of talking, or it may reflect anxiety about change. As we have mentioned earlier, you may need to interrupt conversation of this kind and to educate such clients into the appropriate role of a client in counselling.

You and the client get into a transference–countertransference entanglement

There may be occasions in every counselling relationship where some transference and/or countertransference is operating. Psychodynamic practitioners would say that there always is. Where it is obviously one way it can be dealt with either by the counsellor's vigilance and interpretation, or by resorting to supervision. But when there is simultaneously strong transference and countertransference you may experience difficulties. Suppose that you and your client begin to get angry or irritable with each other, in the sense of 'getting on the wrong side of each other'; perhaps it becomes hard to maintain very much adult-to-adult communication; or perhaps there are simply times when the relationship becomes clearly difficult. In such cases, definitely take this to supervision. But also deal with it by referring to the adult reflection process, part of the working alliance. Discover if there is anything you have done that has offended your client or triggered strong feelings in the client. Remember that it is more your responsibility than the client's to maintain a mature adult perspective. If you notice that you become defensive, watch this and step outside it. It is quite appropriate to apologize to clients if you have made an error, for example. Encourage clients to move into their 'observing ego' at these times, by showing empathy. And don't forget that even within counselling, none of us gets on with everyone – all of us however well trained or however much therapy we have had ourselves, have human limitations.

You experience overpowering (for example erotic) countertransference

Countertransference takes many forms and in its most unhelpful form needs to be dealt with by the counsellor's own therapy and supervision. But it also provides useful information about the client. In the case of an erotic countertransference (which is, we believe, far more common than people realize – see Mann, 1999) you need to learn to distinguish between what comes from you, what comes from the client, and what is mutual. If you are distracted by such feelings towards your client, there is a problem. If, after discussing this in supervision, you cannot make progress with it, you may have to consider referring your client elsewhere. But first, consider whether there is any way in which your client elicits these feelings, and where you think this may be the case, share this sensitively with the client. Don't 'blame' the client for it but ask whether he or she is aware of strong feelings between you. Some counsellors, particularly those who can confidently be themselves in the counselling process, may bring these feelings into the open at an appropriate time and make good therapeutic use of them. If you are in doubt about your ability to do this, try to put it aside until you have discussed it in supervision. Feelings of this kind are understandable; where they become intrusive or overpowering, you need to think hard. Don't berate yourself for having them but don't keep them to yourself either.

You and the client get into a collusively superficial relationship

You may sometimes be tempted to take it easy with a particular client. Perhaps you feel that someone is too fragile to push in the beginning, so you hold off, and the holding off becomes a pattern that is hard to break. Perhaps you like the client and have a similar background; and therefore you value their company. Or, as a beginning counsellor, you may experience an anxiety to keep the client. (Unfortunately, the need that trainees have for accruing hours of practice can lead to such anxiety.) It can be a natural temptation, after losing one client because you were 'too hard', to react by being very soft and unchallenging. In all such instances, remind yourself that this is not, after all, a social relationship and that non-possessive warmth does not mean 'being nice' to clients. You and they are meeting together to effect concrete changes in clients' attitudes and lives.

Summary

Impasses can manifest in various ways. Look for signs that your client is more focused on you, others or circumstances, than on personal change. In cases where you and your client arouse strong feelings in each other, be sure to discuss this in supervision and if necessary to consider referral elsewhere if these feelings cannot be contained or used therapeutically.

PART VI
ENDING COUNSELLING

83 Initiate preparation for termination

In the introduction to his book, Flegenheimer (1982) quotes from Malan (who is echoing Samuel Johnson): 'Being under sentence of termination doth most marvelously concentrate the material.' In other words, in brief therapy many practitioners capitalize on the fact that clients know that they do not have all the time in the world. They are aware from the very beginning that they had better focus on their concerns and maintain their motivation. Some counsellors will emphasize this 'sentence of termination' at the contracting stage in order to ensure that there is no misunderstanding. Indeed, some practitioners use a 'countdown' system of reminding clients at each session of how many sessions have gone by and how many remain. We are aware that such a practice is disliked by many counsellors, but it is practised successfully by many counsellors working from psychodynamic, behavioural and other perspectives.

Budman and Gurman (1988) make a point of reminding clients that counselling is not the centre of their lives and that learning goes on apart from counselling and after it. Termination is thus close to the surface throughout the counselling process. We noted, earlier, differences between time-limited, brief and open-ended counselling. However, if you are working within a brief counselling contract, there will often be no countdown and therefore no explicit awareness of termination to come. There is sometimes a temptation to let the subject of termination slide. We suggest that you raise the subject and keep it appropriately alive. One direct way of challenging clients' objections that they cannot possibly think about termination is to raise the reality issue that counsellors sometimes move jobs; what would your client do if you moved to another part of the country? Of course, in very brief counselling this is an unlikely occurrence; you simply would not take on new clients if you were about to move.

When is the best time to raise the subject of termination? Obviously timing will depend on individual circumstances. In general (in non-time-limited counselling) you would do well to be sensitive to signs that the counselling process is firmly under way before talking much about termination. Perhaps after your client has achieved significant progress with two or three goals, you might allude to increased hope for a better future. Don't get into a clumsy attempt to persuade your clients that they are ready to consider termination when they are clearly distressed or averse to discussing ending. But, equally, don't put the subject off indefinitely. Some clients, particularly those who are highly motivated or whose problems are well defined, may positively invite discussion of termination. They may see it as encouraging, as confirming the manageability of their problems and as showing them the 'light at the end of the tunnel'. If your clients are at the action or maintenance stages we have discussed earlier, they may welcome discussion of termination because they may well want to make and consolidate progress fairly quickly.

Kupers (1988) has looked closely at the subject of termination in both short- and long-term therapies. He concludes that termination is a complex issue and that in practical terms clients often move from one therapy experience to another anyway, thus making strict definitions of termination difficult. Amada (1983) suggests that many brief therapies, beginning with an apparently well-defined problem focus, actually become long term when it is evident that clients are seeking deeper and more open-ended therapeutic exploration. Our view is that this apparent openness to clients' needs, this flexibility between brief and long-term approaches, had better be scrutinized very carefully. When you initiate discussion of termination with clients, listen to how you present it. Are you convinced that an end is in sight? Do you think that (relatively) brief work with this client is truly appropriate? Are you beginning to like this client, and to be fascinated by her intricate psychological world? Is your client subtly signalling to you that her distress is deeper than you had thought? Is she forming an attachment to you and, if so, is that attachment a necessary and valuable part of a therapeutic process? Or is it a dependency on you and a partial avoidance of the hard work of personal change?

Colin saw a client in a community counselling setting that attempted to limit the number of sessions, for practical reasons. The client first applied for counselling when in crisis. By the time she could be seen the crisis had passed but there was still some useful work to be done that related, broadly, to assertiveness. She made very good progress, working actively between sessions to put what she learned in counselling into practice. Colin initiated discussion of termination by telling her, 'I think you've moved a lot from your original position. Each time we meet you've gained more ground for yourself, and the future looks very promising. What do you think you can get from further counselling that you can't do for yourself?' She replied that coming to counselling felt supportive and helped her to concentrate on her goals. Colin accepted this response and agreed that they would continue to meet for a few more weeks. But he also had a sense that he had become a social focus for her. Many clients find in their counsellors 'the only person I can really talk to'. This is not, in the short term, a bad thing, perhaps, but it can too easily come to complicate the end of counselling. This particular client would probably have continued counselling indefinitely, for very mixed motives, had Colin not persistently reminded her of a need to terminate (for example, by reminding her of why she first came, of how much she had achieved, and by affirming a belief in the time-limited nature of the counselling on offer in that particular setting). She finally agreed to a tapering-off method of coming to an end. See Leigh (1998) and Murdin (1999) for further examples.

Summary

With appropriate timing, introduce the subject of the inevitability and desirability of counselling coming to an end. Explain the advantages of concentrated work, and in doing so examine your own attitudes to termination issues.

84 Promote self-change

We have advocated an approach to counselling that is active for both client and counsellor, yet in the beginning stages you will have provided a lot of the input yourself. Guard against letting this activity take over. Once you feel confident that your clients have substantially grasped and internalized new ways of looking at and dealing with their problems, prepare to hand over the reins of counselling and of change to them. In this sense, the approach we outline here tends to become rather more person-centred as time passes.

When the time has come for this switch from counsellor to client 'leadership', the client is probably at the stage of maintenance (Prochaska and DiClemente, 1984). She needs to secure her gains, experiment with them, apply them to different situations and to make the learning resources for progress her own. Egan (2002) suggests that clients at this stage need 'social support and challenge'. In other words, in order to maintain their progress, they will be helped by reinforcement of their goals from friends, as well as necessary challenge and stimulation. People who have gone through treatment programmes for alcoholism, for example, are often actively encouraged to attend regular meetings of Alcoholics Anonymous. Maintenance implies a careful watch over progress made so far. When we speak of promoting self-change we are not referring to a naive endorsement of positive thinking (for example: 'You don't need this counselling. All you need to do is go out there and get on with life. You can do it if you really want to.'). Don't send your clients on a 'flight into health' but encourage them gradually to continue their journey independently.

There are various means of offering such encouragement. One is the in-session exercise of 'rational role reversal' (Dryden, 1982). In this exercise you ask your client to take the role of the counsellor, while you take up the role of the client. Your client challenges 'your' cognitive errors and assists you in finding better perspectives on her problems. In taking such a lead, she experiences the more rational and coping part of herself, and actively confronts her own doubts. Another way of preparing for self-change is to ask your client to visualize you, her counsellor, sitting on her shoulder, talking to her, whenever she encounters difficulties in everyday life. This is, in effect, offering a 'transitional object' to the client. At those times when she is unsure of her new-found abilities, she may be comforted and helped by the image and memory of you and of the kind of approach you have used together. You can elaborate on this exercise by using the image of a magic lamp that the client rubs in times of difficulty: her counsellor issues from the lamp and she is able to engage in an imaginal consultation. We do stress that such exercises will help some clients better than others, and that they are only interim measures – they are not the ultimate aim of counselling!

Let's look at how you might help clients take on the idea of self-change:

You: OK, now we've been talking about how you felt at the bus stop and at your evening class. What do you think is the common link here?

Client: Well, in both cases I suppose I was embarrassed. I felt as if I'd made a fool of myself.

You: From what we've discussed together, what can you identify in this connection that you might work on?

Client: I was embarrassed. The embarrassment was a feeling of ... I was thinking 'they're looking at me, expecting me to say something friendly, and I can't; they must think I'm stupid'. Something like that.

You: Take that further.

Client: They may not have thought anything of the kind. There wasn't any evidence of that, no. I automatically expected them to think that when I fumbled for words ... and I suppose I set myself up for feeling bad.

You: And even if they had thought that ... ?

Client: I wouldn't have to feel embarrassed. I could think 'I wonder what they're thinking', or I could ask them, or even if I got embarrassed, that's uncomfortable but not intolerable.

In this dialogue, the counsellor is prompting the client to remember previous work together. Instead of doing the interim steps for her, he provides cues and leaves her to work out the process herself.

She may not do it as he would do it, but in this instance he wants her to see that she can do it to some extent. She arrives at an array of options. Feeling acutely embarrassed is not inevitable for her. This process could have gone on, perhaps, to look at how she might dispute with herself when another problematic situation arises. But this is a first step.

How do you promote self-change when you are using other models? Ryle's (1990) cognitive analytic therapy has built-in self-change assignments (questionnaires, written and other tasks) and is strictly time-limited. We have already looked closely at the whole subject of homework in Part IV, but here it is worth noting that Macaskill (1985: 140) argues 'that homework assignments are conceptually and technically consistent with current models of brief dynamic psychotherapy and, furthermore, that setting homework assignments offers substantial therapeutic benefits in terms of maintaining a focus, evolving a sound therapeutic alliance, enhancing motivation and reducing termination difficulties.' Analytically oriented counsellors may have a particular interest in the ways in which some clients resist the notion of self-change. There is a difference between understanding such resistance, of course, and helping the client to overcome it. In the context of brief counselling you cannot afford to let your client slowly work through such resistance. Ryle's model (in common with other brief psychodynamic models) discourages the forming of fantasies of eternal dependence on the counsellor.

Summary

Progressively encourage clients to take over the process of change. Show them how to internalize what they have learned already. Use various exercises if they are helpful to your clients. Demonstrate how the approach you have used together can be used *in situ*. Reflect on your own orientation and the weight you place on clients' independence.

---

85 Address the subject of relapse prevention

While engendering hope is usually an important part of counselling, addressing the likelihood of relapse is perhaps just as important. Relapse is the full or partial return to a previous, undesired level of functioning (Leiper, 2001). As we have already noted, change is rarely, if ever, linear. It is much more often a matter of a great many advances and a great many (minor or major) relapses. By now you may well have introduced the subject to your client.

Since you are concerned that clients will maintain their gains after counselling, you need to address possible future pitfalls now, while there is still time and commitment from the client. Bring this subject up with an awareness of the client's stage of change. If the client is at the contemplative stage, it is inappropriate, of course. But when the client has made changes and perhaps consolidated some of them, it may be time to introduce the subject. 'What can you foresee that might stop you from maintaining these gains?' you might ask. 'I'm really keen to see you develop your gains even further and I'm wondering what possible obstacles might lie in your path in the future' is another way to put it. Discussion of relapse and its prevention is not a matter of painting a gloomy scenario but of being realistic and prepared.

Having established with your client that relapse is a common experience for most people in counselling, explain the significance of anticipating its occurrence. Ask the client to imagine and identify what obstacles in himself, in others and in his circumstances might contribute towards relapse. Help him to visualize the kinds of setting in which he might be tempted to succumb to his former habit, or to abandon his new set of beliefs. Who might assist him in his future downfall? What little signs might there be that relapse is imminent? Actively encourage him to use imagery to foresee relapse situations. Introduce the idea of rehearsal for possible relapse and its management. Suggest to the client that relapse is not awful and in fact is an opportunity to test the reality of his gains in counselling. If appropriate, actively encourage the client to seek out situations in which he will be tested. Show him how to use such situations as cues for problem solving.

There are objections to a relapse prevention intervention. Some people claim that it dampens hope. Indeed, there are conditions that are so stubborn (particularly addictions) that counsellors working in those fields may rely on a vision of complete abstinence, emphasizing a 'one-day-at-a-time' approach. This vision seems to stem from the idea that even to contemplate the possibility of relapse is almost to invite it. We agree that addictions like alcoholism and drug abuse are serious and stubborn problems. However, Marlatt and Gordon (1985) have to some extent countered this argument with their concept of the 'abstinence violation effect' (AVE). When someone has remained abstinent from alcohol for a long time, and then one day drinks a glass of wine, they may tell themselves that they've completely messed up all the progress they made; they berate themselves, feel terrible and drink all the more in order to overcome the resulting bad feelings. They may also rationalize, using the 'I may as well be hanged for a sheep as for a lamb' argument. Marlatt and Gordon teach that such 'slips' are small, understandable and forgivable instances of human error. They are not reasons for 'awfulizing', to use a concept from REBT. Note that we are not saying that it is fine to be blasé about clients reverting to their undesirable behaviour. We simply advocate that it be kept in proportion and not be used to make matters even worse. Andrew Solomon (2002) in his harrowing account of his own chronic depression shows that although a mixture of therapy, reading, self-help and friends' support took him through the worst of his depression, he still expects and gets times of depression. This realistic acknowledgement can itself be helpful.

Using the above alcohol example, you might run through this eventuality with a client, having him imagine that drink. Do so as if it were happening in the present to make the experience come alive. What are the circumstances leading up to it? What thoughts run through his mind at the time? What does he tell himself as he does it? How does the problem escalate? What might he do or think differently that would lead to a different outcome? Don't convey the idea that relapse is acceptable or non-problematic, but that instances of it (behaviourally or in experiences of temptation) are likely to occur. Be sensitive to the individual client, his level of understanding and 'ego strength'. Gauge the time and the means for addressing the subject of relapse. Explain to clients that there is often a movement to greater control and better coping skills over time (Prochaska and DiClemente, 1984).

Summary

Appropriately and sensitively introduce clients to the subject of relapse and to the likelihood of its occurring. Demonstrate the importance of anticipation and rehearsal. Use imagery and cognitive restructuring to prepare for relapse. Convey the idea that relapse is not the end of the world, but a chance to test problem-solving skills.

86 Respect the right of a client who wishes to terminate abruptly to do so

Some counsellors believe that there is an ideal way for clients to end their counselling. We do not. We look at different kinds of endings later, but here we want to convey one of the realities of counselling, which is that some clients do terminate 'prematurely'. Another way of saying this is that some clients terminate before their counsellors think they should. Now, if you have picked up cues earlier in the counselling process that your client is doubtful about what progress she is making, or dissatisfied in some other way, you may have had the chance to deal with such issues. But sometimes there are few cues and you find that your client suddenly announces that this is the last session, or she simply doesn't turn up.

If your client does bring up the subject of ending before you think it is appropriate, by all means explore her reasons for wanting to do so. However, do understand the difference between exploring and coercing. Don't subtly persuade her that she really does need further counselling when she obviously doesn't want it. Avoid in any way putting her down or causing bad feelings when it is clear that she has decided to end. Don't be tempted to interpret this as a 'flight into health'. What you may do is convey your understanding, and your willingness to welcome her back later should she wish to return. Some counsellors make a point of telling clients well in advance that there may come a time in counselling when they (the clients) will feel like quitting because of difficulties they may experience in the counselling process.

We have both had personal experiences as clients of counsellors and therapists trying to persuade us that our decision to leave therapy was a misguided and defensive one. Such experiences can be very upsetting for clients, and particularly so for less assertive or less informed clients, who may find it difficult to argue with the counsellor. Counsellors do on occasion have very strong beliefs about their clients' stage of change in counselling, their depth of pathology and need for extensive therapeutic work, which are at odds with their clients' perceptions. If you find yourself wanting to dissuade your client of her resolve to terminate, ask yourself to what extent you are within her, or your own, frame of reference, and whether you are deriving some special satisfaction from this client. Remind yourself that you have contracted to work collaboratively towards the client's goals, and if you are reasonably sure that your client has achieved her goals or is within sight of them, then you can prepare to end gracefully. If you are not confident that this is the case, use the reflection process to solicit the client's view; if she confirms that she has not, after all, substantially achieved her goals, review your work together, take it to supervision, and consider extending the time you have together or a referral if appropriate. We believe that it is not ethical or appropriate to attempt to keep your client in counselling beyond her wishes. The only real exception to this would be temporarily holding on to a client who is endangering herself or others, until the crisis has been resolved or managed satisfactorily.

When a client terminates abruptly, letting you know either directly or indirectly that she is unhappy with your counselling, don't take it personally.

Accept that you may have made a mistake (particularly if you are a beginner) and learn from the experience. Remember that even experienced counsellors have clients who terminate 'prematurely' because the clients do not get on with them. You may, however, need to attend to certain practicalities after termination. If you are unsure whether your client will be returning, we suggest that you write (rather than telephone) in a welcoming manner, letting her know that she can feel free to get in touch. If clients have left owing you money, you will need to send an invoice; in this case, you might say simply that you welcome their contacting you, but in the meantime, here is your invoice. There is no call for any persecutory behaviour! We also suggest that when a client in brief counselling fails to turn up for an appointment, you do not adopt the analytic habit of keeping the space open for the following week: it is unlikely that they will turn up if they have not been in touch. We suggest that you do not make telephone calls because these can be intrusive and do not allow the client time to reflect. You may well persuade clients to return, but you will also, perhaps, be undermining their autonomy. If the case ever arises that you need to cancel a session, you should consider this in advance and seek the client's permission to phone or make alternative arrangements.

Summary

Deal sensitively with clients who terminate before a planned or expected end. Do not try to persuade them to stay or return against their wishes and do not create bad feelings at the end. Do consider exploring reasons if the opportunity presents itself; and consider the advantages and disadvantages of making contact by letter.

87 Reiterate the expectation that counselling will definitely end

You will have made it plain from the beginning that you have a contract for brief counselling. Where your contract is for time-limited work, there will be no doubt about the ending, because it will be reinforced throughout counselling. But where it is not 'date-stamped' (in other words, where you have referred, for example, to ending 'in the summer'), the client may seek to avoid the subject or to extend the time of ending. Discuss the subject clearly. Accept it is as the norm that a contract for brief counselling should terminate within weeks of the expected end, rather than months. There needs to be a very good reason for you to change this, but there may sometimes be such a reason (for example, an unforeseen accident or loss in the client's life near the end of counselling). Some clients do react strongly to endings, perhaps because of 'unfinished business' from their past; in these cases, allow enough time to work on this as an issue in itself.

Look closely at issues of countertransference when you feel unable to face termination as planned. Where resistance to ending is clearly yours, you need either to work on it or to keep it from intruding. But sometimes you will be picking up the client's anxiety about ending. Resist the temptation to protract the counselling. It is sometimes a good idea to warn clients that 'as we approach the end of our work, you may well find that your symptoms return or get worse temporarily'. Because relapse or the fear of a relapse is common towards the end of counselling, clients may wonder if they really are able to continue to make progress on their own, and they may therefore exhibit all their old anxiety responses. Your job in this situation is to emphasize the progress they have made, to manage the ending in such a way that coping skills are reinforced and morbid expectations of inability to cope are minimized.

Your model of working may, of course, affect your approach to ending. You may perhaps interpret your client's resistance to ending as a recapitulation of former losses. This can be a fruitful line of enquiry, but remember that such experiences are not common to all clients. Also remember not to use such instances as reasons, in themselves, to extend counselling. The short-term psychodynamic counsellors (Coren, 2001; Flegenheimer, 1982) do not, on the whole, succumb to lengthening the counselling process; rather, they anticipate and work with the impact of expected loss reactions. You may well need to anticipate such material and raise it earlier and more deliberately than you might in long-term work. You may also need to remind your client of her original goals and help her to review how closely she has come to achieving them. So, barring very exceptional cases, remind the client that the end is in sight and stick to it.

Summary

Repeat the expectation that counselling will definitely end and work explicitly towards this, avoiding any temptation to lengthen the contract, except in rare circumstances.

88 Encourage final feedback

It is a good practice to address the subject of ending explicitly and to include in that discussion a review of the whole counselling experience. Accept that, for some clients, termination is not critical and painful; but still convey the idea that it is useful to look back at what has been learned in counselling and what can be taken further in the client's life. Make it easy for clients to collect their thoughts about counselling and express their feelings towards you. You may find it useful to do this systematically, but you obviously need to be sensitive to individual clients' feelings on ending counselling. So with some clients you may run through a checklist of what they consider has been helpful and unhelpful, and with others you may talk more generally.

Garfield (1989: 98) gives an example of how the client's disappointment with the rate of progress can be discussed in the middle phase of counselling.

Obviously such disappointment is likely to surface before the very end, except perhaps in the case of very compliant and unassertive clients. But you may be faced with certain areas of disappointment at the end. Sometimes a client may say, 'Well, I do feel a lot better on the whole, even though things are still not what I'd hoped'. In such a case, try to elicit the nature of this disappointment. Help the client to spell out exactly how things are better and how they are not. It may turn out that you have failed to address certain areas of the client's concerns in your enthusiasm for looking at other areas.

But it is likely that your client is either minimizing the gains he has made, or is, perhaps, lamenting the fact that life itself is still not problem-free. Tease out the elements of statements of disappointment, acknowledging any genuine dissatisfaction with counselling, but also encouraging the client to take responsibility for himself and for any unrealistic demands that life should meet his needs. To borrow from transactional analysis, when he speaks from his 'Child' at the end of counselling, remind him to maintain an Adult perspective on this. Capitalize on what has been learned in counselling to show your client that he can still make a lot of progress himself after counselling.

Allow and reciprocate both disappointment and gratitude. If your client's temperament is such that he feels very emotional on ending and wishes to be demonstrative, do not discourage this. Depending on your own counselling orientation and your personality, you may be more or less happy to join with your client in emotional feedback. Broadly speaking, the more humanistic practitioners engage freely in spontaneous emotional displays whereas psychodynamic and cognitive behavioural practitioners may be rather more reserved. Our advice is that you respond in a way that is congruent with your own style, your client's style, and the relationship you have built up between you. Avoid a falsely 'professional' or a falsely 'intimate' ending. Genuinely respond, likewise, to any gifts that the client may offer you. While some counsellors do refuse gifts on principle, we believe it is more appropriate to allow clients to give freely if they wish to do so.

Consider what you will do in the event that a client discloses totally new material at this stage. For example, in reviewing the course of counselling, the client may say, 'well, it occurs to me that I've never said much about my sex life' or 'I think I mentioned it once, but I haven't gone much into the time in my life when I was abused'. This may present a real temptation to extend counselling. But you may have picked up earlier your client's tendency to issue 'last minute' statements. If such a disclosure is made, then suggest to the client that this is something it may be important to reflect on and to consider whether she wishes explicitly to work on it at a later time with you, or with another practitioner. Budman and Gurman (1988) emphasize the importance of adhering to present goals and if necessary seeing clients at a later time to address further issues. Don't be afraid that the client will fall apart or that you are failing in your responsibilities as a counsellor by not addressing every issue. There is ample evidence (see, for example, Kupers, 1988) that clients often make their way from one counsellor to another, over the course of years as they feel appropriate, and Cummings and Sayama (1995) explicitly endorse the practice of intermittent therapy. We believe, with Budman and Gurman, that clients may also quite legitimately return for counselling with the same counsellor at different times. A note of caution, here, however. When clients nervously ask you if they can return, should they run into difficulties, consider the wisdom of reminding them how much they have learned, of the extent of their own resources and their ability to cope. Suggest to them that they try out what skills and strategies they have learned, before automatically resorting to further counselling.

Summary

Deliberately encourage discussion of ending and of the counselling process as a whole, including issues of disappointment, gratitude and remaining fears. Remind clients of what they have learned and reinforce their coping skills.

---

89 Consider the advantages and disadvantages of different kinds of endings

There is no one right way to terminate counselling, as we have said. It will be apparent from the rest of this book that there are different approaches to brief counselling and its management. We have mentioned time-limited and brief counselling models. There is also the question of fixed, staggered or tapered endings; of serial counselling (repeated courses of counselling over a span, perhaps, of years – also referred to as intermittent psychotherapy); and of follow-ups. At some stage in your work, you will find it necessary to consider the merits and demerits of each of these methods of ending.

Sledge et al. (1990) discussed the differences between time-limited counselling, where an ending date is fixed in advance and the number of sessions is not negotiable: brief counselling, where there is an understanding that counselling will last a few months, but no specific ending date is set in advance; and open-ended counselling, which involves no discussion of an ending date. Sledge et al.'s study suggests that a strictly time-limited contract reduces the likelihood of people dropping out of counselling. It may, therefore, be particularly containing for some clients who exhibit anxiety about an indefinite period in counselling. Mann (1973) capitalizes on the advantages of a fixed time limit. It gives clients a rather dramatic focus and is likely to shake up ambivalence: clients know they will not get the chance for 'last minute confessions' and delays. Strasser and Strasser (1997) demonstrate the application of existentialist ideas to time-limited therapy. But, equally, time-limited work may not be effective for certain clients – perhaps those who feel heavily pressurized by time constraints in their everyday life. Time-limited work also requires a certain quality of concentration and commitment from practitioners, which may or may not suit your style. Note, too, that cognitive analytic therapy (Ryle, 1990) demands a considerable amount of homework from both client *and* counsellor, in addition to work within the time-limited contract. Time-limited work allows clients to calculate exactly how much it will cost them financially: it also allows counselling agencies to plan services more effectively.

Brief counselling, which has no set ending date, is likely to help clients feel relaxed and able to explore without pressure. You need to convey, in your initial discussions, some idea of how long this kind of contract may run to. You may state this in terms of 'a few months', 'about six months' or 'less than a year' (see Elton Wilson, 1996, for further examples), but however it is explained it is a good idea to reflect on the possibility of any mis-understandings between you and your client. As we have said earlier, most counselling and therapy is in reality brief, lasting a few weeks or months. It can be useful to focus on this, therefore, and to introduce it into conversation with your clients. How do they feel about time constraints? Relieved or anxious? Indifferent? Obviously individual clients react differently. Some clients, told that you would like to see them for a few weeks, may be alarmed at how long counselling will take and that it may imply that they are a 'serious case'. To other clients a few weeks seems like no time at all. These matters should have been discussed early in the counselling process, but they may arise later. You may well wonder, halfway through a counselling con-tract, what the best way to terminate it will be. Remember that clear con-tracting is a critical ethical issue and that peremptory termination that the client objects to may result in a formal complaint.

A time-limited ending presents no dilemma as to how to end. A dis-advantage is that it may cut clients off with no opportunity to experiment with what they have learned. While some time-limited endings may stagger the last few sessions to allow clients to integrate what they have learned, some do not. Date-unspecified brief counselling allows you the flexibility to stagger or taper the final sessions. You might, for example, suggest to your client that she move from weekly to fortnightly sessions, and then to monthly, in order to test for herself how able she is independently to put her new skills into practice. Sometimes this kind of arrangement suits clients in settings like primary care, provided you can manage it. Exactly what kind of ending you propose to each client will depend on client differences that you have become aware of: on the nature and severity of your clients' problems; and on clients' temperaments and learning styles. It is a good practice to combine particular homework assignments with such endings in order to test out gains and consolidate what has been achieved.

Budman and Gurman (1988) are in favour of staggered endings, which allow clients to move their focus from counselling to real life. Their model also emphasizes counselling as a serial process; clients may return at a later date with another issue. Counselling is regarded as a small part of life, appropriate for particular interpersonal, developmental and existential crises. If you are working in this way, perhaps in a clinic setting, or in private practice, we would encourage you to consider its benefits and ethos. This way of working is appropriate to many people, it is cost-effective to clients and some service-providers, but may be more difficult for you as the counsellor to manage. Many counsellors in fact practise sporadic counselling, seeing a cli-ent for a few months, for example, then having a gap, then resuming work for a further period. This is sometimes oriented to different client issues, and sometimes to clients' finances.

You also need to consider the value of follow-up sessions. Some practitioners make a habit of suggesting a single follow-up session three, four or six months after termination. This is in order to check on how firmly clients have consolidated their gains in counselling. It also gives them the opportunity to reflect back on what they have learned. In addition it is experienced by many people as containing – knowing that the counsellor retains an interest in them and is available in the future. It also gives you an opportunity to review your work and to learn what the client found most helpful or unhelpful. One function of such a session can be to act as a booster, reinforcing previous gains in counselling. Consider the value of offering such 'top-up' sessions either on a one-off basis or from time to time.

We trust that this variety of endings conveys our belief that there is not a right way to end. There is sometimes a certain mystique in some models of counselling, or in some training institutes, about correct and immutable ways of beginning and ending. Our preference is to remain sensitized to the needs of each client and to make judgements regarding such arrangements that will best suit clients' temperaments, learning styles, expectations and wallets! We realize that there are pressures on counsellors in certain settings (not least in private practice) either to terminate promptly with clients or to keep clients for a long period of time. We would urge practitioners and service managers and funders to consider the value of flexibility to meet clients' real needs. Invite your clients' opinions on the best kinds of endings for them when it is apparent that they have some understanding of how counselling works and when they have achieved at least some of their goals.

Summary

Examine the advantages and disadvantages of various ways of ending your work with clients, and base your decisions on clients' needs. Balance your own preferences against the possible advantages of date-specific and staggered endings; consider serial counselling, and follow-up sessions.

---

90 Let the client know that ending counselling sometimes (but not inevitably) engenders feelings of loss

Psychodynamic counsellors in particular may be inclined to anticipate loss reactions in their clients as the end is approached. They will also look for significant client reactions to holidays and breaks. Our position is that experiences of loss and separation vary considerably from client to client. This is the position, too, of Garfield (1989), who suggests that for most clients in brief counselling endings are natural, non-troubling events. Given the brevity of brief counselling, it is likely that very intimate bonds will not occur frequently: or that those strong bonds which do occur will be modified by an emphasis on goalsetting and problem solving. Do not add to clients' problems by encouraging them to become dependent on you. We do not advocate aloofness, but we concur here with Mahrer (1989a) who places the emphasis in counselling on the clients being in touch with their own inner world and making changes in their real life, and not on forming a special relationship with the counsellor. If you follow Budman and Gurman's (1988: 11) view that 'being in the world is more important than being in therapy', you will convey this attitude to clients throughout the counselling process. If you are committed to a long-term, transference-based model of counselling or therapy, you are likely to emphasize the nature of the relationship with you and quite possibly de-emphasize clients' progress in their everyday life.

In spite of what we have said here, some clients will experience the end of counselling as difficult. It may restimulate old experiences of painful partings. Or it may be that clients are unconvinced that they will be able to cope without you. Clients' progress is sometimes deceptive; people may do very well in counselling while they have you to confer with, but feel bereft and unprepared at the prospect of losing you. In this case, your task is to remind clients how much they have achieved, how much they have learned to generalize to different situations, and how important it is to test out those gains in real life. If you have emphasized homework, for example, you have prepared the ground for your clients to work on their own concerns confidently. If you have not used homework or other means of encouraging the client to work towards independence outside of the counselling session, find a way of helping the client to work on her own concerns.

One means of encouraging the expression of feelings on ending is written work which reviews what has happened in counselling. The cognitive analytic practice of the client and counsellor writing 'goodbye letters' to each other is an excellent example of this (Appendix 7). It is a channel for clients to order their feelings and to put them into perspective. You may devise your own ways of dealing with strong feelings on ending. If you work humanistically, strong feelings may feature prominently in your work and may help the client to regard strong feelings as normal and acceptable, and not as threats to their integrity or ability to cope. Some counsellors (such as Mearns and Thorne, 1999) may readily display their own feelings of loss and sadness on ending, thus communicating to clients that it is perfectly acceptable to experience and show those feelings, and that one can survive them! The key here is, of course, to be flexible towards your clients' needs, while being true to your own way of working.

Summary

Do not expect all clients to go through the same reactions to ending counselling. Encourage clients to use what comes up at the end for further learning opportunities. Accept whatever genuine, strong feelings are displayed by clients at the end.

91 Help clients to use what they have learned to look positively towards the future

Budman and Gurman (1988: 11) state their belief that the brief therapist 'accepts that many changes will occur "after therapy" and will not be observable to the therapist'. They are content to help clients on their way, rather than nursing them through a mythical, once-and-for-all therapy process. Similarly, if you practise a form of counselling that is brief and which has faith in the adult developmental perspective of learning, then you will probably often be in a position where you are not witness to dramatic and gratifying changes in your clients. It is obviously easier to convey a faith in your clients' ability to continue to put their learning gains into operation 'after counselling' if you yourself believe in such a process.

Melges (1982) actually makes the sense of the future central in his model of future-oriented psychotherapy, arguing that clients' temporal distortions play a large part in their psychopathology. He uses a form of brief eclectic therapy, which strives to correct distorted views of the future. You may not have such an orientation, but all counselling models implicitly aim at changing an unsatisfactory past or present into a more satisfying present or future. Models like transactional analysis work on the premise that lifelong scripts can be changed by present 'redecisions' and by achieving full contact with the here and now.

All models of counselling should have an inbuilt mechanism for making clients their own counsellors. Some models do this explicitly. Rational emotive behaviour therapy, which relies heavily on teaching clients to monitor and challenge their irrational thinking, places a lot of weight on homework assignments, for example. Perhaps person-centred counselling aims at the same ends in its own way, by engendering self-acceptance and continuing congruence. Gendlin (1984: 76), for example, discusses the concept of 'the client's client'. Gendlin explains how a client learns to focus on his 'felt sense' so that he achieves mastery of 'process steps' in counselling, which constitute a 'carrying forward' of new experience. The client becomes his own client and his own counsellor. We have discussed earlier how it is sometimes useful for some clients to use an image of the counsellor temporarily. At the ending phase this may be appropriate for some clients, but it is obviously more desirable that most clients should have truly internalized the means to coping or living more fully.

Reinforce your client's hopes and expectations for further change by referring to the nature of learning: people do not stop learning as soon as they leave a particular situation. Many people learn more outside or after they leave school, for example, than they learned while there. People learn formally how to drive while having driving instruction, but the real learning – coping with driving alone and unprotected by 'L' plates – is done after passing the test. It may be helpful to use such analogies with doubtful clients. Recalling our earlier references to client differences you may also find it useful to make a point like this with clients who are, for example, 'medical modellers' (Richert, 1983) by referring to appropriate literature from educational or counselling psychology, which confirms that learning continues beyond the formal learning situation. You need to gauge your statements about the future to the client's situation in life; it may not be appropriate to insist with clients who are very old, for example, that they have a great deal to look forward to. In such a case, rethink and rephrase your intention: 'you have come a long way' or 'it looks as if you've found some of that peace you've been looking for' may be more fitting.

Summary

Help your clients to look forward by reminding them of what they have achieved; how they have dealt with obstacles and what they have gained mastery of. Sensitively encourage clients to reconsider their view of time.

---

92 Evaluate your clients' progress at the end of counselling and learn what you can from working with them

If you have practised using the reflection process throughout counselling, regularly asking for feedback from the client, then you have in fact been evaluating your work and your client's progress. Questions directed at how well your approach is working for the client, and how helpful your relationship is, for example, constitute elements of process research. Unfortunately this is not in any way foolproof, because your client may not like to offend you, may be unaware of certain negative factors, and so on. But it is a good indication of how counselling is progressing. We have also suggested that you might use a simple progress chart (Section 79). These methods will give you and your client a fair idea of how counselling is going.

It can be very useful for you to evaluate an entire counselling process after it has ended. Garfield (1989) recommends that you carry out a specific evaluation of your work, for example by using or devising appropriate forms (Appendix 8). The value of such evaluation lies in what can be learned from unique cases and in getting into the habit of reasonably objective self-assessment. Garfield suggests in particular that counsellors attend to the presenting complaint in their post-counselling evaluations because there is a temptation to address everything but this. You may dislike the idea of formally evaluating your work, but we consider that if you devise your own means of doing such research, you are likely to learn a lot from it. Questions you might like to ask yourself include: did the client attain or closely approach his goals? Did the client change measurably? Was the client satisfied? How is the client's achievement to be explained? What could have been more helpful? Were there particular errors I made as a counsellor? What were my particular strengths and contributions? What have I learned from working with this person? Do any continuing professional development needs arise from this evaluation?

We have said that it is better to accept that you will sometimes make mistakes, rather than compounding the problem by berating yourself for making them. We don't suggest that you become blasé about errors but that you keep them in proportion. Also, like many highly experienced practitioners, learn to live with and learn from therapeutic failures (Kottler and Carlson, 2002). We also commend the practice of ironing out errors when possible by using the reflection process. Show your clients that you can get things wrong, or that you are open to correction; let them know that you have their interests at heart more than any preoccupation with professional perfectionism. You should pay attention to client differences here – not all will welcome disclosures of your imperfection. Sachs (1983) concluded a study of negative outcomes in brief therapy by finding that counsellor errors clearly predicted such outcomes. Davis (1989) drew the conclusion from this that you would do well to attend to minimizing errors rather than striving for perfection. You can minimize errors by closely monitoring your counselling (for example, by tape-recording), by regularly taking your work to supervision, and by regularly inviting feedback from clients. Do this in a spirit of open learning, rather than of defensive anxiety, and you are very likely to reduce errors considerably. Also, we hope that by using a text such as this you will become aware of what works well for your style of counselling, what you may be avoiding, and what you can most usefully take to supervision. You may well disagree with some of what you read here, and if such disagreement at least provokes thought and further evaluation, then we believe we have achieved our purpose in writing this book.

Summary

Find a method of evaluating your counselling that helps you to develop the habit of assessing your work and helps you to reduce errors. Learn what you can from working with each client and refer your reflections to supervision.

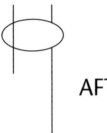

AFTERWORD

After you have completed your initial training and begun practising as a counsellor, new questions will become meaningful for you. We hope that the practical advice in this book will stimulate you to reflect on your work. The combination of putting training into practice and taking practice issues to supervision is the key development for beginners. But as you progress, you will want to know what is happening in the field generally. The literature base of counselling and psychotherapy is now extensive and it is impossible to make definitive recommendations but here are a just a few. The fifth edition of the *Handbook of Psychotherapy and Behavior Change* (Lambert, 2003) is a key source of research information on many aspects of therapy and counselling, and you are advised at least to have a look at the variety of topics covered there and their implications for practice. (Look out for future editions of this.) Remember when you do so, however, always to balance such findings against the individual needs and realities of each of your clients. Research has been promoted very well by BACP and it is well worth your while to read *Counselling and Psychotherapy Research*, as well as any other journals you can access.

You may also find the *Diagnostic and Statistical Manual* (fourth edition, text revised, 2000) a useful source of information on the classification of psychological disturbances. Many counsellors dislike the very idea of classification, and there is certainly a case for being critical of many of the classifications in the DSM IV TR, but it is instructive to become aware of psychiatric terminology. You might also look at the *International Classification of Diseases* (10th edition), which is an alternative source of classification produced by the World Health Organization. It is increasingly important that you are aware of developments in the field of evidence-based practice, some of which are accessible via NICE clinical guidelines. Where your interest is in establishing local professional contacts or looking for counsellors to whom you might refer clients, consult the *Counselling and*

Psychotherapy Resources Directory of the British Association for Counselling and Psychotherapy.

As a counterpoint to this book, if you wish to reinforce your critical thinking you might look at John Rowan's (2005) *The Future of Training in Psychotherapy and Counselling*. Rowan would no doubt regard our book as in the instrumental mode of counselling. He is ambivalent about such approaches for their perceived narrowness and their, as he sees it, 'falling into the fallacy of the clockwork client' (p. 4). On the other hand, he admits that 'most therapists, most of the time, find themselves working in this way, simply because that is what most clients want, most of the time' (p. 4). We hope we have conveyed that we believe, similarly, that this is the case but that you should also remain open to the possibilities of relational depth and complexity. In this way, 'integrative' is a lifelong quest but 'practical' is usually urgent.

We wish you well in your practice in what is now becoming the recognized profession of counselling.

APPENDIX 1
EXPLAINING WHAT
COUNSELLING IS

There is still a great deal of confusion about the identity of counselling, as well as conflict. Counsellors sometimes believe that by using terms familiar to themselves (for example, person-centred, psychodynamic, and so forth) they are necessarily conveying something meaningful to clients. Sometimes they even believe that uninformative silences or 'rabbinic' questions are legitimate responses to clients' requests for clarification. Here, we suggest some of the phrases you might consider when explaining what counselling is. Which you use, adapt or combine, will depend partly on your own beliefs, training and practice, but they should also address the needs, spoken and unspoken, of each of your clients.

- Counselling is a confidential and ethically protected relationship with a trained and qualified practitioner who will take your personal concerns seriously.
- There are different counselling styles or approaches. Some are more non-directive and the counsellor will mainly listen or strive to understand your deepest feelings; others are more active and perhaps directive and the counsellor may make suggestions or ask you to try certain activities.
- Knowing which direction to take (for example, exactly what to talk about in each session) depends largely on you, on your intuition about what is most important, current or vital, but your counsellor may also prompt you or make suggestions. Don't just wait for the counsellor to initiate things; and don't treat your sessions as 'just a chat'.
- Counselling is mainly based on listening, understanding and responding; in other words, it is a psychological therapy. Depending on training, each counsellor may emphasize thoughts, feelings or actions. Many counsellors will address all these dimensions.
- Counselling aims to help you understand yourself better and improve the parts of your life that have become stuck or painful. But it isn't always

smooth, predictable and painless; it will require patience and commitment on your part, as well as skill and knowledge on the part of the counsellor.

- Counselling is a disciplined, ethical and professional activity but it is quite different from medicine, law, accountancy, and so on. This is because it focuses on each individual and their unique cluster of concerns, it includes emotions, and it sometimes works via feelings that are stirred up between you and your counsellor.
- Counselling is a fallible activity. Counsellors are closely supervised. They should be ready to hear your views about the process of counselling and you have avenues for making complaints if not satisfied.

Further discussion can be found in Bates (2005), Feltham (1995), and Feltham and Lambert (2006).

APPENDIX 2
STAGES OF CHANGE
QUESTIONNAIRE

Stages of change scale

Name:

Each statement describes how a person might feel about his or her problems. Please indicate the extent to which you tend to agree or disagree with each statement. In each case, make your choice in terms of how you feel right now, not what you have felt in the past or would like to feel.

There are FIVE possible responses to each of the questionnaire items:

1 = Strongly Disagree (SD)

2 = Disagree (D)

3 = Undecided (U)

4 = Agree (A)

5 = Strongly Agree (SA)

Circle the number that best describes how much you agree or disagree with each statement.

		SD	D	U	A	SA
1	As far as I'm concerned, I don't have any problems that need changing.	1	2	3	4	5
2	I think I might be ready for some self-improvement.	1	2	3	4	5
3	I am doing something about the problems that had been bothering me.	1	2	3	4	5

		SD	D	U	A	SA
4	It might be worthwhile to work on my problems.	1	2	3	4	5
5	I'm not the problem one. It doesn't make much sense for me to be here.	1	2	3	4	5
6	It worries me that I might slip back on problems I have already changed, so I am ready to work on my problems.	1	2	3	4	5
7	I am finally doing some work on my problems.	1	2	3	4	5
8	I've been thinking that I might want to change something about myself.	1	2	3	4	5
9	I have been successful in working on my problems but I'm not sure I can keep up the effort on my own.	1	2	3	4	5
10	At times my problems are difficult, but I'm working on them.	1	2	3	4	5
11	Working on problems is pretty much of a waste of time for me because the problems don't have to do with me.	1	2	3	4	5
12	I'm working on my problems in order to better understand myself.	1	2	3	4	5
13	I guess I have faults, but there's nothing that I really need to change.	1	2	3	4	5
14	I am really working hard to change.	1	2	3	4	5
15	I have problems and I really think I should work on them.	1	2	3	4	5
16	I'm not following through with what I had already changed as well as I had hoped, and I'm working to prevent a relapse of my problems.	1	2	3	4	5
17	Even though I'm not always successful in changing, I am at least working on my problems.	1	2	3	4	5
18	I thought once I had resolved my problems I would be free of them, but sometimes I still find myself struggling with them.	1	2	3	4	5
19	I wish I had more ideas on how to solve my problems.	1	2	3	4	5
20	I have started working on my problems but I would like help.	1	2	3	4	5
21	Maybe someone will be able to help me.	1	2	3	4	5

Thanks for buying on Amazon Marketplace. To provide feedb
To contact the seller, please visit www.amazon.co.uk/seller/2nd

Quantity	Product Details
1	**Brief Counselling: A Practical Guide for Begin** Merchant SKU: 03352194554-509 ASIN: 03352194554 Listing ID: 0116L439307 Order-item ID: 17065422640195

Delivery address:
Charlotte Jane Owens
Bwthyn Gwyn
Swan Lane
Mold
Flintshire
CH7 4AT
United Kingdom

C
S
B
S

Order ID: 736-0132609-9425908
Thank you for buying from 2ndhandbook on Amazon Marketplace

		SD	D	U	A	SA
22	I may need a boost right now to help me maintain the changes I've already made.	1	2	3	4	5
23	I may be part of the problem, but I don't really think I am.	1	2	3	4	5
24	I hope that someone will have some good advice for me.	1	2	3	4	5
25	Anyone can talk about changing; I'm actually doing something about it.	1	2	3	4	5
26	All this talk about psychology is boring. Why can't people just forget about their problems?	1	2	3	4	5
27	I'm working to prevent myself from having a relapse of my problems.	1	2	3	4	5
28	It is frustrating, but I feel I might be having a recurrence of a problem I thought I had resolved.	1	2	3	4	5
29	I have worries but so does the next person. Why spend time thinking about them?	1	2	3	4	5
30	I am actively working on my problems.	1	2	3	4	5
31	I would rather cope with my faults than try to change them.	1	2	3	4	5
32	After all I had done everything to try and change my problems, every now and again they come back to haunt me.	1	2	3	4	5

Scoring of the stages of change scale

- The following are pre-contemplation items: 1, 5, 11, 13, 23, 26, 29, 31.
- The following are contemplation items: 2, 4, 8, 12, 15, 19, 21, 24.
- The following are action items: 3, 7, 10, 14, 17, 20, 25, 30.
- The following are maintenance items: 6, 9, 16, 18, 22, 27, 28, 32.

The scale is designed to be a continuous measure. Thus, subjects can score high on more than one of the four stages.

Because the scale is still being validated, it is available only for research purposes. Therefore, to date there have been no cut-off norms established to determine what constitutes high, medium or low on a particular stage. And, again, the stages are considered to be continuous and not discreet.

APPENDIX 3
OPINIONS ABOUT
PSYCHOLOGICAL PROBLEMS
QUESTIONNAIRE: CAUSES OF
PSYCHOLOGICAL PROBLEMS

Opinions about psychological problems

This questionnaire has two parts. The first asks about how you view the causes of your problems; the second asks how you think these problems can be helped.

Causes of psychological problems

People have different views about what causes psychological problems. The following questions ask for your opinion of the causes of your own problems. There are no right or wrong answers: your own opinion is what counts. Please indicate how much you agree or disagree with each statement by using the following scale. Circle one number for each statement.

Disagree strongly	Disagree moderately	Disagree mildly	Agree mildly	Agree moderately	Agree strongly
−3	−2	−1	+1	+2	+3

My problems are caused by

		Disagree strongly	Disagree moderately	Disagree mildly	Agree mildly	Agree moderately	Agree strongly
1	Feelings that are buried out of sight.	−3	−2	−1	+1	+2	+3
2	Illogical beliefs.	−3	−2	−1	+1	+2	+3
3	Other people not accepting me for who I am.	−3	−2	−1	+1	+2	+3

	Disagree strongly	Disagree moderately	Disagree mildly	Agree mildly	Agree moderately	Agree strongly
4 Becoming too anxious in certain situations.	−3	−2	−1	+1	+2	+3
5 A disorder of the brain or nervous system.	−3	−2	−1	+1	+2	+3
6 Worrying too much about what other people think of me.	−3	−2	−1	+1	+2	+3
7 Exaggerating the importance of things that may happen.	−3	−2	−1	+1	+2	+3
8 Unemployment or an unsatisfactory job.	−3	−2	−1	+1	+2	+3
9 Events that happened in childhood.	−3	−2	−1	+1	+2	+3
10 Having learnt bad habits over the years.	−3	−2	−1	+1	+2	+3
11 An inherited physical cause.	−3	−2	−1	+1	+2	+3
12 Repeating old patterns in relationships with other people.	−3	−2	−1	+1	+2	+3
13 Hiding feelings from friends or family.	−3	−2	−1	+1	+2	+3
14 Lack of money.	−3	−2	−1	+1	+2	+3
15 Running away from responsibilities.	−3	−2	−1	+1	+2	+3
16 Repressing basic human impulses.	−3	−2	−1	+1	+2	+3
17 Thinking about myself too much.	−3	−2	−1	+1	+2	+3
18 Having learnt the wrong reactions to certain situations.	−3	−2	−1	+1	+2	+3
19 Unsatisfactory means of transport.	−3	−2	−1	+1	+2	+3
20 Not paying attention to my feelings.	−3	−2	−1	+1	+2	+3
21 Making harsh judgements of myself.	−3	−2	−1	+1	+2	+3
22 A lack of will power.	−3	−2	−1	+1	+2	+3

	Disagree strongly	Disagree moderately	Disagree mildly	Agree mildly	Agree moderately	Agree strongly
23 Not accepting myself for who I am.	−3	−2	−1	+1	+2	+3
24 Conflicting feelings about my parents when I was young.	−3	−2	−1	+1	+2	+3
25 Dissatisfaction with the community I live in.	−3	−2	−1	+1	+2	+3
26 Not having a realistic view of the good and the bad things that have happened.	−3	−2	−1	+1	+2	+3
27 Conflicts in my unconscious mind.	−3	−2	−1	+1	+2	+3
28 Illness, such as colds or flu.	−3	−2	−1	+1	+2	+3
29 The state of the economy.	−3	−2	−1	+1	+2	+3
30 Unrealistic thinking.	−3	−2	−1	+1	+2	+3
31 Rewards or punishments received in the past.	−3	−2	−1	+1	+2	+3
32 A conscience that won't let me alone.	−3	−2	−1	+1	+2	+3
33 Not liking myself.	−3	−2	−1	+1	+2	+3
34 Having unrealistic expectations.	−3	−2	−1	+1	+2	+3
35 Something going wrong with my body.	−3	−2	−1	+1	+2	+3
36 Not understanding what I really feel inside.	−3	−2	−1	+1	+2	+3
37 Laziness.	−3	−2	−1	+1	+2	+3
38 Not having learnt the right ways to cope with certain situations.	−3	−2	−1	+1	+2	+3
39 Not being true to myself.	−3	−2	−1	+1	+2	+3
40 Other people being unreasonable.	−3	−2	−1	+1	+2	+3

	Disagree strongly	Disagree moderately	Disagree mildly	Agree mildly	Agree moderately	Agree strongly
41 Putting myself down for no reason.	−3	−2	−1	+1	+2	+3
42 Poor housing.	−3	−2	−1	+1	+2	+3
43 The wrong balance of chemicals in my body.	−3	−2	−1	+1	+2	+3
44 Bad luck or fate.	−3	−2	−1	+1	+2	+3
45 Having learnt wrong ways of doing things from someone else.	−3	−2	−1	+1	+2	+3
46 Unsatisfactory relationships with other people.	−3	−2	−1	+1	+2	+3
47 It's impossible to explain the cause of my problems.	−3	−2	−1	+1	+2	+3

If you think there are other important causes not listed above, please add them here:

Opinions about psychological problems

My problems are caused by

Psychodynamic

1   Feelings that are buried out of sight.

9   Events that happened in childhood.

12   Repeating old patterns in relationships with other people.

16   Repressing basic human impulses.

24   Conflicting feelings about my parents when I was young.

27   Conflicts in my unconscious mind.

32   A conscience that won't let me alone.

Humanistic/interpersonal

3   Other people not accepting me for who I am.

13   Hiding feelings from friends or family.

20   Not paying attention to my feelings.

23   Not accepting myself for who I am.

33   Not liking myself.

36 Not understanding what I really feel inside.

39 Not being true to myself.

46 Unsatisfactory relationships with other people.

Behavioural

4 Becoming too anxious in certain situations.

10 Having learnt bad habits over the years.

18 Having learnt the wrong reactions to certain situations.

31 Rewards or punishments received in the past.

38 Not having learnt the right ways to cope with certain situations.

45 Having learnt wrong ways of doing things from someone else.

Cognitive

2 Illogical beliefs.

6 Worrying too much about what other people think of me.

7 Exaggerating the importance of things that may happen.

21 Making harsh judgements of myself.

26 Not having a realistic view of the good and the bad things that have happened.

30 Unrealistic thinking.

34 Having unrealistic expectations.

41 Putting myself down for no reason.

Organic

5 A disorder of the brain or nervous system.

11 An inherited physical cause.

28 Illness, such as colds or flu.

35 Something going wrong with my body.

43 The wrong balance of chemicals in my body.

Social/economic

8 Unemployment or an unsatisfactory job.

14 Lack of money.

19 Unsatisfactory means of transport.

25 Dissatisfaction with the community I live in.

29   The state of the economy.

42   Poor housing.

Naive

15   Running away from responsibilities.

17   Thinking about myself too much.

22   A lack of will power.

37   Laziness.

40   Other people being unreasonable.

44   Bad luck or fate.

47   It's impossible to explain the cause of my problems.

APPENDIX 4
OPINIONS ABOUT
PSYCHOLOGICAL PROBLEMS
QUESTIONNAIRE: HELP FOR
PSYCHOLOGICAL PROBLEMS

Opinions about psychological problems

Help for psychological problems

People have different views about what may help psychological problems. The following questions ask for your opinion of how your own problems could be helped. There are no right or wrong answers: your own opinion is what counts. Please indicate how much you agree or disagree with each statement by using the following scale. Circle one number for each statement.

Disagree strongly	Disagree moderately	Disagree mildly	Agree mildly	Agree moderately	Agree strongly
−3	−2	−1	+1	+2	+3

A good way to help my problems would be

		Disagree strongly	Disagree moderately	Disagree mildly	Agree mildly	Agree moderately	Agree strongly
1	Taking the attitude that I should count my blessings, rather than looking on the dark side of things.	−3	−2	−1	+1	+2	+3
2	Having an expert show me how to think in a more logical way.	−3	−2	−1	+1	+2	+3
3	Getting tablets to regulate my mood.	−3	−2	−1	+1	+2	+3

		Disagree strongly	Disagree moderately	Disagree mildly	Agree mildly	Agree moderately	Agree strongly
4	Learning to pay attention to my feelings.	−3	−2	−1	+1	+2	+3
5	Discussing the problems with someone in an honest, person-to-person way.	−3	−2	−1	+1	+2	+3
6	Understanding the childhood origins of the problems.	−3	−2	−1	+1	+2	+3
7	Having an expert teach me better ways of reacting to certain situations.	−3	−2	−1	+1	+2	+3
8	Getting medication.	−3	−2	−1	+1	+2	+3
9	Better housing.	−3	−2	−1	+1	+2	+3
10	Having an expert point out the meaning of my dreams and fantasies.	−3	−2	−1	+1	+2	+3
11	An improvement in the economy.	−3	−2	−1	+1	+2	+3
12	Examining, with an expert, what situations make the problems better or worse.	−3	−2	−1	+1	+2	+3
13	Talking to an expert about my relationship with my parents when I was young.	−3	−2	−1	+1	+2	+3
14	Having someone listen to my feelings without giving advice.	−3	−2	−1	+1	+2	+3
15	Worrying less about what other people think of me.	−3	−2	−1	+1	+2	+3
16	Learning to live with the problems, rather than trying to change them.	−3	−2	−1	+1	+2	+3

	Disagree strongly	Disagree moderately	Disagree mildly	Agree mildly	Agree moderately	Agree strongly
17 Being shown by an expert how to change my outlook on the problems.	−3	−2	−1	+1	+2	+3
18 Learning to accept myself for who I am.	−3	−2	−1	+1	+2	+3
19 Taking my mind off myself.	−3	−2	−1	+1	+2	+3
20 Having medical treatment to put the chemicals of my body back into balance.	−3	−2	−1	+1	+2	+3
21 A better community to live in.	−3	−2	−1	+1	+2	+3
22 Learning the skills needed in difficult situations.	−3	−2	−1	+1	+2	+3
23 Putting my bad feelings aside, so I can feel more cheerful.	−3	−2	−1	+1	+2	+3
24 Tackling the problems in a planned, step-by-step way.	−3	−2	−1	+1	+2	+3
25 Learning to think more realistically.	−3	−2	−1	+1	+2	+3
26 Having other people change, rather than changing myself.	−3	−2	−1	+1	+2	+3
27 Having an expert teach me specific ways to change my behaviour.	−3	−2	−1	+1	+2	+3
28 Discovering what I really feel inside.	−3	−2	−1	+1	+2	+3
29 Deciding to 'keep a stiff upper lip'.	−3	−2	−1	+1	+2	+3
30 Talking about my feelings to someone I trust.	−3	−2	−1	+1	+2	+3
31 Learning to think differently about the problems.	−3	−2	−1	+1	+2	+3

	Disagree strongly	Disagree moderately	Disagree mildly	Agree mildly	Agree moderately	Agree strongly
32 Having an expert analyse my unconscious reasons for doing things.	−3	−2	−1	+1	+2	+3
33 Keeping busy, so as not to think about the problems.	−3	−2	−1	+1	+2	+3
34 Hearing from other people that I am doing well or trying hard.	−3	−2	−1	+1	+2	+3
35 Getting a satisfactory job.	−3	−2	−1	+1	+2	+3
36 Learning to judge myself less harshly.	−3	−2	−1	+1	+2	+3
37 Talking to someone who listens closely to what I'm really saying.	−3	−2	−1	+1	+2	+3
38 Realizing how I repeat old patterns in relationships with other people.	−3	−2	−1	+1	+2	+3
39 Deciding to 'grin and bear it'.	−3	−2	−1	+1	+2	+3
40 Getting tablets.	−3	−2	−1	+1	+2	+3
41 Getting physically fit and healthy.	−3	−2	−1	+1	+2	+3
42 Having an expert point out that how I think about myself can sometimes be wrong.	−3	−2	−1	+1	+2	+3
43 Better means of transport.	−3	−2	−1	+1	+2	+3
44 Coming to understand feelings or impulses that I'm not aware of.	−3	−2	−1	+1	+2	+3
45 Having more money.	−3	−2	−1	+1	+2	+3
46 Using will power to overcome the problems.	−3	−2	−1	+1	+2	+3

	Disagree strongly	Disagree moderately	Disagree mildly	Agree mildly	Agree moderately	Agree strongly
47 There's nothing that can be done to help my problems.	−3	−2	−1	+1	+2	+3

If you think there are other ways in which your problems could be helped, please add them here:

Opinions about psychological problems

Treatment

A good way to help my problems would be

Psychodynamic

6   Understanding the childhood origins of the problems.

10   Having an expert point out the meaning of my dreams and fantasies.

13   Talking to an expert about my relationship with my parents when I was young.

32   Having an expert analyse my unconscious reasons for doing things.

38   Realizing how I repeat old patterns in relationships with other people.

44   Coming to understand feelings or impulses that I'm not aware of.

Humanistic/interpersonal

4   Learning to pay attention to my feelings.

5   Discussing the problems with someone in an honest, person-to-person way.

14   Having someone listen to my feelings without giving advice.

18   Learning to accept myself for who I am.

28   Discovering what I really feel inside.

30   Talking about my feelings to someone I trust.

37   Talking to someone who listens closely to what I'm really saying.

Behavioural

7   Having an expert teach me better ways of reacting to certain situations.

12   Examining, with an expert, what situations make the problems better or worse.

22   Learning the skills needed in difficult situations.

24   Tackling the problems in a planned, step-by-step way.

27   Having an expert teach me specific ways to change my behaviour.

34   Hearing from other people that I am doing well or trying hard.

Cognitive

2   Having an expert show me how to think in a more logical way.

15   Worrying less about what other people think of me.

17   Being shown by an expert how to change my outlook on the problems.

25   Learning to think more realistically.

31   Learning to think differently about the problems.

36   Learning to judge myself less harshly.

42   Having an expert point out that how I think about myself can sometimes be wrong.

Organic

3   Getting tablets to regulate my mood.

8   Getting medication.

20   Having medical treatment to put the chemicals of my body back into balance.

40   Getting tablets.

41   Getting physically fit and healthy.

Social/economic

9   Better housing.

11   An improvement in the economy.

21   A better community to live in.

35   Getting a satisfactory job.

43   Better means of transport.

45   Having more money.

Naive

1   Taking the attitude that I should count my blessings, rather than looking on the dark side of things.

16   Learning to live with the problems, rather than trying to change them.

19   Taking my mind off myself.

23   Putting my bad feelings aside, so I can feel more cheerful.

26   Having other people change, rather than changing myself.

29   Deciding to 'keep a stiff upper lip'.

33   Keeping busy, so as not to think about the problems.

39   Deciding to 'grin and bear it'.

46   Using will power to overcome the problems.

47   There's nothing that can be done to help my problems.

Background information

1. Name:

2. Age:

3. Sex: M F

4. Location (where are you filling out this questionnaire?):

5. What psychological problems were you thinking about while you were answering this questionnaire?

6. What problems are you currently seeking help for (if different from question 5 above)?

Thank you for completing this questionnaire.

APPENDIX 5
POSSIBLE REASONS FOR
NOT COMPLETING
HOMEWORK
ASSIGNMENTS
QUESTIONNAIRE

Questionnaire for client to complete

The following is a list of reasons that various clients have given for not doing their self-help assignments during the course of therapy. Because the speed of improvement depends primarily on the amount of self-help assignments that you are willing to do, it is of great importance to pinpoint any reasons that you may have for not doing this work. It is important to look for these reasons at the time that you feel a reluctance to do your assignment or a desire to put off doing it. Hence, it is best to fill out this questionnaire at that time. If you have any difficulty filling out this form and returning it to the therapist, it might be best to do it together during a therapy session. (Rate each statement by ringing 'T' (True) or 'F' (False). 'T' indicates that you agree with it; 'F' means the statement does not apply at this time.)

1	It seems that nothing can help me so there is no point in trying.	T / F
2	It wasn't clear; I didn't understand what I had to do.	T / F
3	I thought that the particular method the therapist had suggested would not be helpful. I didn't really see the value of it.	T / F
4	It seemed too hard.	T / F
5	I am willing to do self-help assignments, but I keep forgetting.	T / F
6	I did not have enough time. I was too busy.	T / F
7	If I do something the therapist suggests I do it's not as good as if I come up with my own ideas.	T / F
8	I don't really believe I can do anything to help myself.	T / F

9   I have the impression the therapist is trying to boss me around or   T / F
     control me.

10   I worry about the therapist's disapproval. I believe that what I do just   T / F
     won't be good enough for him/her.

11   I felt too bad, sad, nervous, upset (underline the appropriate word(s)) to   T / F
     do it.

12   It would have upset me to do the homework.   T / F

13   It was too much to do.   T / F

14   It's too much like going back to school again.   T / F

15   It seemed to be mainly for the therapist's benefit.   T / F

16   Self-help assignments have no place in therapy.   T / F

17   Because of the progress I've made these assignments are likely to be of   T / F
     no further benefit to me.

18   Because these assignments have not been helpful in the past, I couldn't   T / F
     see the point of doing this one.

19   I don't agree with this particular approach to therapy.   T / F

20   OTHER REASONS (Please write them.)

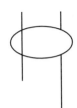

APPENDIX 6
ADVANTAGES AND
DISADVANTAGES OF
PRESENT AND DESIRED
BEHAVIOUR INVENTORY

Advantages/benefits of present behaviour

Short-term advantages/benefits

For yourself

1_____
2_____
3_____
4_____
5_____
6_____
7_____
8_____
9_____
10_____

For the other person

1_____
2_____
3_____
4_____
5_____
6_____
7_____
8_____
9_____
10_____

Long-term advantages/benefits

For yourself

1_____
2_____
3_____
4_____

For the other person

1_____
2_____
3_____
4_____

5_____   5_____
6_____   6_____
7_____   7_____
8_____   8_____
9_____   9_____
10_____   10_____

Disadvantages/costs of present behaviour

Short-term disadvantages/costs

For yourself   For the other person
1_____   1_____
2_____   2_____
3_____   3_____
4_____   4_____
5_____   5_____
6_____   6_____
7_____   7_____
8_____   8_____
9_____   9_____
10_____   10_____

Long-term disadvantages/costs

For yourself   For the other person
1_____   1_____
2_____   2_____
3_____   3_____
4_____   4_____
5_____   5_____
6_____   6_____
7_____   7_____
8_____   8_____
9_____   9_____
10_____   10_____

Advantages/benefits of desired behaviour

Short-term advantages/benefits

For yourself

1_____

2_____

3_____

4_____

5_____

6_____

7_____

8_____

9_____

10_____

For the other person

1_____

2_____

3_____

4_____

5_____

6_____

7_____

8_____

9_____

10_____

Long-term advantages/benefits

For yourself

1_____

2_____

3_____

4_____

5_____

6_____

7_____

8_____

9_____

10_____

For the other person

1_____

2_____

3_____

4_____

5_____

6_____

7_____

8_____

9_____

10_____

Disadvantages/costs of desired behaviour

Short-term disadvantages/costs

For yourself

1_____
2_____
3_____
4_____
5_____
6_____
7_____
8_____
9_____
10_____

For the other person

1_____
2_____
3_____
4_____
5_____
6_____
7_____
8_____
9_____
10_____

Long-term disadvantages/costs

For yourself

1_____
2_____
3_____
4_____
5_____
6_____
7_____
8_____
9_____
10_____

For the other person

1_____
2_____
3_____
4_____
5_____
6_____
7_____
8_____
9_____
10_____

APPENDIX 7
SPECIMEN 'GOODBYE
LETTERS'

Goodbye letter from a client in cognitive analytic therapy to her therapist

Dear Barney,

These weeks of therapy have not been what I expected. I was worried that there would not be time enough to sort things out. I wanted the opportunity to talk exhaustively about all the things that had upset me in the past. It took a while for me to realize that this was not necessary and perhaps not even desirable. I found the middle sessions very difficult and felt quite discouraged about failure to get in touch with my hurt about my childhood. For me, the real revelation, the unexpected, was learning about self-sabotage. Before commencing therapy I wrote a list of some things I wanted to understand. The first point was why I was never properly prepared for examinations; it is really quite shocking to realize that I deliberately hurt myself because fundamentally I feel unworthy. A related point was why I feel that I respect myself, and am confident in spite of evidence to the contrary. My major worry is that I will continue to spoil my chances. I feel that self-sabotage is deeply rooted and that it will take tremendous, sustained effort to combat it. I think it may be a long and uphill battle. The very positive thing that has emerged from therapy is the re-emergence of a 'lust for life'. There are so many things I want to enjoy, I have recovered a feeling of leaving therapy. Last week I felt ready for it, this week the fear that I may backslide is more prominent. If I'm honest I would like to have the continuous support of regular sessions until I feel more confident that I'm not going to undo the good work. Having said this, though, I do not feel I am about to be abandoned, the three-month follow-up session is a considerable solace. My relationship with my boyfriend still needs improving. As regards to the future, I want to continue to feel good about myself, to feel increasingly confident and to feel secure with this confidence, i.e. to know that it is a solid base and is not dependent upon props such as other people's opinions of me, or my career, etc. In brief, I want to be happy and autonomous and to feel that I have taken life in both hands. Perhaps I need some structured means of monitoring my progress by myself so that any backsliding can be arrested at the early stages.

Thank you, you've really helped me cut through the crap and to feel good and excited again.

Yours sincerely

Jasmine

Goodbye letter from a therapist to a client in cognitive analytic therapy

Dear Ingrid,

Looking back at the time when you first came to therapy, you may recall your expectations of some miraculous cure for the frigidity both you and your husband put forth as being the major obstacle to your joint pursuit of happiness. Well, no miracles have taken place, yet now you feel like a sexually capable person – a far cry from feeling finished or burnt out and desperately seeking for miracles. More importantly, you have gained a sense of independence and of being very worthy to be respected by others. How were these changes brought about? The essential thing was that you gradually came to realize that frigidity was only the 'tip of the iceberg', the final expression of a whole constellation of pressures within the context of your important relationships. It both reflected the existence of a crucial problem in your life and a 'solution', however awkward or self-defeating the latter was. The problem consisted in establishing your independence while at the same time resentfully and placatingly committing yourself to your parents and to your husband without risking a choice. Frigidity, as a solution to this, enabled you to postpone making a choice without feeling responsible for this postponement. Now you don't need this any more; you have become your own agent, you have seen that you can be both tender and caring, and assert your own needs. What cut across the stalemate you were in, not daring to make any move, was the reinvestment in the positive aspects of yourself. You identified and worked upon the false dilemmas, the unobtrusive traps, the subtle snags which, you came to see, had dominated your way of dealing yourself and the others, and had kept you enmeshed in that wasteland of inertia, dissatisfaction, guilt and anger. Now you feel confident enough to renegotiate the terms of your relationship with your mother and with your husband. Perhaps this is what makes me, on my part, feel happy and optimistic about your future, whatever it may be.

Yours sincerely

Basil

APPENDIX 8
CASE EVALUATION
FORM

Case

Sex

Age

Referred by

Therapist

Supervisor

No. of interviews seen

No. of missed appointments

Referral or treatment problem(s)

Possible changes at termination

Recommendations for this case (if any)

Rating scales

Amount of change in client

Please rate the amount of change you believe has occurred in this client since he/she started therapy. Please do not rate on this scale the final level of adjustment of the client. Rather, please rate the amount of change or difference in functioning you believe has occurred in this client since the beginning of therapy, regardless of how well or badly adjusted you believe the client currently is and how much or how little work might remain to be done in order for the client to be considered completely healthy and well functioning.

1. Client has changed markedly for the worse.
2. Client has changed somewhat for the worse.
3. Client has changed slightly for the worse.
4. Client has shown essentially no change.
5. Client has changed slightly for the better.
6. Client has changed somewhat for the better.
7. Client has changed markedly for the better.

REFERENCES

Albee, G.W. (1990) The futility of psychotherapy, *Journal of Mind and Behavior*, 11(3 and 4): 369–84.

Amada, G. (1983) The interlude between short- and long-term psychotherapy, *American Journal of Psychotherapy*, 37: 357–64.

Amato, R. and Bradshaw, R. (1985) An exploratory study of people's reasons for delaying or avoiding helpseeking, *Australian Psychologist*, 20(1): 21–31.

BACP (2002) *Ethical Framework for Good Practice in Counselling and Psychotherapy*. Rugby: British Association for Counselling and Psychotherapy.

BACP (2005) *Guidelines for Online Counselling and Psychotherapy*, 2nd edn. Rugby: British Association for Counselling and Psychotherapy.

Balint, M., Ornstein, P.O. and Balint, E. (1972) *Focal Psychotherapy*. London: Tavistock.

Bates, Y. (ed.) (2005) *Shouldn't I Be Feeling Better By Now? Client Experiences in Therapy*. Basingstoke: Palgrave.

Bayne, R. (1999) The counselling relationship and psychological type, in C. Feltham (ed.) *Understanding the Counselling Relationship*. London: Sage.

Bell, R.H. (2002) *Understanding African Philosophy: Cross-Cultural Approaches to Classical and Contemporary Issues*. New York: Routledge.

Bellack, A.S. and Hersen, M. (1987) *Dictionary of Behavior Therapy Techniques*. Oxford: Pergamon.

Blackburn, I.-M. and Davidson, K. (1990) *Cognitive Therapy for Depression and Anxiety*. Oxford: Blackwell.

Blanton, B. (1996) *Radical Honesty*. New York: Dell.

Bolton, G., Howlett, S., Lago, C. and Wright, J.K. (eds) (2004) *Writing Cures: An Introductory Handbook of Writing in Counselling and Psychotherapy*. London: Brunner-Routledge.

Bond, T. (2000) *Standards and Ethics for Counselling in Action*, 2nd edn. London: Sage.

Bond, T. and Sandhu, A. (2005) *Therapists in Court*. London: Sage/BACP.

Bordin, E.S. (1979) The generalizability of the psychoanalytic concept of the working alliance, *Psychotherapy: Theory, Research and Practice*, 16(3): 252–60.

Brandt, L.W. (1982) *Psychologists Caught*. Toronto: University of Toronto Press.

Bryant-Jeffries, R. (2005) Head-centred versus heart-centred trainees, *Counselling and Psychotherapy Journal*, 16(5): 9.

Buber, M. (1947) *Between Man and Man*. London: Routledge & Kegan Paul.

Budman, S.H. (1990) The myth of termination in brief therapy, in J.K. Zeig and S.G. Gilligan (eds) *Brief Therapy: Myths, Methods and Metaphors*. New York: Brunner/Mazel.

Budman, S.H. and Gurman, A.S. (1988) *Theory and Practice of Brief Therapy*. London: Guilford.

Carr, A. (2004) *Positive Psychology: The Science of Happiness and Human Strengths*. London: Brunner-Routledge.

Carter, M.F. (2005) Time-limited therapy in a community mental health team setting. *Counselling and Psychotherapy Research*, 5(1): 43–7.

Casement, P. (1985) *On Learning from the Patient*. London: Tavistock.

Casement, P. (2002) *Learning from our Mistakes: Beyond Dogma in Psychoanalysis and Psychotherapy*. London: Routledge.

Chamberlain, L.L. and Butz, M.R. (eds) (1998) *Clinical Chaos: A Therapist's Guide to Nonlinear Dynamics and Therapeutic Change*. Philadelphia, PA: Brunner/Mazel.

Clark, J. (ed.) (2002) *Freelance Counselling and Psychotherapy: Competition and Collaboration*. London: Brunner-Routledge.

Clarkson, P. (1990) A multiplicity of psychotherapeutic relationships, *British Journal of Psychotherapy*, 7(2): 148–63.

Clarkson, P. (2003) *The Therapeutic Relationship*, 2nd edn. London: Whurr.

Colson, D., Lewis, L. and Horwitz, L. (1985) Negative outcome in psychotherapy and psychoanalysis, in D.T. Mays and C.M. Franks (eds) *Negative Outcome in Psychotherapy and What To Do About It*. New York: Springer.

Coren, A. (2001) *Short-Term Psychotherapy: a Psychodynamic Approach*. Basingstoke: Palgrave.

Cummings, N. and Sayama, M. (1995) *Focused Psychotherapy: A Casebook of Brief, Intermittent Psychotherapy Throughout the Life Cycle*. New York: Brunner/Mazel.

Daines, B., Gask, L. and Usherwood, T. (1997) *Medical and Psychiatric Issues for Counsellors*. London: Sage.

Davanloo, H. (1985) Short-term dynamic psychotherapy, in H. Kaplan and B.J. Sadock (eds) *Comprehensive Textbook of Psychiatry*. Baltimore, MD: Williams & Wilkins.

Davis, J. (1989) Issues in the evaluation of counsellors by supervisors, *Counselling*, 69: 31–7.

Davy, D. and Cross, M. (2004) *Barriers, Defences and Resistance*. Maidenhead: Open University Press.

Day, R.W. and Sparacio, R.T. (1989) Structuring the counselling process, in W. Dryden (ed.) *Key Issues for Counselling in Action*. London: Sage.

Dinnage, R. (1988) *One To One: Experiences of Psychotherapy*. London: Viking.

Dryden, W. (1982) *Social Problems: Treatment from a Rational-Emotive Perspective*. London: Institute for RET.

Dryden, W. (ed.) (1989) *Key Issues for Counselling in Action*. London: Sage.

Dryden, W. (1990) *Rational-Emotive Counselling in Action*. London: Sage.

Dryden, W. (1991) *Dryden on Counselling, Vol. 1: Seminal Papers*. London: Whurr.

Dryden, W. (1992) *The Dryden Interviews*. London: Whurr.

Dryden, W. and Feltham, C. (1995) *Counselling and Psychotherapy; A Consumer's Guide*. London: Sheldon.

Durlak, J.A. (1979) Comparative effectiveness of paraprofessional and professional helpers, *Psychological Bulletin*, 86(1): 80–92.

Ecker, B. and Hulley, L. (1996) *Depth-Oriented Brief Therapy*. San Francisco, CA: Jossey-Bass.

Egan, G. (2002) *The Skilled Helper*, 7th edn. Pacific Grove, CA: Brooks/Cole.

Elton Wilson, J. (1996) *Time-Conscious Psychological Therapy*. London: Routledge.

Embleton Tudor, L. (1997) The contract boundary, in C. Sills (ed.) *Contracts in Counselling*. London: Sage.

Fairbairn, S. and Fairbairn, G. (eds) (1987) *Psychology, Ethics and Change*. London: Routledge & Kegan Paul.

Feltham, C. (1995) *What is Counselling? The Promise and Problem of the Talking Therapies*. London: Sage.

Feltham, C. (1997) *Time-Limited Counselling*. London: Sage.

Feltham, C. (ed.) (1999) *Understanding the Counselling Relationship*. London: Sage.

Feltham, C. (2004) *Problems Are Us: Or Is It Just Me?* Felixstowe: Braiswick.

Feltham, C. (2006) Conceptualising clients' problems, in C. Feltham and I. Horton (eds) *Sage Handbook of Counselling and Psychotherapy*, 2nd edn. London: Sage.

Feltham, C. and Lambert, P. (2006) Client experiences, in C. Feltham and I. Horton (eds) *Sage Handbook of Counselling and Psychotherapy*, 2nd edn. London: Sage.

Fennell, M. (1999) *Overcoming Low Self-Esteem: A Self-help Guide to Using Cognitive Behavioural Techniques*. London: Robinson.

Flegenheimer, W.V. (1982) *Techniques of Brief Psychotherapy*. New York: Aronson.

Frances, A., Sweeney, J. and Clarkin, J. (1985) Do psychotherapies have specific effects? *American Journal of Psychotherapy*, 39(2): 159–74.

Fransella, F. and Dalton, P. (2000) *Personal Construct Counselling in Action*, 2nd edn. London: Sage.

Gardner, H. (1993) *Frames of Mind: The Theory of Multiple Intelligences*, 2nd edn. London: Fontana.

Garfield, S.L. (1989) *The Practice of Brief Psychotherapy*. Oxford: Pergamon.

Garfield, S.L. and Bergin, A.E. (eds) (1986) *Handbook of Psychotherapy and Behavior Change*, 3rd edn. Chichester: Wiley.

Gendlin, E.T. (1984) The client's client: the edge of awareness, in R.F. Levant and J.M. Shlien (eds) *Client-Centered Therapy and the Person-Centered Approach*. New York: Praeger.

Gendlin, E.T. (1996) *Focusing-Oriented Psychotherapy: A Manual of the Experiential Method*. New York: Guilford Press.

Gilbert, P. (ed.) (2005) *Compassion: Conceptualisations, Research and Use in Psychotherapy*. London: Routledge.

Glasser, W. (1984) *Take Effective Control of your Life*. New York: Harper & Row.

Greenberg, L.S., Rice, L.N. and Elliott, R. (1993) *Facilitating Emotional Change: The Moment-by-Moment Process*. New York: Guilford.

Greenberger, D. and Padsesky, C.A. (1995) *Mind Over Mood: A Cognitive Therapy Treatment Manual for Clients*. New York: Guilford.

Guinagh, B. (1987) *Catharsis and Cognition in Psychotherapy*. New York: Springer-Verlag.

Hall, E., Hall, C., Stradling, P. and Young, D. (2005) *Guided Imagery: Creative Interventions in Counselling and Psychotherapy*. London: Sage.

Hayes, S.C., Follette, V.M. and Linehan, M.M. (eds) (2004) *Mindfulness and Acceptance: Expanding the Cognitive-Behavioural Tradition*. New York: Guilford.

Heron, J. (1992) *Feeling and Personhood: Psychology in Another Key*. London: Sage.

Heron, J. (2001) *Helping the Client: A Creative Practical Guide*, 5th edn. London: Sage.

Higgs, J. and Titchen, A. (eds) (2001) *Practice Knowledge and Expertise in the Health Professions*. Oxford: Butterworth-Heinemann.

Hill, C.E. (1989) *Therapist Techniques and Client Outcomes*. London: Sage.

Hobson, R.E. (1985) *Forms of Feeling: The Heart of Psychotherapy*. London: Tavistock.

Holmes, J. and Lindley, R. (1989) *The Values of Psychotherapy*. Oxford: Oxford University Press.

Horowitz, M., Marmar, C., Krupnick, J., Wilner, N., Kaltreider, N. and Wallerstein, R. (1984) *Personality Styles and Brief Psychothrerapy*. New York: Basic Books.

Howard, G.S., Nance, D.W. and Myers, P. (1987) *Adaptive Counseling and Therapy*. San Francisco: Jossey-Bass.

Howard, K.I., Kopta, S.M., Krause, M.S. and Orlinsky, D.E. (1986) The dose-effect relationship in psychotherapy, *American Psychologist*, 41: 159–64.

Ivey, A.E., Ivey, M.B. and Simek-Downing, L. (1987) *Counseling and Psychotherapy: Integrating Skills, Theory and Practice*. Englewood Cliffs, NJ: Prentice-Hall International.

Jinks, G. (2006) Specific strategies and techniques, in C. Feltham and I. Horton (eds) *Sage Handbook of Counselling and Psychotherapy*, 2nd edn. London: Sage.

Kabat-Zinn, J. (1990) *Full Catastrophe Living*. New York: Delta.

Kopp, S.B. (1974) *If You Meet the Buddha on the Road, Kill Him!* London: Sheldon.

Koss, M.P. and Butcher, J.M. (eds) (1986) Research in brief psychotherapy, in S.L. Garfield and A.E. Bergin (eds) *Handbook of Psychotherapy and Behavior Change*, 3rd edn. Chichester: Wiley.

Kottler, J.A. and Carlson, J. (eds) (2002) *Bad Therapy: Master Therapists Share Their Worst Failures*. London: Routledge.

Kupers, T.A. (1988) *Ending Therapy*. London: New York University Press.

Lago, C. and Smith, B. (eds) (2003) *Anti-discriminatory Counselling Practice*. London: Sage.

Lambert, M.J. (ed.) (2003) *Bergin and Garfield's Handbook of Psychotherapy and Behavior Change*, 5th edn. San Francisco, CA: Jossey-Bass.

Lazarus, A.A. (1981) *The Practice of Multimodal Therapy*. New York: McGraw-Hill.

Lazarus, A.A. and Fay, A. (1990) Brief psychotherapy: tautology or oxymoron? In J.K. Zeig and S.G. Gilligan (eds) *Brief Therapy: Myths, Methods and Metaphors*. New York: Brunner/Mazel.

Leigh, A. (1998) *Referral and Termination Issues for Counsellors*. London: Sage.

Leiper, R. (2001) *Working Through Setbacks in Psychotherapy: Crisis, Impasse and Relapse*. London: Sage.

Levant, R.F. and Schlien, J.M. (eds) (1984) *Client-Centered Therapy and the Person-Centered Approach*. New York: Praeger.

Lewis, M.K., Rogers, C.R. and Shlien, J.M. (1959) Two cases of time-limited client-centered psychotherapy, in A. Burton, (ed.) *Case Studies of Counseling and Psychotherapy*. New York: Prentice-Hall.

Lowry, J.L. and Ross, M.J. (1997) Expectations of psychotherapy duration: how long should psychotherapy last? *Psychotherapy: Theory, Research, Practice, Training*, 34(3): 272–7.

Macaskill, N. (1985) Homework assignments in brief psychotherapy, *British Journal of Psychotherapy*, 2(2): 134–41.

Mahrer, A.R. (1988) The briefest psychotherapy, *Changes*, 6(3): 86–9.

Mahrer, A.R. (1989a) *Experiential Psychotherapy: Basic Practices*. Ottawa, Canada: Ottawa University Press.

Mahrer, A. R. (1989b) *Dreamwork in Psychotherapy and Self-Change*. New York: Norton.

Mahrer, A. (1996) *The Complete Guide to Experiential Psychotherapy*. New York: Wiley.

Malan, D.H. (1975) *A Study of Brief Psychotherapy*. London: Plenum.

Mann, D. (1999) *Erotic Transference and Countertransference*. London: Routledge.

Mann, J. (1973) *Time-limited Psychotherapy*. Cambridge, Mass.: Harvard University Press.

Marlatt, G.A. and Gordon, J. (eds) (1985) *Relapse Prevention*. New York: Guilford Press.

Maroda, K. (1991) *The Power of Countertransference*. Northvale, NJ: Aronson.

Mays, D.T. and Franks, C.M. (1985) *Negative Outcome in Psychotherapy and What to do about it*. New York: Springer.

McLeod, J. (1997) *Narrative and Psychotherapy*. London: Sage.

Mearns, D. and Cooper, M. (2005) *Working at Relational Depth in Counselling and Psychotherapy*. London: Sage.

Mearns, D. and Thorne, B. (1999) *Person-Centred Counselling in Action*, 2nd edn. London: Sage.

Melges, F.T. (1982) *Time and the Inner Future: A Temporal Approach to Psychiatric Disorders*. New York: Wiley.

Milner, J. and O'Byrne, P. (2002) *Brief Counselling: Narratives and Solutions*. Basingstoke: Palgrave.

Molnos, A. (1995) *A Question of Time: Essentials of Brief Dynamic Psychotherapy*. London: Karnac.

Murdin, L. (1999) *How Much Is Enough? Endings in Psychotherapy*. London: Routledge.

Neenan, M. and Dryden, W. (2004) *Cognitive Therapy: 100 Key Points and Techniques*. London: Brunner-Routledge.

Neimeyer, G. J. (ed.) (1993) *Constructivist Assessment: A Casebook*. Newbury Park, CA: Sage.

Nelson, M.L. (2002) An assessment-based model for counselling strategy selection, *Journal of Counseling and Development*, 80(4): 416–21.

Nelson-Jones, R. (1989) *Effective Thinking Skills*. London: Cassell.

Norton, K. and McGauley, G. (1998) *Counselling Difficult Clients*. London: Sage.

Omer, H. (1990) Enhancing the impact of therapeutic interventions, *American Journal of Psychotherapy*, 44(2): 218–31.

Orlinsky, D.E. and Howard, K.I. (1986) Process and outcome in psychotherapy, in S.L. Garfield and A.E. Bergin (eds) *Handbook of Psychotherapy and Behavior Change*, 3rd edn. Chichester: Wiley.

Palmer, S. (ed.) (2002) *Multicultural Counselling; A Reader*. London: Sage.

Palmer, S. and McMahon, G. (1997) *Client Assessment*. London: Sage.

Patten, M.I. and Walker, L.G. (1990) Marriage Guidance Counselling I: what clients think will help, *British Journal of Guidance and Counselling*, 18(1): 28–39.

Perraton Mountford, C. (2005) One size does *not* fit all, *Counselling and Psychotherapy Journal*, 16(5): 43–5.

Perry, S. (1989) Treatment time and the borderline patient: an underappreciated strategy, *Journal of Personality Disorders*, 3(3): 230–9.

Pipes, R.B., Schwartz, R. and Crouch, P. (1985) Measuring client fears, *Journal of Consulting and Clinical Psychology*, 53(6): 933–4.

Preston, J., Varzos, N. and Liebert, D. (1995) *Every Session Counts: Making the Most of Your Brief Therapy*. San Luis Obispo, CA: Impact.

Prochaska, J.O. and DiClemente, C.C. (1984) *The Trans Theoretical Approach*. Homewood, IL: Dow Jones-Irwin.

Regan, A.M. and Hill, C.E. (1992) Investigation of what clients and counsellors do not say in brief therapy, *Journal of Counseling Psychology*, 39(2): 168–74.

Reid, W.H., Balis, G.U. and Sutton, B.J. (1997) *The Treatment of Psychiatric Disorders*, 3rd edn, revised for DSM IV. Bristol, PA: Brunner/Mazel.

Rice, L.N. (1984) Client tasks in client-centered therapy, in R.F. Levant and J.M. Shlien (eds) *Client-Centered Therapy and the Person-Centered Approach*. New York: Praeger.

Richert, A. (1983) Differential prescription for psychotherapy on the basis of client role preferences, *Psychotherapy: Theory, Research and Practice*, 20(3): 321–9.

Robertiello, R.C. and Schoenewolf, G. (1987) *101 Common Therapeutic Blunders: Countertransference and Counterresistance in Psychotherapy*. Northvale, NJ: Aronson.

Rogers, C.R. (1990) *On Becoming a Person*. London: Constable.

Rosenbaum, R., Hoyt, M.F. and Talmon, M. (1990) The challenge of single-session therapies; creating pivotal moments, in R.A. Wells and V.J. Gianetti (eds) *Handbook of the Brief Psychotherapies*. New York: Plenum.

Rosenthal, H.G. (ed.) (1998) *Favorite Counseling and Therapy Techniques: 51 Therapists Share Their Most Creative Strategies*. Washington, DC: Accelerated Development.

Roth, A. and Fonagy, P. (ed.) (2005) *What Works for Whom? A Critical Review of Psychotherapy Research*, 2nd edn. New York: Guilford.

Rowan, J. (1988) The psychology of furniture, *Counselling*, 64: 21–4.

Rowan, J. (1989) *The Reality Game*. London: Routledge.

Rowan, J. (2005) *The Future of Training in Psychotherapy and Counselling: Instrumental, Relational and Transpersonal Perspectives*. London: Routledge.

Ryle, A. (1983) The value of written communications in dynamic psychotherapy, *British Journal of Psychiatry*, 8: 195–8.

Ryle, A. (1990) *Cognitive-Analytic Therapy: Active Participation in Change*. Chichester: Wiley.

Ryle, A. (ed.) (1995) *Cognitive Analytic Therapy: Developments in Theory and Practice*. Chichester: Wiley.

Sachs, J.S. (1983) Negative factors in brief psychotherapy: an empirical assessment, *Journal of Consulting and Clinical Psychology*, 51: 557–64.

Sands, A. (2000) *Falling for Therapy: Psychotherapy from a Client's Point of View*. Basingstoke: Palgrave.

Scott, M. (1989) *A Cognitive-Behavioural Approach to Clients' Problems*. London: Routledge.

Sherman, R.T. and Anderson, C.A. (1987) Decreasing premature termination from psychotherapy, *Journal of Social and Clinical Psychology*, 5(3): 298–312.

Shipton, G. and Smith, E. (1998) *Long-Term Counselling*. London: Sage.

Shlien, J.M., Mosak, H.H. and Dreikurs, R. (1962) Effect of time limits: a comparison of two psychotherapies, *Journal of Consulting Psychology*, 9: 31–4.

Sifneos, P. (1972) *Short-Term Psychotherapy and Emotional Crisis*. Cambridge, MA.: Harvard University Press.

Sills, C. (ed.) (1997) *Contracts in Counselling*. London: Sage.

Sklar, H. (1988) The impact of the therapeutic environment, *Journal of Contemporary Psychotherapy*, 18(2): 107–23.

Sledge, W.H., Moras, K., Hartley, D. and Levine, M.A. (1990) Effects of time-limited psychotherapy on patient drop-out rates, *American Journal of Psychiatry*, 147(10): 1342–7.

Solomon, A. (2002) *The Noonday Demon: An Anatomy of Depression*. London: Vintage.

Stewart, I. (1989) *Transactional Analysis Counselling in Action*. London: Sage.
Stewart, I. and Joines, V. (1987) *T.A. Today*. Nottingham: Lifespace.
Storr, A. (1963) *The Integrity of the Personality*. Harmondsworth: Pelican.
Stout, C. (1991) A methodological approach to differential diagnosis, in K.N. Anchor (ed.) *Handbook of Medical Psychotherapy: Cost-Effective Strategies in Mental Health*. Toronto, ON: Hogrefe & Huber.
Strasser, F. and Strasser, A. (1997) *Existential Time-Limited Therapy: The Wheel of Existence*. Chichester: Wiley.
Striano, J. (1988) *Can Psychotherapists Hurt You?* Santa Barbara, CA: Professional Press.
Strupp, H.H. (1980) Success and failure in time-limited psychotherapy, *Archives of General Psychiatry*, 37: 708–16.
Sugarman, L. (2004) *Counselling and the Life Course*. London: Sage.
Sutherland, S. (1989) *Breakdown*. London: Weidenfeld & Nicolson.
Sutton, C. (1989) The evaluation of counselling: a goal-attainment approach, in W. Dryden (ed.) *Key Issues for Counselling in Action*. London: Sage.
Talmon, M. (1990) *Single-Session Therapy*. San Francisco: Jossey-Bass.
Thompson, R.A. (1996) *Counseling Techniques: Improving Relationships with Others, Ourselves, Our Families, and Our Environment*. Washington, DC: Accelerated Development.
Tosey, P. and Gregory, J. (2002) *Dictionary of Personal Development*. London: Whurr.
Ursano, R.J., Sonnenberg, S.M. and Lazar, S.G. (1991) *Psychodynamic Psychotherapy*. Washington, DC: American Psychiatric Press.
Van Deurzen, E. (2001) *Existential Counselling and Psychotherapy in Practice*, 2nd edn. London: Sage.
Wachtel, P.L. (1993) *Therapeutic Communication: Knowing What to Say When*. New York: Guilford.
Walker, L.G. and Patten, M.I. (1990) Marriage Guidance Counselling II: what counsellors want to give, *British Journal of Guidance and Counselling*, 18(3): 294–307.
Watkins, C.E. jnr (1989) Countertransference: its impact on the counselling situation, in W. Dryden (ed.) *Key Issues for Counselling in Action*. London: Sage.
Wells, R.A. and Gianetti, V.J. (eds) (1990) *Handbook of the Brief Psychotherapies*. New York: Plenum.
West, W. (2004) *Spiritual Issues in Therapy*. Basingstoke: Palgrave.
Willer, B. and Miller, G.H. (1976) Client involvement in goal setting and its relationship to therapeutic outcome, *Journal of Clinical Psychology*, 32(3): 687–9.
Wolberg, L.R. (1980) *Handbook of Short-term Psychotherapy*. New York: Thieme-Stratton.
Yankura, J. and Dryden, W. (1990) *Doing RET: Albert Ellis in Action*. New York: Springer.
Yapko, M.D. (1994) *When Living Hurts: Directives for Treating Depression*. Levittown, PA: Brunner/Mazel.
Zeig, J.K. (1990) Seeding, in J.K. Zeig and S.G. Gilligan (eds) *Brief Therapy: Myths, Methods and Metaphors*. New York: Brunner/Mazel.

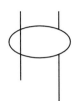

INDEX

involvement in process,
encouragement of 57–8
language use, sensitivity to 58–9
length of sessions for, negotiation of 40,
93
listening for problems within story of,
importance of 47–9
maintenance stage 55
misconceptions, avoidance of 18–19
misunderstandings, avoidance of 12
motivations of, exploration of 16–17,
25
multi-modal profiles of 62–4
multiple problems, recognition of
potentially different stages of 56
naivety, problems of 197
organic problems of 196
orienting to counselling 11–41
pacing, sensitivity to 59–60
passivity in, pitfalls of 57–8
past history of being helped,
exploration of 34–7
perceived needs, elicitation of 19
permission for tape recording 15
'personal growth' agenda of 23
perspective on counselling, elicitation
of 37–9
practical arrangements for, dealing with
39–41
pre-contemplation stage 24–5, 54, 56
pre-therapy relations of 23–4
preconceptions, exploration of 18–20
preparation for first contact with 11–12
present behaviour, advantages and
disadvantages of desired and
207–10
presenting issues, assessment of 20–2
primary problems of, dealing with
49–50
progress of counselling, questions
seeking views on 54
psychodynamic problems 195
questions for elicitation of helpful
information from 50–51
rambling talk of, dealing with 45–7
reappearance of previously overcome
problem 76–7
reasons for referring on 26–7
referral agent, exploration of advice/
impressions given by 18–20
referring on 26–8
risks of counselling for 21

risks of single-session counselling for 33
scheduling for, negotiation of 39–40
self-harm, dealing with problems of
49–50
sensations, problems of 63, 64
session frequency for, negotiation of
39–40
severity of problems 66–7
shyness, problem of 34–5
single-session counselling,
appropriateness for 33
social/economic problems of 196–7
social supports of, assessment of 25
stages of change 24–5, 189–91
target concerns, appropriateness to
120–21
state of change
identification of 54–6
stigmatization of, avoidance of 30
story of, importance of 47–9
suicide risk, dealing with 49–50
talk, facilitation of need to 45–7
tape recording, presentation of issue to
15
telephone enquiries from 11
themes emerging from counselling,
identification of problems within
47–9
therapeutic alliance with, formation of
34–6
therapeutic 'tasks' required of 57–8
therapist's view of counselling,
demonstration to 37–9
time-specific state, exploration of 16–17
unhelpful experiences, dealing with
34–6
unhelpful narrative tendencies of,
responding to 48–9
welcoming approach to 11, 12
'why now?' question for 16–18
cognition problems of clients 63, 64, 196
cognitive analytic therapy 170–71
cognitive behavioural therapy (CBT) 6,
55–6, 57, 81, 114, 148, 149
cognitive inflexibility 52
collaborative assessment 20, 22
commission bias 52
compassion in counselling 149
concerns of clients
assessment of 45–88
identification of unsuccessful attempts
to deal with 74–5

commitment of clients' to carrying
out 125–6
demonstrations of 133–4
distinguish between 'try' and 'do'
125–6
empathy with clients on 134–5
explanation of rationale for specific
119
failures to attempt, discovering
reasons for 132–3
modification or renegotiation of
failed 132–3
'no-lose' nature of 129–30
possible outcomes from 129
problem-solving data from
unsuccessful attempts at 131–2
purpose of, clients' understanding of
124
reasons for not completing,
questionnaire for clients on
205–6
responsibility of clients' for,
encouragement of 133–4
types of 114–17
unsuccessful attempts at, dealing
with 131–2
barriers to progress on, identification of
126–7
behavioural tasks as 116
change through, encouragement of
113–35
checking on 130–32
circumstances of clients, mindfulness of
122
clients' abilities, mindfulness of 121–2
clients' stage of change and target
concerns, appropriateness to 120–21
comments of clients on, elicitation of
119–20
commitment to change, reinforcement
through 113
emotive situations between sessions as
113
evidence for and against 113
feedback from 114
focus of sessions, determination of
homework on basis of 120–21
imagery in 117
integration into therapeutic approach
of 114–17
learning style of clients, mindfulness of
123

mental rehearsal, initiation of 127–8
mobilization of clients and 96
monitoring behaviour as 116
negotiation of, allowing session time
for 118
negotiation of, rather than setting of
119–20
negotiation of, transference issues and
120
obstacles to completion of,
identification of 126–7
past history of clients in, mindfulness of
13
personal learning for therapists from
134–5
process of change and 113
progress checks on 130–32
questionnaires for 116
rationale for, explanation of 113–14,
119
reading assignments for 115
reinforcement of messages concerning
124
relationship-based approaches and 113
sensitivity to needs of clients in respect
of time 118
success criteria, establishment of 128–9
therapists' homework, benefits of 134–5
values of clients, mindfulness of 122
writing assignments for 115
humanistic models of therapy 6, 7
humanistic problems 195–6

imagery
in homework 117
imagery-oriented techniques 100
problems of 63, 64
incompatibility of clients 27–8
inductive work 45–88
influence base, appropriate use of 60–61
intermediaries, use at first contact 11, 12
International Classification of Diseases 184
interpersonal-developmental-existential
(IDE) problems 7, 16
interpersonal problems of clients 63, 64,
195–6
interventions, specific for specific
concerns 83–5
introduction of counselling to clients
38–9

jargon, avoidance of 59